LOW-WAGE WORK IN FRANCE

LOW-WAGE WORK IN FRANCE

Ève Caroli and Jérôme Gautié,
editors

The Russell Sage Foundation Case Studies of Job
Quality in Advanced Economies

Russell Sage Foundation • New York

The Russell Sage Foundation

The Russell Sage Foundation, one of the oldest of America's general purpose foundations, was established in 1907 by Mrs. Margaret Olivia Sage for "the improvement of social and living conditions in the United States." The Foundation seeks to fulfill this mandate by fostering the development and dissemination of knowledge about the country's political, social, and economic problems. While the Foundation endeavors to assure the accuracy and objectivity of each book it publishes, the conclusions and interpretations in Russell Sage Foundation publications are those of the authors and not of the Foundation, its Trustees, or its staff. Publication by Russell Sage, therefore, does not imply Foundation endorsement.

BOARD OF TRUSTEES
Thomas D. Cook, Chair

Kenneth D. Brody	Kathleen Hall Jamieson	Nancy Rosenblum
W. Bowman Cutter, III	Melvin J. Konner	Richard H. Thaler
Christopher Edley Jr.	Alan B. Krueger	Eric Wanner
John A. Ferejohn	Cora B. Marrett	Mary C. Waters
Larry V. Hedges		

Library of Congress Cataloging-in-Publication Data
Low-wage work in France / Ève Caroli and Jérôme Gautié, editors.
    p. cm — (The Russell Sage Foundation case studies of job quality in advanced economies)
    ISBN 978-0-87154-070-6
    1. Unskilled labor—France.　2. Wages—France.　3. Minimum wage—France.　4. Labor market—France.　I. Caroli, Ève.　II. Gautié, Jérôme.
    HD8431.L69　2008
    331.7'980944—dc22

                                                      2007045950

Copyright © 2008 by Russell Sage Foundation. All rights reserved. Printed in the United States of America. No part of this publication may be reproduced, stored in a retrieval system, or transmitted in any form or by any means, electronic, mechanical, photocopying, recording, or otherwise, without the prior written permission of the publisher.

Reproduction by the United States Government in whole or in part is permitted for any purpose.

The paper used in this publication meets the minimum requirements of American National Standard for Information Sciences—Permanence of Paper for Printed Library Materials. ANSI Z39.48-1992.

Text design by Suzanne Nichols.

RUSSELL SAGE FOUNDATION
112 East 64th Street, New York, New York 10021

Contents

	About the Authors	vii
Introduction	The French Story *Robert Solow*	1
Chapter 1	Low-Wage Work: The Political Debate and Research Agenda in France *Ève Caroli and Jérôme Gautié*	16
Chapter 2	Low-Wage Work and Labor Market Institutions in France *Ève Caroli, Jérôme Gautié, and Philippe Askenazy*	28
Chapter 3	Operators in Food-Processing Industries: Coping with Increasing Pressures *Ève Caroli, Jérôme Gautié, and Annie Lamanthe*	88
Chapter 4	Good Jobs, Hard Work? Employment Models for Nurse's Aides and Hospital Housekeepers *Philippe Méhaut, Anne Marie Arborio, Jacques Bouteiller, Philippe Mossé, and Lise Causse*	127
Chapter 5	Housekeepers in French Hotels: Cinderella in the Shadows *Christine Guégnard and Sylvie-Anne Mériot*	168
Chapter 6	Working Hard for Large French Retailers *Philippe Askenazy, Jean-Baptiste Berry, and Sophie Prunier-Poulmaire*	209
Chapter 7	Job Quality and Career Opportunities for Call Center Workers: Contrasting Patterns in France *Mathieu Beraud, Thierry Colin, and Benoît Grasser, with the participation of Émilie Fériel*	254

| Chapter 8 | Summary and Conclusions: Why and How Do Institutions Matter?
Ève Caroli and Jérôme Gautié | 288 |

Index 303

About the Authors

ÈVE CAROLI is professor of economics at University Paris X-Nanterre and senior researcher at EconomiX and the Paris School of Economics.

JÉRÔME GAUTIÉ is professor of economics at the University of Paris 1 Panthéon-Sorbonne, senior researcher at the Centre d'Economie de la Sorbonne.

ANNE MARIE ARBORIO is assistant professor in Sociology at the University of Aix-Marseille I and a member of the Institute of Labor Economics and Industrial Sociology (LEST) in Aix-en-Provence, France.

PHILIPPE ASKENAZY is senior researcher at the CNRS-Paris School of Economics, Deputy-Director of the Centre Pour la Récherche en Économie et ses Applications, and IZA Research Fellow.

MATHIEU BERAUD is assistant professor of economics at the University Nancy 1 (Henri Poincaré), researcher at GREE (Groupe de recherche sur l'education et l'emploi), and director of the associate Céreq (French Center for Research on Education, Training, and Employment) for the Lorraine region.

JEAN-BAPTISTE BERRY is a researcher at the Direction of Research Animation, Studies and Statistics (Ministry of Labor and Social Affairs).

JACQUES BOUTEILLER is labor socioeconomist at the Institute of Labor Economics and Industrial Sociology, Aix-en-Provence.

LISE CAUSSE is a sociologist and researcher at the National Research Center on Qualifications, Marseille.

THIERRY COLIN is assistant professor of economics and business at the University of Nancy 2, and researcher at CEREFIGE and GREE.

ÉMILIE FÉRIEL is a PhD student in economics and member of the laboratory Groupe de Récherche sur l'Education et l'Emploi (University of Nancy 2).

BENOÎT GRASSER is assistant professor of economics and business at the University Nancy 2, and researcher at GREE and CEREFIGE.

CHRISTINE GUÉGNARD is a researcher at the French Center for Research on Education, Training and Employment (Céreq) and at the Institute on Sociology and Economics of Education (Iredu), associated with the French National Center for Scientific Research (CNRS) and the University of Burgundy.

ANNIE LAMANTHE is a sociologist and researcher at the Institute of Labour Economics and Industrial Sociology (LEST) - Cereq's Associated Regional Center in Aix-en-Provence, France.

PHILIPPE MÉHAUT is senior researcher at the CNRS, Institute for Labor Economics and Industrial Sociology (LEST) in Aix-en-Provence.

SYLVIE-ANNE MÉRIOT is a sociologist and researcher at the Céreq, the French Center for Research on Education, Training and Employment.

PHILIPPE MOSSÉ is an economist, senior researcher, and director of the Institute of Labor Economics and Industrial Sociology, Aix-en-Provence.

SOPHIE PRUNIER-POULMAIRE is assistant professor at the University of Paris 10-Nanterre.

ROBERT SOLOW is Institute Professor Emeritus at the Massachusetts Institute of Technology and a Nobel laureate in economics.

INTRODUCTION

The French Story

Robert Solow

By any reasonable standard definition of "low-wage work," about a quarter of American wage earners are low-wage workers. The corresponding figure is smaller, sometimes much smaller, in other comparable advanced capitalist countries. This fact is not very good for the self-image of Americans. It does not seem to be what is meant by "crown(ing) thy good with brotherhood, from sea to shining sea." The paradox, if that is the right word, is the starting point for the extensive study of which this book is an important part. What are the comparative facts, what do they mean, and why do they turn out that way?

A foundation dedicated from its beginning to "the improvement of social and living conditions in the United States of America" has to be interested in the nature of poverty, its causes, changes, consequences and possible reduction. Low-wage work is not the same thing as poverty, still less lifelong poverty. Some low-wage workers live in families with several earners, and share a common standard of living, so they may not be poor even while working such jobs. Some low-wage workers are on a reasonably secure track that will eventually move them to better paid jobs, so they are not poor in a lifetime sense. But some low-wage workers are stuck with very low income for a meaningful length of time. For them, low-wage work does mean poverty in the midst of plenty.

Of course, the incidence of poverty can be reduced by transfer payments outside the labor market. Nevertheless, in a society that values self-reliance, and in which productive work confers identity and self-respect as well as the respect of others, income redistribution unconnected or wrongly connected with work is not the best solution except in special cases. In that kind of society, ours for instance, the persistence of low-wage work is felt as a social problem on its own. It first has to be understood if we are to find satisfactory ways to diminish its incidence or alleviate its effects.

One obvious basis for low-wage work is low productivity, which may be primarily a characteristic of the worker, as is often simply assumed, or may be primarily a characteristic of the job. If it inheres in the job, equity could be achieved by passing the job around, so to speak, like boring committee assignments or military service, but that would have no aggregate effect. Wherever low pay originates, however, raising productivity provides a double benefit: it diminishes the amount of low-wage work to be done, and it increases the useful output of the whole economy.

Low productivity, and therefore low-wage work, tends to reproduce itself from generation to generation. This is an important additional reason why a high incidence of low-wage work is a "social condition" that needs to be improved. Growing up in a chronically low-wage family limits access to good education, good health care, and to other ladders to social mobility. So a persistent high incidence of low-wage work, when confined to a relatively small group, contravenes the widely accepted social goal of equal opportunity.

These are among the reasons why, in 1994, the Russell Sage Foundation inaugurated a major program of research on the nature, causes, and consequences of low-wage work and the prospects of low-wage workers. This initiative replaced a successful but more conventional program of research on poverty. It was called, rather grandly, *The Future of Work*. One of its key motivations was the need to understand how poorly educated, unskilled workers could cope with an economy in which most jobs were becoming technologically advanced, and therefore more demanding of cognitive power and refined skills.

This formulation was intended to call attention both to workers and to jobs, the natural subtext being that low-end jobs might be disappearing faster than low-skilled workers. This potential disparity presented the danger that low-wage workers could be stranded in an economy that had no use for them. The research mandate was interpreted quite broadly.

The Future of Work program was, as a matter of course, focused on the United States. It produced a large body of useful and original research, some of which was collected and summarized in the 2003 volume *Low-Wage America: How Employers Are Reshaping Opportunity in the Workplace*, edited by Eileen Appelbaum, Annette Bernhardt, and Richard Murnane. One of the refreshing aspects of these studies was precisely that the needs and capacities of employers shared the stage in the low-wage labor market with the abilities and motivations of workers.

One interesting hypothesis that emerged from this work was the notion that employers have significant discretion about the way they organize their use of low-skilled workers and the value they put on the continuity and productivity of their work force. The extreme versions came to be labeled "low-road" and "high-road" modes of organization. At the low-road extreme lie employers such as the typical car-wash, whose workers are regarded as casual labor, interchangeable parts that can be picked up off the street freely under normal labor-market conditions. There is no advantage in doing otherwise. At the other extreme are employers who regard their unskilled workers as an asset whose productive value can be increased by more training and longer attachment to the firm.

The point of this distinction was the belief that in some market situations both styles can be viable. An employer's place on the continuum is not uniquely determined by technology and the intensity of competition in the product market. Satisfactory profits can be earned by somewhat higher- and somewhat lower-road modes of organization; in some industries, examples of both can be found coexisting.

Of course, the nature of the technology and the competitive intensity in the industry are important determinants of labor-market outcomes. That is not in doubt. In some situations, however, there may be scope for several levels of wages and job quality for unskilled workers. It is important here to note that job quality covers much more than the current wage and benefits paid; it includes the length and slope of the internal wage scale, the degree of job security, the training offered and the possibilities of promotion within the firm, small creature comforts, the pace of the work itself, the autonomy and ergonomic character of the work, and so on. Each of these has a cost to the firm and a value to the workers, and the two are not always the same.

It hardly needs arguing that these elements of job quality can be important for the satisfaction and self-respect attached to a job. It then becomes important to the researcher to understand the broad factors that govern the typical choices made by employers. These may include historical precedents, legislation, the working of the educational system, collective bargaining, and other "institutional" biases.

At this stage of the argument, the advantages of a comparative cross-country study stand out. Most of those broadly institutional factors cannot be studied empirically within the United States because they change so slowly in time, and because there is not much locational variation. One cannot actually see them at work in a still snapshot. One can speculate and make thought-experiments, but that is not the same thing. So the idea sprouted within the Russell Sage Foundation in 2003 that it might be very useful to observe systematically how the fate of low-wage labor differs across a sample of European countries. Not any countries will do: one wants countries with somewhat different but not radically different political and institutional histories; but they must be at the same level of economic development as the United States if lessons are to be learned that could be useful in the United States. In the end, the countries chosen included the three indispensable large countries—France, Germany, and the United Kingdom—and two small northern European countries—Denmark and the Netherlands. The choice was consciously limited to Europe in order to avoid the complication of drastically different sociopolitical systems. A competition was held, and a local team selected for each of these five countries.

The planners of the project framed it in such a way that would sharpen the inferences that could be made from cross-country comparisons. Most centrally, five target jobs were chosen as objects of close study, the same five in each country. They were nurses' assistants and cleaners in hospitals, housekeepers in hotels, checkout clerks and related occupations in supermarkets and retail stores specializing in electrical goods, packagers, machine tenders and other unskilled occupations in two branches of food processing, namely confectionary and meat products, and low-skilled operators in call centers. (This last choice took advantage of an already ongoing international study of the call-center industry.) These are all low-wage jobs in the United States. The fact that some of them are not low-wage jobs in some of the five countries is an example of the value of cross-country comparisons. The simple fact invites, or rather compels, the question: Why not?

Each national team was asked to compile a statistical overview of low-wage work in its country, with special but not exclusive attention to the five target jobs. The team was also asked to complement the routine data with a survey of the historical, legislative, educational and other institutional infrastructure that is believed to underlie its own particular ways of dealing with low-end jobs and low-skilled workers. The final part of each country report is a series of case studies of each of the target jobs, including interviews with employers, managers, workers, union representatives and other participants. (When temporary work agencies were used to provide some or all of the relevant workers, they were included in the interviews wherever possible.) The national teams met and coordinated their work in the course of the research. This book is the report of the France team.

There will be one more stage to complete the project. A six-country group of participants, including Americans, will prepare an explicitly comparative volume, job by job. They will try to fathom what deeper attitudinal, institutional, and circumstantial factors might explain the sometimes dramatic differences in the way these six modern nations engage with the problem of low-wage work.

One big, somewhat unexpected, finding is the one mentioned in the first paragraph of this introduction. The six countries differ substantially in the incidence of low-wage work. ("Incidence" is defined as the fraction of all workers, in the country or in a specific sector, who fall into the low-wage category.)

There is an interesting and important definitional issue that arises immediately. Uniformly in Europe (and elsewhere), a low-wage worker is anyone who earns less than two-thirds of the national median wage (usually the gross hourly wage, if only for data-availability reasons). This obviously makes the incidence of low-wage work an index of the inequality or dispersion of the wage distribution: multiplying or dividing everyone's wage by ten leaves the number of low-wage workers unchanged. The same applies to the measurement of poverty. In the United States, the poverty line is an absolute income. It was initially chosen as an empirical compromise, never entirely appropriate and less so as time passes, but nevertheless an absolute income. The United States has no corresponding definition for low-wage work, but the same approach could be taken. There are arguments to be made on both sides of this issue; for the purposes of this project, the choice of a low-wage threshold makes little practical difference. We use the European definition because that is the way their data are collected.

There is yet another practical reason to use the European definition. As noted, the two-thirds-of-median index simply reflects the degree of wage dispersion: a low incidence of low-wage work means a relatively compressed wage distribution, at least in the lower tail. This measure makes international comparisons more meaningful.

Comparing absolute real wages between the United States and other countries is problematic because pensions, health care, payroll taxes, employer contributions and other such benefits and deductions are handled differently in different systems. Relative comparisons are subject to similar distortions, but considerably less so.

Here are the basic facts. In 2005, the incidence of low-wage work was 25 percent in the United States, 22.1 percent in the United Kingdom, 20.8 percent in Germany (2004), 18.2 percent in the Netherlands (2004), 12.7 percent in France (2002) and 8.5 percent in Denmark. The range is obviously very wide.

In a way, that is helpful, because figures like this cannot be interpreted to the last decimal. Here is one interesting example of an unexpected twist. It turns out that the Dutch are the part-time champions among these countries, with a significantly larger fraction of part-time workers than elsewhere. This appears to be a voluntary choice, not something compelled by the unavailability of full-time work. Part-time workers tend to be paid lower hourly wages than full-time workers in the same or similar jobs, even in countries where it is against the law to discriminate against part-timers. The incidence measures given in the preceding paragraph are based on a head-count: 18 percent of all Dutch workers earn less than the low-wage threshold. One could with reason ask instead what fraction of the hours worked in the Netherlands falls into the low-wage category; the answer is about 16 percent. The fact that the hours-based incidence is lower would be common in all countries, but the difference is particularly large in the Netherlands.

A key issue is the degree of mobility out of low-wage work that characterizes each country's system. The seriousness of the "problem" turns almost entirely on the transitory nature of low-wage work. It is impossible to be precise about inter-country differences, because the data are sketchy and definitions vary. It is clear, however, that there are substantial differences among the countries, although mobility is fairly substantial everywhere, if only because younger workers eventually propel themselves into better jobs. The Danes appear to have the shortest residence times in low-wage work. For Americans the take-away lesson is that the self-image of an extremely mobile society is not valid, at least not in this respect.

Of course, there are many uniformities—often just what you would expect—among these countries in the pattern of low-wage work. The "concentration" of low-wage work in any subgroup of the population is defined as the incidence in that subgroup divided by the incidence among all workers. For instance, any subgroup with a higher incidence than the country at large will have a concentration index bigger than 1. This is the case for workers in the service sector of the economy, for women, for young people, for part-timers, and for those with little education. In most instances, the particular sectors we have picked out for study have a high concentration index; together, retail trade and "hotels and catering" have a concentration ratio of about 3 in the Netherlands. The categories mentioned obviously overlap, but the data do not permit us to zero in statistically on young part-time secondary-school-only women working in supermarkets. Nevertheless, the odds are very high that they fall into the low-wage category.

The cross-country differences are more interesting, however, because they at least offer the possibility that we can find explanations for them in the circumstances, institutions, attitudes and policies of these basically similar economies. It is important that these are basically similar economic systems with broadly similar labor markets. They differ in certain historically established social norms, institutions and policies. One can hope to figure out which of these fairly small differences underlie the observed variation in the conditions of low-wage work. This would be difficult or even meaningless if we were comparing radically different economic systems.

Here is one example of commonality that illustrates the point. In some of the target jobs, in several instances and several countries, there has been a noticeable increase in the intensity of competition in the relevant product market. Low-cost German chains compete with Dutch food retailers. Large food retailers, domestic and foreign, put pressure on meat processing and confectionary prices in every country. The spread of international hotel chains—along with the availability of exhaustive price comparisons on the internet—has made the hotel business more competitive. In all such instances, business firms respond to intensified competition by trying to lower their own unit costs (as well as by product differentiation, quality improvement, and other devices).

The urgent need to reduce costs seems almost invariably—though not exclusively—to involve particular pressure on the wages of low-skilled workers. It is not hard to understand why this should happen in every country, precisely because they are all advanced capitalist market economies. The main reason is that low-wage workers usually have very little "firm-specific human capital." That is to say, since they have few skills of any kind, they have few skills that are difficult to replace for the firm that employs them. If they quit in response to wage reductions, they can be replaced with little cost, especially in a slack labor market. Low-wage workers have few alternatives, so they cannot defend themselves well. For similar reasons, they have little political power and usually little clout with their trade unions, if they have any union protection at all. Firms seeking profit will respond similarly, though not identically in every detail. Country-specific institutions can modify the response, but not entirely.

A closely related common factor has to do with "flexibility." Partly because technology now permits it, and partly because a globalized market now demands it, business firms find that their level of production has to fluctuate seasonally, cyclically and erratically. Sometimes it is not so much the total but the composition of production that has to change, often with short notice. Under those circumstances, it is an advantage if the firm can vary its employment more or less at will; otherwise, underutilized labor constitutes an unproductive cost. The low-end labor force is likely to bear the brunt of this adjustment, for the same reasons already mentioned in connection with wage pressure. Low-wage workers cannot do much to defend themselves against or prepare themselves for these vicissitudes, other than to try for even lower-wage part-time jobs or to resort to public assistance.

There is always a possibility that observed cross-country variation in low-wage employment practices are somehow "natural," in the sense that they can be traced to underlying differences that were not chosen and could not be changed, such as geographical or topographical characteristics, resource availability, or perhaps even some irreversible bit of historical evolution. That does not seem to be what is happening in these six countries. In many instances, cross-country differences are the result of legislation, with minimum wage laws being an obvious example. A more unusual example, at least to Americans, is the fact that many European governments, such as those in France and the Netherlands, can and do extend certain collective bargaining agreements to cover employers and workers in the industry who were not parties to the bargaining itself. In this way, even comparatively small union density can lead to much broader coverage by union agreements.

This need not be an unalloyed benefit to workers. Companies have been known to arrange to bargain with a small, weak union and then press for the resulting favorable agreement to be generalized. But the practice may also reflect a desire by employers to eliminate large wage differentials as a factor in inter-firm competition. It is interesting that when the abolition of this practice of extending collective bargaining agreements was proposed in the Netherlands, the employers' federation opposed the proposal. It is a toss-up which event seems more outlandish to an American: the practice of mandatory extension or that employers should oppose abolishing it.

Explicit legislation is not the only source of institutional differences that affect the low-wage labor market. All sorts of behavioral norms, attitudes, and traditions on both sides of the labor market can have persistent effects. The country narratives describe many such influences. For example, the German report outlines a distinctive system of wage determination and labor relations, based on diversified high-quality, high-value-added industrial production, along with "patient," mostly bank-provided, capital, and participation of employee representatives in company supervisory boards.

This system may be coming to an end, undermined by international competition—especially from the ex-communist countries of eastern Europe, including the reunification of Germany—and shifts in public opinion and political power. It is still a matter of controversy among specialists whether the traditional system had become unsustainable or simply unsustained. The German "mini-job," low wage, frequently incurring lower non-wage employment costs in practice, and limited to very short hours per month, is an example of a device to encourage both demand and supply for certain kinds of low-wage work.

This introduction is not the place for a detailed description of each national system. The individual country narratives will provide that. It is important, however, to underline the fact that the components of each national system often hang together in some way. It may not be possible to single out one component and think: "That looks clever; why don't we try it in our country?" The German mini-job, for example, is occupied mostly by women, and may work the way it does because the social welfare apparatus in Germany is still organized around the notion of the single-breadwinner family. The concept of a labor relations "system" may suggest tighter-fitting than the facts justify; a word like "pattern" might be more accurate. But the basic point remains.

The four continental countries in the study correspond in a general way to the common notion of a "European social model" in contrast with the more individual-responsibility oriented approach of the United States. The post-Thatcher United Kingdom probably falls somewhere in between. It would be a bad mistake, however, to ignore the differences among Denmark, France, Germany, and the Netherlands. To do so would be to miss the variety of conditions for low-wage labor that is possible for advanced capitalist market economies. Only the briefest characterization is possible here, but the individual reports are quite complete.

The Danish "flexicurity" system has achieved the status of a buzzword. The idea is to allow wages and job quality to be determined in an unregulated labor market (except for considerations of health and safety, of course) but to combine this flexibility with a very generous safety net, so that "no Dane should suffer economic hardship." For this system to be workable, the rules of the safety net have to push most recipients into whatever jobs are available. Even so, the system is likely to be expensive. Apparently the *lowest* marginal income tax rate is 44 percent (which is higher than the *highest* rate in the U.S.). One would need to know more about the details of the tax system in order to understand the content of any such comparison, but the details are unlikely to reverse the presumption that Danes are less tax-averse than some others.

To describe the Danish labor market as "unregulated" means only that there is very little intervention by the government. In fact, the labor market is regulated through centralized negotiations between representatives of employers and employees, who have very wide scope. For example, there is no statutory minimum wage, but a minimum labor scale is negotiated by the "social partners." It (almost) goes without saying that there is some evasion of this scale in traditional low-wage sectors, including some covered in the case studies. One reason why this is tolerated is that many of the affected workers are young people, especially students, who are only engaged in low-wage part-time work as a transitory phase. Denmark is a country that is low on university enrollments but high on vocationally-oriented post-secondary, non-university education.

There is a neat contrast here with France, which lives up to its reputation as a rather bureaucratically organized society. As the French report says, "Low hourly wages are fixed in France—perhaps more than in any other country—at the political level, not through collective bargaining agreements, and these wage rates are set in a centralized, not decentralized, manner. Thus, the legal minimum wage plays a crucial role in France." Since 1970, the SMIC (minimum interbranch growth wage) is indexed not only to inflation but also to the growth of overall productivity and wages. The intent was specifically to resist what was felt to be a tendency in the market toward excessive wage inequality.

The SMIC has been set at a fairly high level, and one consequence of this has been the disappearance of some unskilled jobs, to be replaced by unemployment (especially long-term unemployment), participation in active labor market policies, and withdrawal from the labor force. Other forces have been at work, however—urban land-use regulation in food retailing, for example—so the simple-minded causal connection between the SMIC and high unemployment is not exact. France is also distinguished by having a trade union movement that is rather strong at the national level, but has very little presence on the shop floor. This may account for some evasion of labor market regulations at the low end.

The low-wage labor market in the United Kingdom is especially interesting because it is an example of changes in institutions and outcomes brought about in a relatively short time by deliberate acts of policy. The Thatcher government chose as a matter of principle to weaken or eliminate preexisting supports for the occupants of low-quality jobs, and to undermine the ability of the trade union movement to compress the wage distribution. As a result, the incidence of low-wage work increased in the late 1970s and after. The Blair government, looking for a work-based solution to the problem of poverty, undertook measures to increase the supply of low-wage workers, but it also introduced a (fairly low) National Minimum Wage in 1999. The net outcome appears to have been a steady increase in the incidence of low-wage work from the late 1970s until the mid-1990s, and a leveling-off since then.

In effect, the United Kingdom has changed from a system rather like the other continental European countries to something much closer to the United States. The incidence of low-wage work has then followed the same trajectory. Of course, other economic factors, common to many countries, were also at work.

The Netherlands occupies a position somewhere between the Nordic model and the United States model, but not in a simple average sense. Many of the institutions are peculiarly Dutch; together they are described as the "Polder" model. One of its features is the important extent to which organizations representing employers, the government, and labor act jointly to regulate the labor market and much else, sometimes in a very detailed way. For instance, the minimum wage for young workers is substantially lower than for adults. The proliferation of part-time jobs, many of them occupied by students and young people, may be a consequence of this in part, though it may have other roots as well.

It is striking to an outsider that these tripartite institutions are more than merely regulatory. They are described as "deliberative," and apparently much of the serious public discussion of issues underlying socioeconomic policy takes place within them. This fact may make fairly tight regulation palatable to the Dutch public. The system has had considerable success; for example, the national unemployment rate fell from over 10 percent in 1984 to under 4 percent in 2001, when the widespread recession supervened. As will be seen in the Dutch report, however, it has its problems.

The purpose of these brief vignettes is definitely not to provide a summary of the pattern evolved in each of these countries with respect to low-wage job quality. That information is to be found in each of the separate country studies. The goal of this introduction is to illustrate the important general point that there are several viable systems of labor-market governance, including the mode of management of the low-wage labor market. The issue is not uniquely determined by the needs of a functioning market economy, or by technology, or by the imperatives of efficient organization. The system in place in each country has evolved in response to historical circumstances, cultural preferences, political styles and fashion in economic and social ideas. One cannot avoid noticing that relatively small countries, like Denmark and the Netherlands in our sample, and the other Nordic countries, Austria and perhaps Ireland outside it, seem more able than large countries to create and maintain the amount of trust that is needed for tripartite cooperation. This observation begs the question as to whether successful policy aimed at improving the relative status of low-wage workers may require a degree of social solidarity and trust that may be beyond larger, more diverse populations.

There are certainly many common influences as well: the response to intensified competition; the role of women, immigrants, and minorities; limitations on productivity; and so on. But there is no unique or best pattern. It even seems likely that the same "principles" of organization, applied in different institutional contexts, would eventuate in quite different practices. Some of this may emerge in the detailed comparative volume that is still to come.

The lowness of low wages and the place of low-wage workers in society are to a much greater extent national political issues in France than in the other countries engaged in this study. This institutional fact perhaps reflects traditional French bureaucratization, but its significance extends far beyond that. Discussion of the minimum wage in France often focuses on "inclusion." The idea is that the function of the minimum wage is not merely to provide an income that makes it possible, say, to have a physiologically adequate diet but one that underpins a socially tolerable standard of living. The initial attempt at a legal minimum wage in 1950 was indexed to inflation, but it soon fell behind the advance of the general wage level. (Remember that the minimum wage in the United States is not even indexed to inflation, so it will tend to fall even further behind the median standard of living; it is revised only at politically convenient intervals, which are often long intervals.)

Since 1970, the minimum wage in France (the SMIC) has been tied not only to inflation but to productivity, so that it will tend to rise approximately in parallel with the general wage level. The attitudinal difference behind this decision explains why the European definition of low-wage work is a purely relative one, unlike the "poverty line" notion in the United States: when the "low-wage" cutoff is set at two-thirds of the median national wage, it automatically moves in step with the median. In fact, in France the low-wage cutoff is only a few percentage points higher than the SMIC. Thus, anyone who advances beyond a minimum-wage job is very likely to leave the low-wage category. The fairly low incidence of low-wage work in France must reflect this political decision to keep the SMIC fairly high; it is almost illegal to fall very far below the low-wage threshold.

Other aspects of the French system of regulation of the labor market seem to be consistent with what has just been described. For example, the trade unions operate almost entirely at the national political level. Even at their most powerful, they have had very little presence in the workplace, so that job quality issues that slip between the legislative cracks are more likely to be ignored than in systems where there is local bargaining or an effective grievance mechanism. Even regulations that are part of labor law may not be well enforced. Perhaps for this reason, union membership is very low, and any kind of industrial action is possible only in parts of the public sector, like education and transportation.

It is an important part of the picture that unemployment has been chronically high in France for a couple of decades. One line of (partial) causality may run from a high minimum wage to high unemployment among the unskilled. The missing jobs simply are not viable at the going wage. One sees this effect not only in the absence of very low-end jobs in food retailing (a large source of low-wage work in the United States) but also in the more general fact that some French industries are more capital-intensive than the corresponding industry in the United States, indicating a market-induced substitution of capital for labor.

But causality also runs the other way. Long periods of high unemployment force more highly qualified workers to compete for unskilled jobs, leaving no room for the unskilled who might otherwise fill them. The latter may then be relegated to casual or illegal jobs or to living outside the labor market altogether. The chances of leaving this rock-bottom status get smaller the longer one stays in it. The unemployment pool may then come to contain a large fraction of very long-term unemployed.

The contributors to this volume suggest a further ramification. It appears that French workers report an even greater feeling of job insecurity—"precariousness"—than the data suggest they should. This malaise may reflect the understanding that loss of a job, even for accidental reasons, could all too easily lead to a long spell of unemployment and permanent deterioration of one's labor market prospects.

Although the incidence of low-wage work in France is quite low, the pattern is similar to the other countries in the study. Above-average rates of low-wage work are most common among women, the young, and those with little or no educational qualification. It is hard to say anything about ethnic differences because it is official policy not to make that statistical distinction among French nationals. But nationals of other European Union countries have a slightly higher incidence, and nationals of non-EU countries have an even higher incidence. The differences among occupations and sectors are the standard ones.

The French study is particularly interesting precisely because the

French economy is managed so differently from the American economy (and to a slightly lesser extent, from the other continental European countries included in the comparative study). Although France's persistently high unemployment is outside the scope of this study, there is still a lot be learned from the country and its economy about the possible versions of modern capitalism and their special characteristics.

CHAPTER 1

Low-Wage Work: The Political Debate and Research Agenda in France

Ève Caroli and Jérôme Gautié

The impact on the low-skilled/low-pay labor market of economic factors such as technical change, globalization, and, to a lesser extent, changes in financial markets has been scrutinized by many research works both in the United States and Europe. France is no exception in having been exposed to these global trends: new technologies have spread rapidly during the last decades, both the exports and imports ratio to GDP were twice those of the United States in the mid-2000s, and foreign investors, particularly pension funds, are very active on the French stock market. But the same factors may not generate the same labor market outcomes in France as are seen in other countries; the impact of these factors may depend on the institutional context.

Indeed, compared to the United States, the French labor market displays very specific features: a high legal minimum wage, strong employment protection legislation, and a highly restrictive immigration policy are only the most obvious differences. How do French firms respond to economic pressures in such a context, and what have been the consequences for low-wage workers? Can we find differences in strategies and outcomes when we compare French firms to American or other European firms?

A few years ago, *Low-Wage America* by Eileen Appelbaum, Annette Bernhardt, and Richard Murnane (2003) drew on extensive fieldwork to provide a very detailed picture of the lower reaches of the American job market. The present volume addresses the same issues for France, drawing on comparative research from four other European countries: Denmark, Germany, the Netherlands, and the United Kingdom. It aims at highlighting the role of national institutions in shaping the employment and working conditions of low-wage workers—defined as earning less than two-thirds of the median hourly wage.

From this point of view, France stands as a good comparison point given that its labor market institutions are in stark contrast to American ones. As a consequence, the pay and working conditions of low-wage workers are likely to be very different in these two countries. This introduction sets the scene by describing the main features of the French labor market. Its aim is also to contribute to an understanding of how these features have shaped the social and political debate on low-wage work in France, which is quite different from that debate in the United States.

A KEY FACTOR: THE MINIMUM WAGE

Low hourly wages are fixed in France—perhaps more than in any other country—at the political level, not through collective bargaining agreements, and these wage rates are set in a centralized, not a decentralized, manner. Thus, the legal minimum wage plays a crucial role in France.

THE MINIMUM WAGE POLICY IN THE POST–WORLD WAR II ERA

There has long been political concern at the central government level about low wages in France. From a historical perspective, the political and social issues at stake turn on integrating the working class into society and on maintaining the stability of the republican regime. As in many other European countries, these issues have also reflected the strength of left-wing and labor movements since the second half of the nineteenth century, as well as the weakening of the political system in the wake of the wars and crises running from 1914 to 1945 (for a comparative historical analysis, see Alesina and Glaeser 2004). In the aftermath of World War II, in 1950, the first national legal minimum hourly wage (the Minimum, Interbranch, Guaranteed Wage, or SMIG), indexed to inflation, was introduced. It was conceived as a "fair wage" that would balance the relationship between the wage earner and the employer in the face of disequilibria that could favor the latter, and also as a "decent wage," with an explicit reference to needs.[1]

In 1970 this minimum wage was transformed into the SMIC (salaire minimum interprofessionnel de croissance, or interprofessional, index-linked growth minimum wage), which is automatically indexed not only to inflation but also partially to real growth.[2] The

SMIC was brought in because the SMIG had not allowed the fruits of growth to be distributed equitably: at the end of the 1960s, France suffered from record wage inequalities among the OECD countries (the 90/10 pay ratio had reached more than 4; see Piketty 2003). The implementation of the SMIC relied on a political and social consensus according to which a decent wage should be defined not only in absolute but also in relative terms and thus low wages should benefit from growth and be indexed to the average wage increase. This is a major difference with the American minimum wage. It should also be remembered that, unlike in the United States, poverty is defined in relative terms in France, as it is in many other European countries—the poverty line being defined as a percentage of the standardized, median income.

The introduction of the SMIC was followed by strong minimum wage growth in both relative and real terms: the French minimum wage real value doubled between 1970 and 2005, whereas in the United States the real value of the federal minimum wage was 34 percent lower in 2005 than in 1970. Overall, at the beginning of 2006, the monthly purchasing power of a full-time minimum wage earner was nearly 45 percent higher in France than in the United States (at the federal minimum wage level). Yet, most French workers believe that the purchasing power of the minimum wage is still too low.

It should also be remembered that besides the SMIC there is a means-tested "basic income" in France (revenu minimum d'insertion [RMI]).[3] The RMI benefit is computed as the difference between a reference threshold and the resources of the household (including family benefits).[4] It amounted to about 40 percent of the full-time, monthly SMIC (net of social contributions) in 2006; at that rate, it limits the development of very poorly paid work.

Overall, both the SMIC and the RMI are representative of the well-documented difference in attitudes toward poverty and inequality between France (and most European countries) and the United States (see Alesina and Glaeser 2004).

"FRANCE JOBLESS" COMPARED TO "AMERICA PENNILESS"?

Another key difference between the French and the American labor markets is the level of unemployment: during the last two decades it has been about twice as high in France as in the United States (around 10 percent compared to around 5 percent).[5] France is also characterized by a strong compression at the bottom of the wage distribution and by a limited number of low-wage workers, as we will see in chapter 2.[6] Does the low number of low-wage workers not simply stem from the fact that many workers who should earn low wages are priced out of the labor market?

This question has been much debated in France in recent years. Some indicators indeed suggest that there may be a shortage of low-skilled jobs, leading to a crowding-out of people who would otherwise be low-wage workers. The unemployment rate among the low-skilled is high, and the number of jobs in the sectors in which low-skilled labor is concentrated is relatively low (especially compared to the United States). Production processes also appear to be particularly capital-intensive in France. An indicator of this is the record high rate of hourly labor productivity. This may also be the outcome of a selection effect if a substantial proportion of potentially low-productivity workers are crowded out of the labor market.

Besides unemployment, many potential low-wage workers are on active labor market policy schemes. Others benefit from various social allowances (such as public early retirement schemes, basic income support, and so on). It should be noted, however, that these are partly "functional equivalents" of incapacity benefits, which cover a large share of the working-age population in other European countries (especially the United Kingdom and the Netherlands).

A HIGHLY REGULATED LABOR MARKET?

France is without doubt the country that best illustrates the contrast between (continental) European labor markets and the American market: the former have numerous rules and regulations protecting workers, whereas the latter is characterized by (nearly) unlimited flexibility. On closer inspection, however, this distinction as it applies to France and the United States is not quite so clear. France has among the lowest rates of unionization in the OECD. At the same time its unions appear to be powerful, but only at certain levels. State regulation in France is extensive compared to other OECD countries, but it is often contradictory and badly applied.

POWERFUL UNIONS?

Seen from outside, French industrial relations appear highly paradoxical. Any foreigner who gets caught up in a public transport strike in Paris or a major demonstration may indeed conclude that France is the last remaining industrialized country to experience massive labor movement mobilizations.[7] The unions would surely have appeared powerful and highly politicized to such a visitor. And yet, union membership rates are very low (and clearly lower than in the United States). Overall, about 8 percent of the labor force is unionized, and only 5 percent in the private sector.

So what is the reality behind the figures? Because union membership is high in certain key parts of the public sector (transport, energy, education, tax collection), industrial disputes can block or strongly disrupt the functioning of the economy. In the private sector too, the unions are more powerful than such low membership levels would allow in other countries. This follows from the rules governing labor representation and the legal extension of collective bargaining agreements across branches. Overall, the unions do play an important role in regulating the labor market.

However, given the state of industrial relations in France (divisions among unions, poor relations between unions and management), negotiations at the branch and national levels are not as active as they could be—especially concerning low wage rates. As a result, the state (that is, the law) often has to intervene when negotiations break down. Massive strikes may also be seen as a symptom of unions' failure to promote their views at the political level—and therefore as another sign of their weakness.

Moreover, at a more decentralized level, the unions are relatively absent in the workplace, for historical reasons, compared not only to other European countries but even to the United States. They are also often divided. Consequently, in many companies (and not just small firms) unions do not exercise their functions of being a countervailing power or controlling the application of rules and laws. Overall, if France ranks very high in terms of the union protection index, unions are weak at the firm level.[8]

The Central (and Contested) Role of Labor Law

The weakness of industrial relations and the strength of the law go together in France, but it is not easy to determine which is the cause and which is the consequence: they tend to reinforce each other.[9] Regulations (codified in the Labor Code, which is more than two thousand pages long) abound in all areas, including employment protection, working time, and hygiene and safety. But there seems to be a gap between the formal institutional framework and effective regulation.

Overregulation may have something to do with this, to the extent that it may lead to a lack of clarity and poor enforcement. There are many rules, but at the same time many exceptions or derogations to these rules. The labor standards and the employment protection legislation (EPL) are a good illustration of this. French EPL is considered among the most stringent in the OECD (see OECD 2004). However, in almost all sectors there exist special labor contracts, or derogations to the rules guiding the two traditional and well-protected types of contract—open-ended contracts and fixed-term contracts. Overall, there are more than fifteen labor contracts in France, and these serve to raise actual labor flexibility far beyond what could be expected when considering standard indicators of EPL.

The laws on the reduction of working time (implementing the thirty-five-hour working week), adopted at the end of the 1990s, provide a good example of the complexity and lack of transparency in French labor law. Taken as a whole, the texts of the two main laws (the so-called Aubry laws of 1998 and 2000, named after the minister of labor, Martine Aubry) run to several thousand pages. While many employers complain about them, these laws actually include numerous adjustments and adaptations to allow for greater flexibility.

Overall, in many areas of labor regulation rules seem to lead both to greater flexibility and to more rigidity. As a result, it should be noted that it is very difficult to construct indices that properly measure the way existing rules constrain the functioning of the French labor market.

Furthermore, even when the rules are clear, they are often not respected, and the state does not always give itself the resources to enforce them. Indeed, the number of labor inspectors is limited (about one for every 1,100 firms), so that controls and sanctions are few and often low. This problem is compounded by the weakness or even absence of unions in the workplace.

THE RESEARCH AGENDA AND THE POLITICAL AND SOCIAL DEBATES: A DIFFERENT FOCUS

All these features help to explain why social and political concerns are different in France and in the United States. In the latter, much attention is paid to the problem of low-wage workers in connection with the "working poor" phenomenon, whose causes are partly different in France than in the United States. In France the working poor are more often part-time workers or workers facing precariousness (such as alternating periods of employment and non-employment). When the worker is employed full-time and continuously, the minimum wage is often sufficient to escape poverty. In the United States, the fact that a significant share of the working poor have full-time jobs and are continuously employed throughout the year, explains the attention paid there to the problem of insufficient hourly wages (and therefore the ongoing debate about the minimum wage level and "living wages").

More generally, in the United States analyses of the labor market refer mainly to wages and incomes. For example, studies on changes in the nature of employment (occupations) in the economy tend to classify jobs by wage levels, and increasing earnings inequality is a key issue (see, for instance, Autor, Katz, and Kearney 2006). In contrast, in France—where inequalities have remained relatively stable in the past two decades—research has concentrated much more on employment levels (and symmetrically on unemployment). Interest in low wages and "the working poor" is less strong and more recent. Also, studies on trends in occupations classify them by skill levels (or "qualifications" according to the classification of the Institut National de la Statistique et des Études Économiques [INSEE], or National Institute for Statistics and Economic Studies) rather than by earnings levels. Attention focuses in particular on unemployment and on the matching of workers with jobs according to their skills. This is of great importance given that constraints on many young and educated workers force them to take unskilled jobs. As a result, research has focused more on "low-skilled" (or "unskilled") jobs rather than on "low-wage" workers (for a comprehensive survey of the issue, see, for instance, Méda and Vennat 2005).

Another key difference is the focus on the job instability and insecurity issue, induced by the proliferation of so-called atypical (that is, nonpermanent) work contracts. Indeed, this "precariousness" issue pervades all discussion on labor and social policy in France, whereas it is much less of an issue in Northern Europe and the United States (Barbier 2004).

THE OUTLINE OF THE BOOK

The aim of this volume is to tackle the low-wage work issue in the French context. More specifically, we investigate to what extent the pay and working conditions of low-wage workers are influenced by national and local institutions, either directly or in response to changing economic conditions.

Chapter 2 tackles this issue at the macro level. As a first step, it provides an overview of low-wage work in France. The incidence of low-wage work in France is rather limited (about 12 percent), and if anything, it is on a declining trend. As in many countries, low-wage jobs are concentrated in the service sector and in low-skilled occupations, and women, young workers, and foreigners are particularly affected. Moreover, high work intensity and bad working conditions (compared to other European countries) characterize low-skilled/low-paid jobs. The second part of the chapter investigates the potential impact of labor market institutions on the incidence and characteristics of low-wage work. The minimum wage plays, of course, a crucial role, but labor market regulations and industrial relations also come up as important factors. Another characteristic of the French labor market is the high and persistent rate of unemployment. The last part of the chapter investigates the reasons why this model of high (hourly) wages, high work intensity, and low employment has remained so stable until now. Strict immigration policy and social benefits play an important role, and strong social distrust seems to have been an obstacle to any deep structural reforms to date.

Aside this general overview of the French low-wage labor market, our research is based on case studies carried out in five sectors. These sectors have been chosen because of their importance in the lower end of labor markets, in both Europe and the United Sates. The methodology is very similar for all sectors: seven to eight firms were visited in each sector, and interviews were carried out with managers, workers' representatives, and a sample of workers in all firms. Overall, a total of 40 establishments were studied and more than 530 employees were interviewed, mostly in 2005.

Chapter 3 presents the food-processing sector. Given its great diversity, we focus on two subsectors, meat processing and confectionery. Food manufacturing is the only manufacturing sector in our sample, and it is quite representative of the French employment model. The share of low-wage work is small despite the large number of low-skilled workers. The sector is facing increasing competitive pressure and rising flexibility requirements. However, none of the firms in our sample has implemented "social dumping" strategies. Compensation is under pressure, but many firms have also tried to cut costs by computerizing their production process and introducing new forms of work organization, especially multitasking. This has had contradictory effects on workers: on the one hand, physical labor is not as hard, but on the other, some work intensification has taken place, which was not compensated by wage increases.

Interestingly, some of these features can also be found in the hospital sector (chapter 4). The study focuses on nurses' aides and hospital service workers, among whom the proportion of low-wage workers is very low. This is partly due to the fact that the sector is highly regulated, in terms of both product (health regulations) and employment (the leading role of the public sector). Overall, nurses' aides and hospital service workers are more highly skilled in France than in the United States, and their jobs appear to be rather attractive. But segmentation is a structural feature of employment in this sector: employers regularly use an important stock of nonpermanent workers, who are waiting to get open-ended contracts. Economic conditions are changing along with the technological change and increasing competition between private and public hospitals and within the public sector. Hospitals adjust to these changes by increasing productivity through mechanization of certain tasks and rising work intensity. Outsourcing is also used but remains marginal. As in the food-processing sector, the traditional employment model is still dominant.

The situation is somewhat different in the hotel sector (chapter 5), where the proportion of low-wage workers is much higher. As for hospital service workers in the previous chapter, the study focuses on housekeepers. Almost all employees in these jobs are women—many of them of foreign origin—and they are paid wages that hardly enable them to support a family. They also have very few career prospects, and long working hours as well as undeclared work are characteristics of their jobs. A lack of labor regulations is one of the reasons why housekeepers fare so much worse in the hotel sector than in the hospital sector. Labor regulations are much less favorable in this sector than in others owing to the weakness of collective bargaining and to sector-specific employer dispensations from the Labor Code resulting from the very low rate of unionization and the strong lobbying power of employers. Overall, hotel housekeeper jobs are both insecure and low-paid. These workers hardly benefit from technological improvements and continuous training, even though in some hotels management has been making some positive initiatives.

Chapter 6 takes us into the retail sector, where the proportion of low-wage workers is also quite high on average. The focus is on cashiers, delicatessen sales staff in large food retailers, and electrical/electronics sales staff. The pay conditions of workers in these jobs appear to be very different across types of stores. Hard-discount food stores offer rock-bottom wages, but most large retailers pay relatively high hourly wages. In the electrical and electronics sector, high demand for efficient sales staff and incentive pay schemes has pushed wages up. But in food retailing a different mechanism is at play. The "high roads" are supported by high legal entry barriers, which generate rents for firms. Some of these rents are redistributed to workers to compensate them for the demanding work requirements—in particular, the imposition of part-time schedules, the very high labor productivity, and the often harmful working conditions. So, despite very low rates of unionization and no specific labor market regulations, hourly wages are not so low in many large retail stores.

Chapter 7 deals with the most recent of all these employment sectors, namely, call centers. The main focus of the study is on operators in in-house call centers in the bank/insurance and utilities subsectors, where the incidence of low-wage work is rather limited. Branch-level institutions are still being developed, but national institutions play a key role in accounting for the rather high level of wages. First, many workers are covered by the favorable collective agreements covering the bank and utilities sectors. Second, the high level of the French minimum wage has led many call centers to specialize in high-value-added activities; because these can involve rather complex tasks, operators must have a minimum level of social skills and communication competence. To attract such workers, wages cannot be too low, especially since the level of mental strain remains very high for operators. In contrast, a high incidence of low-wage work and classical forms of bad working conditions prevail at independent call centers, where the institutional environment is much looser.

In chapter 8, we conclude by offering a synthesis of our findings.

We are particularly grateful to Annette Bernhardt, and Tom Cook, who reviewed first drafts of the book. We also thank all the members of the French team, including Christine Erhel, Gilbert Lefèvre, and François Michon (who are not co-authors of the following chapters), as well as Gerhard Bosch, Aixa Cintrón-Valdez, Geoff Mason, Ken Mayhew, Niels Westergaard-Nielsen, Wiemer Salverda, Christopher Tilly, Eric

Wanner, and an anonymous referee for useful comments and suggestions. We are also grateful to Nicholas Sowels for translation and rewriting assistance for chapters 1, 2, 3, 6, 7, and 8. The usual disclaimer applies.

NOTES

1. This concept of a "decent wage" may be linked to the notion of a "living wage" in the United States.
2. More precisely, the SMIC is indexed to consumer prices (for rises of 2 percent or more) and must be raised every year by at least half of the increase in the hourly wage rate of all blue collar workers.
3. Every French resident age twenty-five or more is entitled to this social allowance.
4. For instance, in January 2006 the reference benefit was €433 (US$617) for a single person, €650 (US$926) for a couple, and €909 (US$1,295) for a couple with two children.
5. See Krugman (1994).
6. This is a direct consequence of a high minimum wage in relative terms.
7. In March 2006, one to three million people marched in France against a law making labor contracts for young people more flexible. The law was finally withdrawn.
8. The union protection index is an average of indicators of protection, such as the extension of collective agreements, requirements for works councils, the nonreplacement of striking workers, and the legality of sympathy strikes (see Siebert 2005, 4).
9. Note that this reinforcing effect may be one factor in the path dependency phenomenon put forward by Juan Botero and his colleagues (2004) to account for the permanence of legal systems in general and in particular the civil law tradition in France.

REFERENCES

Alesina, Alberto, and Edward L. Glaeser. 2004. *Fighting Poverty in the United States and Europe: A World of Difference.* Oxford: Oxford University Press.

Appelbaum, Eileen, Annette Bernhardt, and Richard J. Murnane, editors. 2003. *Low-Wage America.* New York: Russell Sage Foundation.

Autor, David, Lawrence F. Katz, and Melissa S. Kearney. 2006. "The Polarization of the U.S. Labor Market." Working paper 11986. Cambridge, Mass.: National Bureau of Economic Research (January).

Barbier, Jean-Claude. 2004. "A Comparative Analysis of 'Employment Precariousness' in Europe." In *Learning from Employment and Welfare Policies in Europe*, edited by Marie-Thérèse Letablier, *Cross-National Research Papers* (European Research Center) 7(3, May).

Botero, Juan, Simeon Djankov, Rafael La Porta, Florencio C. Lopez-de-Silanes, and Andrei Shleifer. 2004. "The Regulation of Labor." *Quarterly Journal of Economics* 119(4, November): 1339–82.

Krugman, Paul. 1994. "Europe Jobless, America Penniless?" *Foreign Policy* 95(Summer): 19–34.

Méda, Dominique, and Francis Vennat. 2005. *Le Travail non qualifié: Permanence et paradoxes* [*Unqualified Work: Permanence and Paradoxes*]. Paris: Editions La Découverte.

Organization for Economic Cooperation and Development (OECD). 2004. "Employment Protection Regulation and Labor Market Performance." In *OECD Employment Outlook 2004* (July).

Piketty, Thomas. 2003. "Income Inequality in France, 1900–1998." *Journal of Political Economy* 111(5): 1004–42.

Siebert, W. Stanley. 2005. "Labor Market Regulation: Some Comparative Lessons." *Economic Affairs* 25(3, September): 3–10.

CHAPTER 2

Low-Wage Work and Labor Market Institutions in France

Ève Caroli, Jérôme Gautié, and Philippe Askenazy

This chapter presents an overview of the low-wage labor market in France. The presentation is intended to provide background information for the following industry chapters and to highlight the specifics of the French low-wage labor market from a comparative perspective.

The first section presents the main characteristics of the French low-wage labor market and its evolution during the past decade. It highlights the high level of unemployment and the small proportion of low-wage workers compared to the United States as well as to some other European countries. The next section investigates the role of the minimum wage in reaching this "equilibrium" and discusses how French firms cope with the cost of labor. Some empirical evidence suggests that increasing capital and work intensity is one of the main strategies, with a subsequent deterioration in working conditions. Another solution, however, lies in withdrawing from activities that are low-skilled and potentially low-wage and labor-intensive. That discussion is followed by a section in which the role of employment protection and industrial relations is scrutinized. Although employment protection legislation (EPL) appears to be quite stringent in France at a global level, workers in the low-skilled segment of the labor market are actually rather poorly protected. There is indeed a gap between EPL in theory and practice. We relate this to the very peculiar nature of industrial relations: whereas unions are fairly powerful at the national level, they are weak and often absent at the local firm level. The local weakness of unions also contributes to bad working conditions. The following section investigates the sustainability of the French model. Financial support to the unemployed is a key element of the system, along with a strict immigration policy that aims to reduce pressure on the labor market. Such solutions are now being questioned, however, owing to their high financial cost.

Nevertheless, political support for the French model remains rather strong, and that explains why France has still not moved to an American (much more flexible) or Danish (based on "flexicurity") type of labor market. The concluding section summarizes the argument.

UNEMPLOYMENT AND LOW WAGES IN FRANCE

The French labor market is characterized by a high and persistent level of unemployment and by a reduced incidence of low-wage work.

A High and Persistent Level of Unemployment

High Unemployment From the beginning of the 1990s until the mid-2000s, employment growth in France was not very different from the rest of the European Union, but it lagged behind the United States (see table 2.1).

There are two reasons for this lack of employment dynamism. The first one has to do with the rather slow growth in GDP experienced by Europe in general, and by France in particular. There is much debate on the origins of this slow growth—and in particular on the lack of contra-cyclical policy in continental Europe compared to what has been done in the United States and the United Kingdom since the mid-1990s (see Aghion and Howitt 2006).[1] The second reason for the lack of employment dynamism lies in the low job content of growth, despite the long-term change in the structure of employment in favor of services, which are usually more labor-intensive than the manufacturing sector. While total employment has increased by some 25 percent since 1970, employment in the manufacturing sector has decreased by 29 percent. Employment in the service sector accounted for 72.8 percent of total employment in 2005, compared to 23 percent for manufacturing and construction and 3.8 percent for agriculture.

The lack of employment creation, combined with positive growth of the labor force, has generated mass unemployment: the rate of unemployment in France has been almost double that of the United States since the mid-1990s. This high rate of unemployment corresponds to small flows in and out of unemployment and, correspond-

Table 2.1 Annual Growth Rates of Real GDP, Employment, and Labor Force in France, the EU-15 and the United States, 1993 to 2005

	1993 to 2003	2004	2005
France			
GDP	2.2%	2.1%	1.4%
Employment	1.2	0.0	0.4
Unemployment	10.8	10.0	9.9
Labor force	0.9	0.2	0.2
EU-15			
GDP	2.3	2.0	1.5
Employment	1.1	0.9	0.9
Unemployment	8.8	8.1	7.9
Labor force	0.9	1.0	0.7
USA			
GDP	3.2	4.2	3.5
Employment	1.4	1.1	1.8
Unemployment	5.3	5.5	5.1
Labor force	1.3	0.6	1.3

Source: OECD, *Employment Outlook* (2006).

ingly, a large proportion of long-term unemployed: 42.5 percent of the unemployed had been so for more than twelve months in 2005, compared to only 22.4 percent in the United Kingdom and 11.8 percent in the United States.[2] Such a high rate induces important risks of exclusion from the labor market, in particular for unskilled workers.

At the lowest end of the skill distribution, unemployment is indeed rather high in absolute terms in France: 12.1 percent for workers with less than a secondary education (see table 2.2). However, it is not so high in relative terms: about 20 percent higher than the average unemployment rate in France (compared to about 100 percent higher in the United States). Moreover, it should be noted that both the participation rates and the employment rates of low-educated workers are higher in France than in the United States, largely because the share of low-educated workers in the labor force is much higher in France (as discussed later in the chapter) and these workers are more concentrated in middle-aged generations.

Another characteristic of the French labor market is that the employment rate is very low at both ends of the age distribution: fewer

Table 2.2 Employment, Unemployment, and Labor Force Participation in France and the United States, 2005

	Employment Rate (Percent of Population)		Labor Force Participation (Percent of Population)		Unemployment Rate (Percent of Labor Force)	
	France	United States	France	United States	France	United States
Whole population fifteen to sixty-four years old	62.3	71.5	69.1	75.4	9.9	5.1
Gender						
Men	67.8	77.6	74.5	81.8	9.0	5.1
Women	56.9	65.6	63.8	69.2	10.9	5.2
Age						
Fifteen to twenty-four years old	26.0	53.9	33.7	60.8	22.8	11.3
Twenty-five to fifty-four years old	79.6	79.3	87.2	82.8	8.7	4.1
Fifty-five to sixty-four years old	40.7	60.8	43.6	62.9	6.8	3.3
Education (2003)						
Less than upper secondary education	59.6	56.5	67.8	63.1	12.1	10.5
Upper secondary education	75.4	72.8	81.5	77.2	7.6	5.6
Tertiary education	81.7	82.0	87.1	84.7	6.2	3.3

Source: OECD, *Employment Outlook* (2006).

than 26 percent of people below age twenty-five and 41 percent above age fifty-five are employed. The low level of labor market participation at both ends of the age distribution is due to continuing initial education for the youngest group and early retirement for the oldest one. The unemployment rate of younger workers is also very high—22.8 percent compared to an average of 9.9 percent in 2005—especially among the least-skilled. This is not the case for older workers: the unemployment rate was 6.8 percent in 2005 among fifty-five- to sixty-four-year-olds. Overall, the French employment regime seems to be characterized by a high employment rate only among middle-aged workers and by, to a large extent, exclusion of the youngest and oldest groups from the labor market.

Increasing Employment by Sharing Work? Since the end of the 1990s, an attempt has been made to increase employment through the sharing of hours worked. In 1996, 1998, and 2000, three laws were successively passed to reduce legal working time (the so-called Robien law in 1996 and the Aubry I and II laws in 1998 and 2000). The latter two laws stipulate that the legal working time cannot exceed 35 hours per week on average over one year and the amount of yearly overtime is strongly contingent (with a maximum of 130 hours per worker). These laws were relaxed in 2003, when the number of legal overtime hours was brought up to 180.

Overall, this legislation brought down the number of hours actually worked per week from 38.9 in 1993 to 35.6 in 2003, thus reinforcing the long-term trend toward a decrease in the number of hours worked (see table 2.3). In 2005 the average number of hours worked per person in dependent employment was 1,446—substantially below the average number of hours worked in the United Kingdom and the United States.

However, part of this long-term decrease is also due to the increasing number of individuals working part-time (less than thirty-five hours per week): from 1990 to 2005, the proportion of part-timers in the working population went up from 10 to 17.2 percent (see table 2.4). This increase is almost entirely due to women: 30.8 percent of women worked part-time in 2005 (compared to only 5.7 percent of men). One characteristic of part-time work in France is that it is quite long: 30.3 percent of part-timers work more than thirty hours per week, so that the proportion of employed workers working less than thirty hours per week (the OECD definition of part-time work) was only 12 percent in 2005. Nevertheless, on average 28.7 percent of French part-timers are underemployed in the sense that they would like to work more. This is the case for 27.5 percent of women and

Table 2.3 Numbers of Hours Worked per Dependent Worker

	France	Germany	Netherlands	Denmark	United Kingdom	United States
1979	1,711	—	1,591	—	1,750	1,839
1994	1,564	1,465	1,388	1,420	1,693	1,850
2005	1,446	1,372	1,322	1,420	1,652	1,809

Source: OECD, *Employment Outlook* (2006).

Table 2.4 Part-Time Work, 2005

	Total	Men	Women
Proportion of part-time workers	17.2%	5.7%	30.8%
Proportion of part-timers according to weekly working time			
Less than fifteen hours	15.8	17.4	15.5
Fifteen to twenty-nine hours	53.4	54.2	53.3
Thirty hours and more	30.3	27	31.1
Unknown	0.5	1.4	0.1
Proportion of part-timers by main occupation			
Managers, teachers, intellectual professions	8.4	3.9	16.0
Intermediate professions	14.9	4.7	25.3
Clerks	31.8	10.0	37.8
Blue-collar workers	8.9	4.5	27.0
Share of underemployment among part-timers	28.7	34.1	27.5
Managers, teachers, intellectual professions	25.1	28.6	16.5
Intermediate professions	27.5	29.2	18.3
Clerks	37.3	37.7	32.0
Blue-collar workers	39.2	42.7	34.0

Source: Authors' compilation from Enquête Emploi (French Labor Force Survey), 2005.

34.1 percent of men. This proportion is particularly high among blue-collar workers and clerks: 34 percent of blue-collar female part-timers (and 42.7 percent of men) and 32 percent of clerk female part-timers (and 37.7 percent of men) wish to work more.

Overall, the French labor market is characterized by only a rather small proportion of the working-age population being actually employed. This is mainly due to a low participation rate at younger and older ages and to a high rate of unemployment. Moreover, a substantial proportion of part-time workers would like to work more, particularly those at low occupational levels. These characteristics suggest that *employment is in short supply, especially at the bottom end of the skill distribution.*

THE REDUCED INCIDENCE OF LOW-WAGE WORK

Changes in Low-Wage Employment over Time Low-wage workers are defined here as workers earning less than two-thirds of the median hourly wage, defined as the basic wage plus all bonuses and premiums earned on a monthly or yearly basis.[3] The data we use come from the Enquête Emploi (French labor force survey) or the Declarations Annuelles des Données Sociales (Annual Reports of Social Data, or DADS).[4] The median wage is computed on *before-tax* hourly wages (net of social contributions), excluding apprentices. This restriction is made in order to take into account the fact that the low level of apprentices' wages partly corresponds to a sharing in the cost of training between employers and trainees.

By 2002 the low-wage cutoff amounted to €5.58 per hour (see table 2.5). This is equivalent to $6.18 if using the euro-dollar purchasing power parity computed at consumer prices in August 2006 and to $5.91 if using the "Big Mac" purchasing power parity for year 2004.[5] This cutoff is very close to the minimum wage (only 5.5 percent higher in 2002), and since 1995 both wages have grown at a very similar rate: 2.7 percent per year on average for the low-wage cutoff—in nominal terms—compared to 2.8 percent for the minimum wage.

With this threshold, the proportion of low-wage earners in France in 2002, at 12.2 percent, was lower than in the mid-1990s (see table 2.6, specification 1).

To test whether the exclusion of apprentices from our sample makes a big difference, we recomputed the proportion of low-wage workers for the whole salaried population (specification 2). The proportion of low-wage earners is very close to that obtained with specification 1. It is slightly higher because most apprentices are low-wage earners. In theory, this effect could be counterbalanced by the fact that the corresponding cutoff wage is lower when apprentices are included, which reduces the proportion of workers below the low-wage threshold. However, as shown in table 2.2, the former effect dominates the latter. The proportion of low-wage workers is still a little bit higher when weighting wages by the number of hours worked (specification 3). This amounts to computing the proportion of hours worked that are paid below the low-wage threshold. In this computation, the cutoff is above that corresponding to specification 2. This is no surprise given that part-timers' hourly wages tend to be lower than those of full-timers. Thus, weighting by hours worked yields a higher median wage, hence a greater share of people below the low-wage threshold.

Table 2.5 Minimum Wage and Low-Wage Cutoff, 1995 to 2002 (Before Tax, Net of Social Contributions)

	1995	1996	1997	1998	1999	2000	2001	2002
Hourly minimum wage								
Nominal rate (in euros)	4.37	4.48	4.66	4.75	4.81	4.97	5.17	5.29
Annual growth rate	—	2.5%	4%	1.9%	1.3%	3.3%	4%	2.3%
Hourly cutoff wage								
Nominal rate (in euros)	4.62	4.71	4.76	4.86	4.93	5.11	5.32	5.58
Annual growth rate	—	1.9%	1.1%	2.1%	1.4%	3.7%	4.1%	4.9%

Source: Authors' compilation from Enquête Emploi and Ministry of Labor.
Notes: Wages net of employees' social contributions were about 80 percent of gross hourly wages during the period. The hourly cutoff wage is computed on all wage earners except apprentices.

One striking point, however, is that, whatever specification we use, the share of low-wage earners remains quite low in France compared to other European Union countries (see table 2.7). France's share of low-wage earners is lower than in all partner countries except Denmark.

Table 2.6 Incidence of Low-Wage Work, 1995 to 2002

Low-Wage Earners in the Whole Workforce	1995	1996	1997	1998	1999	2000	2001	2002
Low-wage cutoff equals two-thirds of the median hourly wage, excluding apprentices	13.7%	13.5%	13.6%	12.6%	11.7%	12.6%	11.6%	12.2%
Low-wage cutoff equals two-thirds of the median hourly wage of all workers	14.5	14.2	14.4	13.4	11.8	13.2	12.1	12.7
Low-wage cutoff equals two-thirds of the median hourly wage of all workers, weighted by the number of hours worked	14.1	14.0	14.3	13.3	12.7	14.0	12.7	13.1

Source: Authors' compilation from Enquête Emploi.

A second characteristic of low-wage workers in France is that, whatever the specification, their share has declined over the past decade (see table 2.6). Part of this decline is due to the reduction in legal working time: in a vast majority of firms, monthly wages remained constant, particularly at the lowest end of the distribution, which ended up with a 11 percent increase in hourly wages. This increase is likely to have brought a number of formerly low-paid workers above the low-wage threshold. Moreover, since 2002 the share of low-wage workers is likely to have further decreased. The gross, hourly minimum wage increased by more than 20 percent in nominal terms between 2002 and 2006, owing to several increases, partly related to the implementation of the laws on the reduction in working time. Given that the median wage is unlikely to have increased by such a large amount over the period, the share of low-wage workers was probably far below 12 percent in 2006. The anticipated slowing of increases in the minimum wage in the coming years may induce a progressive growth of low-wage work in France.

It should be noted that the extent of undeclared low-wage work (which leads to an underestimation of the actual figures) remains an open question. It seems to play an important role in some sectors, such as hotels and restaurants, construction, and domestic services (notably housemaids and other domestic help). The high tax wedge due mainly to social contributions (see discussion in the next section) affects both the demand and the supply of undeclared low-wage work. In addition, the small number of labor inspectors (also discussed later in the chapter) may encourage underreporting of low-wage work. Unfortunately, we have no reliable statistics on this issue, and therefore no evidence that this phenomenon is more important in France than in other comparable European countries.

Overall, the incidence of low-wage work appears to be smaller in France than in the United States and in many other European Union countries, except Denmark.

The Incidence of Low-Wage Work According to Workers' Characteristics
On average, low-wage work is more frequent among women than among men: in 2002, 17 percent of women were low-wage earners, compared to only 8 percent of men (see table 2.8). The incidence of low-wage work decreased for both groups between 1995 and 2002, but the gap in the risk of low pay by gender has remained stable over time: in 2002 the share of low-wage earners among women was 39

Table 2.7 Employees Below Low Pay Threshold in the United Kingdom, France, Germany, the Netherlands, and Denmark

	France	Germany	Netherlands	Denmark	United Kingdom
Year	2002	2004	2002	2002	2002
Employees below low pay threshold	12.7%	20.8%[a]	17%	8.5%	22.1%
Data source	Enquête Emploi	GSOEP	LSO	CCP/IDA	ASHE
Definition of low pay threshold	Two-thirds median hourly wage net of social contributions, all employees	Two-thirds median gross hourly wage, all employees except apprentices	Two-thirds median gross hourly wage, all employees	Two-thirds median gross hourly wage, all employees except apprentices	Two-thirds median gross hourly wage, all employees

Source: Mason, Mayhew, and Osborne (2008).

Note: GSOEP = German Socio-Economic Panel; LSO = Loonstructuuronderzoek (Dutch survey of earnings structures); CCP/IDA = Center for Corporate Performance/Integrated Data Base for Labor Market Statistics; ASHE = Annual Survey of Hours and Earnings.

[a] Weighted average computed using two different low-wage thresholds for West and East Germany.

Table 2.8 Incidence of Low-Wage Work, by Workers' Characteristics

	1995	2002
Average incidence of low-wage work	13.7%	12.2%
Gender		
Men	9.2	8.0
Women	19.0	17.0
Age		
Less than twenty-six years old	35.3	26.1
Twenty-six to thirty-five years old	13.1	10.7
Thirty-six to forty-five years old	10.7	10.6
Forty-six to fifty-five years old	9.5	10.3
Fifty-six and older	13.6	12.9
Education		
Tertiary education	3.8	4.4
Less than twenty-five years old	19.4	17.6
Twenty-five to fifty-four years old	3.0	3.7
Fifty-five and older	3.4	3.1
High school	10.6	11.7
Less than twenty-five years old	39.3	31.8
Twenty-five to fifty-four years old	6.9	8.5
Fifty-five and older	4.1	6.4
Lower secondary	13.5	12.7
Less than twenty-five years old	40.1	29.8
Twenty-five to fifty-four years old	11.2	11.3
Fifty-five and older	8.1	10.9
No diploma	23.2	21.9
Less than twenty-five years old	52.4	38.8
Twenty-five to fifty-four years old	21.6	21.1
Fifty-five and older	21.0	20.2
Nationality		
French	13.3	11.8
Born in France	13.4	11.9
Born in the European Union	15.1	11.3
Born outside of the European Union	11.5	10.3
Foreigners (European Union)	16.8	16.1
Foreigners (non-European Union)	22.7	21.0

Source: Authors' compilation from Enquête Emploi.

percent higher than average, identical to 1995. It should be noted that if the low-pay threshold were calculated on a monthly basis (two-thirds of the median monthly wage), the gender gap would be even higher because of part-time work (see previous section).

As could be expected, younger workers are much more affected by low-wage work than older ones. This is particularly true for those under the age of twenty-five: in 2002 the incidence of low pay in this age group was as high as 26.1 percent. This high incidence of low pay is partly due to student jobs, which are particularly low-paying and account for 10.6 percent of employment in this age group: the incidence of low-wage work among working students reached 31 percent in 2002. The proportion of low-wage workers then decreases with age, going down to 10.3 percent for forty-six- to fifty-five-year-olds before rising again for older workers.

The incidence of low-paid work is much higher among workers with no diploma (80 percent higher than average in 2002) than among workers with a lower secondary diploma (almost at the average level). It is even lower, of course, among workers with a high school (baccalaureate) diploma (slightly below average) and lowest for workers with some tertiary education (one-third of the average level).

One interesting point is that between 1995 and 2002 the share of low-wage earners increased in the two most-educated groups while decreasing among the least-educated. This does not seem to be due to a composition effect driven by the entry of younger and more-educated workers into the low-wage labor market. Indeed, the incidence of low-wage work has decreased for workers with a high school diploma or some tertiary education who are less than twenty-five years old. In contrast, it has increased for older, educated workers, in particular those between twenty-five and fifty-four years old. This may be due to a "waiting list" effect: in a situation of high unemployment, some educated workers eventually accept low-paid jobs because they cannot find anything better.

Finally, foreign workers are more affected by low-wage work than native French. This is particularly the case for non-European Union foreign workers, among whom the incidence of low-wage work reached 21 percent in 2002, compared to only 11.8 percent for French nationals. A similar, although smaller, gap exists between French workers and foreign workers from the rest of the European Union. One interesting point is that the proportion of low-wage workers is very similar among French nationals, be they native French or born in other countries. Part of the gap in the proportion of low-wage workers among French nationals and foreign workers is due to the fact that foreign workers tend to be overrepresented in unskilled occupations, which are those with the highest incidence of low-wage work: 18 percent of foreign workers from the European Union and 29 percent of non-European Union foreign workers are unskilled, blue-collar workers, compared to only 11 percent for French workers. They are also less educated: more than 50 percent of all foreign workers had no diploma in 2002, compared to 19 percent among French workers. Foreign workers are also particularly numerous in services to households (domestic services as well as hotels and restaurants): about 15 percent of all foreign workers were employed in this sector in 2002, compared to only 7 percent of French workers. As evidenced in the next section, these are low-wage-intensive sectors.

The Incidence of Low-Wage Work According to Job Characteristics The proportion of low-wage earners is much higher among part-time workers than among full-timers: the risk of low pay was more than double the average for employees working fifteen to twenty-nine hours per week in 2002, compared to 27 percent lower than average for full-timers (see table 2.9). However, the proportion of low-wage earners was not very different across part-timers, ranging from 30.7 percent for workers working very short hours to 27.1 percent for workers employed more than thirty hours a week.

The incidence of low wages is very small among managers, supervisors, and foremen. It is substantially below average in skilled blue-collar occupations, and it decreased between 1995 and 2002. In contrast, the incidence of low pay is much higher than average for clerks in both years, and it is, of course, the highest in unskilled, blue-collar occupations : 20.2 percent in 2002. For this last group, however, the risk of low pay has sharply decreased over time: it was only 66 percent higher than average in 2002, compared to almost twice the average in 1995. In contrast, it should be noted that the proportion of low-wage earners increased between 1995 and 2002 for managers, supervisors, and foremen, even if it remained quite marginal.

As expected, the incidence of low wages is much higher for workers on fixed-term rather than open-ended contracts (27.7 percent and 10.1 percent, respectively). The gap is also quite sizable for tempo-

Table 2.9 Incidence of Low-Wage Work, by Job Characteristics

	1995	2002
Average incidence of low-wage work	13.7%	12.2%
Hours worked		
Full-time	10.2	8.9
Part-time: more than thirty hours per week	24.2	27.1
Part-time: fifteen to twenty-nine hours per week	34.4	29.3
Part-time: less than fifteen hours per week	34.7	30.7
Occupation		
Managers	1.5	2.1
Supervisors and foremen	1.9	3.2
Clerks	22.1	21.1
Skilled blue-collar workers	10.8	9.2
Unskilled blue-collar workers	27.1	20.2
Type of work contract		
Open-ended	11.1	10.1
Fixed-term	33.3	27.7
Temporary agency work	26.4	19.3
Labor market policy schemes	55.4	41.5
Public sector	6.5	6.4
Sector		
Agriculture	38.6	29.2
Manufacturing	8.5	6.2
Construction	9.7	9.4
Services	15.1	13.6
Real estate	27.1	22.0
Household services	41.9	37.6
Retail trade	23.6	18.4

Source: Authors' compilation from Enquête Emploi.

rary agency work (19.3 percent). Of course, the proportion of low-wage earners is highest among people employed on active labor market policy schemes.

There are more low-wage workers in agriculture and services than in construction and manufacturing. Low wages are particularly common in retail trade and real estate activities, and in services dedicated to households the low-wage incidence was as high as 37.6 percent in 2002. In contrast, low wages are quite rare in the public sector (6.4 percent in 2002). Note that the high share of public employment in France (about 23 percent of total employment in 2004, compared to 15 percent in the United States) may contribute to the low incidence of low-wage work at a global level.

The Incidence of Low-Wage Work in the Occupations and Sectors Studied   To determine the incidence of low-wage work in the sectors and jobs under study in this book, we relied on the DADS database. We used this database because the number of observations in the DADS is very large; that enabled us to identify rather disaggregated job-sector cells, which is not feasible with the Enquête Emploi, owing to its much smaller sampling. Given that the DADS dataset does not include information on household services or on the public, noncompetitive sector, the sampling is different from that of the Enquête Emploi. As a result, we recalculate the low-wage cutoff, defined as two-thirds of the median hourly wage (net of social contributions). It should be noted that we do not have reliable data for the call center sector. The jobs and sectors under study are highly heterogeneous (see table 2.10).

With a share of low-wage workers that is well below the national average, hospitals are clearly not a low-wage sector. In the food production sector, low-wage workers are concentrated in artisan shops (which are beyond the scope of our study) and are quite few in the meat-processing and confectionery sectors (7.2 percent and 6.2 percent, respectively). The overall proportion of low-wage workers in the sector decreased sharply between 1995 and 2003 (from 23 to 11.6 percent), mostly because of the increase in the hourly minimum wage that followed the reduction in legal working time (as discussed earlier in this section). The effect was particularly important in this sector because most workers are paid the minimum wage, that is, just below the low-wage cutoff, so that the sharp increase in the hourly minimum wage is likely to have brought them above the cutoff (see next section). In contrast, hotels, especially smaller ones without restaurants, are structurally a low-wage sector, with 21.2 percent of low-wage workers and as many as 26.7 percent of them among lower-skilled employees. The incidence of low wages is also very high in the retail sector (18.0 percent), in particular among cashiers and food vendors. However, there is a big difference between supermarkets

Table 2.10 Incidence of Low-Wage Work in Selected Industries and Occupations, 2003

	1995	2003
Hourly cutoff (net of social contributions), in euros	5.09	6.23
Proportion of low-wage workers	12.7%	10.4%
Food processing	23.0	11.6
Meat industry	16.8	10.1
Meat artisans	35.1	21.8
Meat processing	13.4	7.2
Pastry artisans	34.5	14.1
Confectionery	9.3	6.2
Retail trade in general stores	20.1	18.0
Cashiers	36.8	29.1
Food vendors	25.1	20.4
Electric and electronic goods vendors	5.1	3.3
Supermarkets	24.2	26.4
Hypermarkets	17.3	11.2
Hotels	19.3	20.4
Low-skilled employees	23.4	26.7
Hotels with restaurant	21.1	17.9
Hotels without restaurant	17.6	21.2
Health (private competitive sector)		
Hospitals[a]	5.5	3.5

Source: Authors' compilation from Déclarations Aunnelles des Données Socialess (DADS).
[a] Computed on the basis of the official number of hours worked.

(including hard-discounters) and hypermarkets, which are mainly high-end.

Is Low-Wage Work a Dead End? There have been few studies on the wage mobility and career paths of low-wage workers in France. One exception is a study by the European Commission (2004) that provides comparative data on earnings mobility based on the European Community Household Panel (ECHP) database for the years 1994 to 2001. It takes into account only those workers working fifteen hours per week or more and excludes those in paid apprenticeships or other labor market policy training schemes. Regarding the transition from low pay to higher pay, two main results arise from the period

1994 to 2001 (pooled data). The yearly exit rate out of low-wage employment in France was above the European average: 34.5 percent, compared to 30.7 percent for the EU-15. It is much higher than in Germany (25.4 percent), the United Kingdom (28.0 percent), or even the Netherlands (29.4 percent), but it is notably lower than in Denmark (36.6 percent), which has among the highest scores in the EU-15 (only Portugal, Finland, and Belgium score better). As for the cumulated exit probability, it amounts to about 54 percent after three years (about ten percentage points more than in Germany, five points more than in the United Kingdom, three points less than in the Netherlands, and eleven points less than in Denmark) and about 70 percent after seven years (about twenty percentage points more than in Germany, eight points more than in the United Kingdom, five points less than in the Netherlands, and eight points less than in Denmark).

Thus, the exit rate from low-wage employment appears to be quite high in France with respect to international standards. But this does not necessarily mean that French workers experience important wage mobility or have steep wage profiles. Indeed, the high exit rate from low-wage employment is partly due to the fact that the low-wage threshold is very close to the minimum wage (it was less than 6 percent higher during the last decade, as described earlier in the section), and therefore many low-wage workers are very close to the two-thirds median hourly wage threshold. As a result, many workers may exit from low-wage work without any occupational mobility or (basic) wage mobility, benefiting only from the seniority premium (about 1 percent per year of tenure, until fifteen years of tenure in many sectors) or from other premiums or bonuses related to tenure.

Moreover, wage mobility has substantially decreased over the past twenty years. Using the DADS database, Bertrand Lhommeau (2005) finds that it decreased a lot between the period 1984 to 1991 and the period 1994 to 1998. It slightly increased between 1997 and 2001, but remains much lower than in the 1980s. The two-year exit rate out of low wages (defined as wages below 1.3 times the minimum wage) for full-time workers was, on average, 29.4 percent over the 1984 to 1991 period. It then fell to 21.1 percent in the period 1994 to 1998 and increased with the economic recovery at the end of the 1990s, up to 23.8 percent in the 1997 to 2001 period. This decline in wage mobility cannot be explained only by the economic cycle. In five out of the twelve industries under study, mobility declined significantly over the period, whereas the growth rate of value-added was equal or even higher in the period 1994 to 1998 compared to the period 1984 to 1991.

In terms of living standards, a slowdown in wage mobility may be compensated (as well as induced) by wage increases. Indeed, between 1995 and 2005 the gross hourly minimum wage increased by almost 28 percent in real terms. But it is notable that the monthly earnings of minimum wage earners did not increase by that much. As noticed earlier, the 10 percent reduction in the volume of hours worked induced by the laws on working time was compensated at low-wage levels by an increase in hourly wages. But in many firms these laws also drastically limited the amount of overtime that workers could take on. This contributed to decreasing take-home pay for many workers—all the more considering that overtime is paid at a higher hourly rate—with the relative impact on income being larger at the lower end of the wage distribution. According to Eurostat data, applying purchasing power parities, the monthly minimum wage, at the beginning of 2006, was 45 percent higher in France (for a thirty-five-hour week) than in the United States (given the federal minimum wage), but about 7 percent lower than in the United Kingdom and the Netherlands (for workers older than twenty-six) (see Regnard 2006).

Moreover, low-wage work is not identical to poverty. We consider here two different poverty lines: workers are poor if their monthly income is lower than 40 percent (or 60 percent) of the median monthly income per consumption unit. With this definition of poverty, and using ECHP data, the proportion of working poor amounts to 0.6 percent of the whole working population according to the 40 percent poverty line and 5.2 percent according to the 60 percent line. The corresponding figures for low-wage workers are, of course, higher: 2.5 percent and 16 percent, respectively. However, most low-paid workers are not poor, which means that public support and institutions play a major role in allowing salaried workers to remain above the poverty line, in particular at the bottom end of the wage distribution.

Overall, *France is characterized by a rather low incidence of low-wage work and a high and persistent rate of unemployment.* Does this situation result from a simple trade-off between the number of jobs and the level of wages at the lowest skill levels? It might seem so owing to the key role of the minimum wage at the lower end of the labor market.

THE ROLE OF THE MINIMUM WAGE: FROM A LOWER BOUND TO PRODUCTIVITY ENHANCEMENT

The minimum wage plays a key role in compressing the distribution of wages at the bottom. It also impacts the cost of labor and, hence, the supply of low-paid jobs.

THE MINIMUM WAGE AS A DRIVING FORCE IN THE DETERMINATION OF LOW WAGES

The introduction of a legal, hourly minimum wage in France dates back to 1950. Given that it was not index-linked to GDP real growth, its purchasing power increased much less than the average wage from 1950 to 1968. After the social uprising of 1968, the working of the minimum wage was modified (in 1970) and the SMIC (salaire minimum interprofessionnel de croissance, or interprofessional, index-linked growth minimum wage) was created. According to the law, the SMIC aimed at ensuring "workers with the lowest pay a guaranteed purchasing power and participation in the economic development of the nation" (CSERC 1999).

The consequence of this change was very important: since the beginning of the 1970s, via SMIC increases, the law and the government have become the driving forces in the growth of low wages in France, whereas the role of collective agreements has almost disappeared. It is not easy to disentangle which is the cause and which is the consequence. Actually, branches and firms with workers' representatives have to bargain on wage changes each year, but these negotiations often fail. This failure of the bargaining process partly accounts for the existence and persistence of a high national minimum wage in France. The leading role of the government may therefore be considered the consequence of the failure of the social partners to agree on low-wage levels and increases. But conversely, the fact that the SMIC is set by law is not an incentive for unions and employers' organizations to bargain on low wages.

This leads to a paradoxical situation (unknown in other countries like Belgium and the Netherlands, for instance, where statutory minimum wages also exist): in many industries and in various occupations of the public sector, the lowest wage rates of the job evaluation schemes set by collective agreements at the branch level are below the SMIC level and are therefore irrelevant. The SMIC being a lower bound, workers at the lowest levels of the job classification are paid at the SMIC level and end up earning more than allowed by collective agreements. According to the French Ministry of Labor (January 2005), this is the case in 55 percent of the branch-level collective agreements; the proportion was about 70 percent in 1999. Consequently, the SMIC is a more relevant reference than collective agreements for the remuneration of most low-wage workers.

Since July 2006, the (gross) hourly SMIC has been set at €8.27—that is, €6.49 per hour before tax but after social contributions. At consumer price purchasing power parity, the corresponding wages are $9.16 and $7.19, respectively.[6] The proportion of workers earning the SMIC as their basic wage was 15.1 percent in 2006 (Berry 2007).[7] It may be noted that the purchasing power of the monthly SMIC (net of social contributions for a full-time worker working 39 hours a week) increased by almost 18 percent between 1990 and 2004, while the average real monthly wage (net of social contributions for a full-time worker) increased by only 7.3 percent over the same period.

The existence of the minimum wage is one key explanation for the small number of low-wage workers in France. The SMIC strongly compresses the wage distribution at the bottom with the ratio of the fifth decile to the first decile (D5/D1) of hourly wages being only 1.6 in 2002 compared to 1.9 for the ratio of the ninth decile to the fifth (D9/D5). The sharp increase in the SMIC since the beginning of the 2000s is likely to have further reduced wage inequality.[8]

At the same time, the increase in the SMIC has had little effect on the low-wage cutoff, which is defined with reference to the median wage. Thus, the main effect of the SMIC is to push wages up, toward the cutoff. In this context, many workers may escape low-paid work by only the effect of premiums and bonuses, in particular in relation to seniority (see earlier section). This is even the case for many minimum wage earners. For instance, in 2002 the hourly earnings of 26

Table 2.11 Distribution of Hourly Wages, 1995 and 2002

	1995	2002
D5/D1	1.6	1.6
D9/D1	3.0	2.9
D9/D5	1.9	1.9

Source: Authors' compilation from Enquête Emploi.

percent of the minimum wage earners were at least 30 percent above the hourly minimum wage (Seguin 2006)—well above the low-wage threshold. This is why the proportion of workers earning the minimum wage as a basic wage (about 14.0 percent in 2002) is higher than the proportion of low-wage workers (12.2 percent in 2002).

Overall, the minimum wage has a mechanical effect on the proportion of low-wage workers: *within a wide range of potential variations, the higher the SMIC, the lower the incidence of low-paid work.*

The Minimum Wage and the Cost of Labor

A feature of the French labor market has long been the high relative cost of low-skilled labor compared to the average. At the bottom of the wage distribution, the minimum wage acts as a lower bound under which firms cannot go, but part of the problem also arises from social contributions. As shown in figure 2.1, the ratio of the cost of labor at the level of the SMIC to the cost of labor at the level of the median wage sharply increased between 1968 and the mid-1980s owing to increases in the minimum-to-median-wage ratio. The trend reversed in 1983 with the implementation of the so-called competitive disinflation policy, but the relative cost of labor at the SMIC level was still 47 percent higher at the beginning of the 1990s than in 1968.

To further reduce the cost of low-skilled labor, it was decided to act on the level of social contributions. Since 1993, several reductions in employers' social contributions have been implemented at wage levels close to the SMIC.[9] They brought down the total cost of labor for employers (that is, the sum of the gross wage and the social contributions paid by them) at the level of the SMIC from about 1.40 (gross) SMIC to about 1.14 (gross) SMIC in 2006, so that the relative cost of labor at the SMIC level went back to its early 1970s level (see figure 2.1).

The impact of such measures on the employment prospects of low-skilled workers has, of course, been positive. Low-skilled employment has risen since 1994, whereas it had declined continuously during the previous decade. But it is difficult to assess the number of jobs that were created as a direct consequence of these reforms: econometric estimates vary from 100,000 to 500,000 jobs created between 1993 and 1996.

In the 1990s *the cost of labor was kept under control, particularly at low-skill levels, by means of reductions in employers' social contribu-*

Figure 2.1 The Minimum to Median Wage Ratio, 1959 to 1998

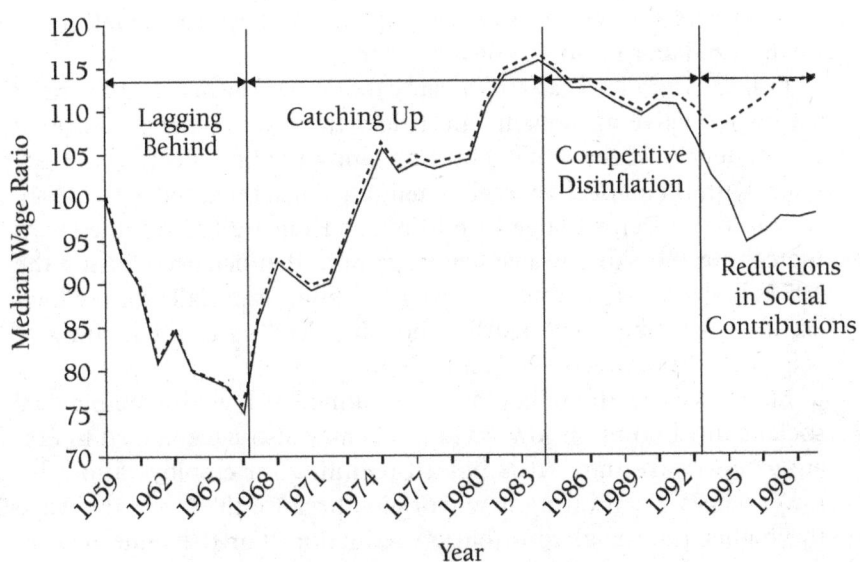

Source: Carcillo and Delozier (2004).

tions. In parallel, firms have developed a variety of strategies to reduce the cost per efficiency unit of labor.

COPING WITH THE COST OF LABOR AT LOW WAGE LEVELS

Flat Wage Profiles Wage profiles appear to be relatively flat at low wage levels. This is indeed the case for many minimum wage earners. According to Sébastien Seguin (2006), in 2002 in firms with ten employees and more, more than 25 percent of workers at the SMIC level had at least ten years of tenure. This means that their basic wage had been "stuck" at the minimum level since they were hired. Of course, various factors help to explain this phenomenon (which is not specific to France), the first one being the low accumulation of human capital in low-skilled jobs. But the high level (in relative terms) of the SMIC as an entry wage may also play a role here. In this case, flat wage careers also reflect a strategy implemented by firms to minimize the cost of labor for low-skilled workers.

Indeed, as noticed earlier, in many industries the lowest wage rates set by collective agreements are below the level of the SMIC. As a consequence, workers may move up along the first levels of the pay scale, with their effective wage remaining constant at the SMIC level. According to Denis Fougère and Francis Kramarz (2001), the sharp increase in the SMIC-to-average-wage ratio that occurred during the 1970s had a negative impact on wage mobility, especially for the lowest deciles of the wage distribution, thus leading to a flattening of wage profiles between 1967 and 1984.[10]

More recently, the policy measures aimed at lowering employers' social contributions at low-wage levels may also have helped to create a "low-wage trap." It is indeed tempting for employers to offer lower wages when hiring new workers, because the lower the wage the higher the social contribution reduction. For the same reason, firms may also keep wage increases as small as possible because at the minimum wage level a 1 percent increase in the gross wage implies a 1.6 percent increase in the total labor cost borne by the employer. This may contribute to explaining the decline in wage mobility at low wage levels since the late 1990s (Lhommeau 2005). However, the evidence of a low-wage trap is not empirically compelling (Sraer 2007), and the role of employers' social contribution exemptions is still in debate.

Whatever their origin, these very flat wage careers are a major source of frustration for workers, as we see in the industry chapters. In some sectors, they even make it difficult for firms to fill vacancies, particularly when working conditions are difficult (such as in the food-processing sector).

Increasing Capital Intensity   A second way for firms to minimize the impact of the cost of labor is to move toward more capital-intensive production processes. Some empirical evidence suggests that this strategy is being used by French firms. The capital-to-GDP ratio is actually higher in France than in most partner countries (see figure 2.2), and it has been steadily increasing in France since 1980, while it has decreased or remained constant in most other countries.

Figure 2.2 Capital-to-GDP Ratio (in Volume)

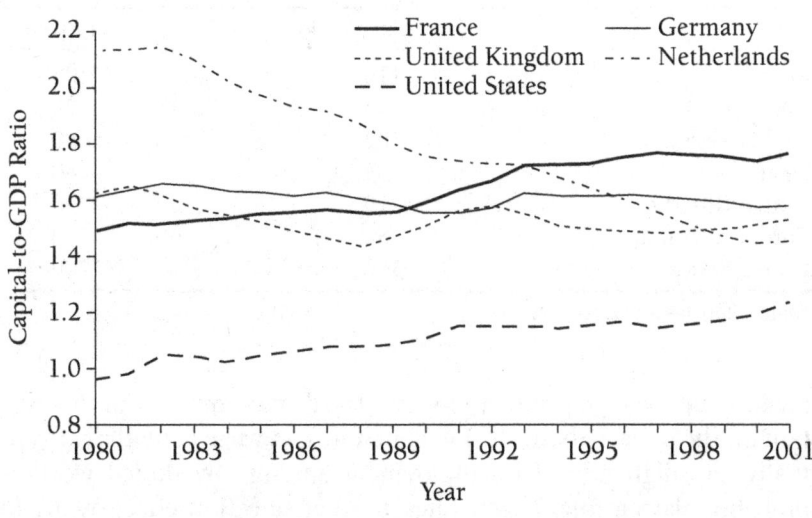

Source: Artus and Cette (2004).

One consequence of the high capital intensity is that labor productivity is high in France (see table 2.12). When measured per hour worked, it is 13 percent above American levels and far above the European Union average. However, given the small number of hours worked, productivity per worker is below that of the United States, as is the case for all European countries.

These aggregate ratios do not seem to result from a sectoral-composition effect. Estimates at the two-digit industry level by Geoff Mason, Brigid O'Leary, Mary O'Mahony, and Kate Robinson (2007) show that both hourly productivity and capital intensity are higher in France than in the United Kingdom and Germany—and even the United States—in sectors that are intensive in low-skilled work, such as textiles, clothing, and leather goods, retail, and hotels and catering.[11]

There are several possible reasons for the high level of hourly labor productivity. Part of it is due to the fact that workers are more efficient while they are working because of the small number of hours they work per week or per year. A second factor has to do with changes in the production structure: firms tend to focus on high-value-added businesses at the expense of low-productivity ones, thus

Table 2.12 Labor Productivity as a Percentage of United States Productivity, 2002

	Per Hour Worked	Per Worker
France	113%	95%
Germany	93	79
Netherlands	102	80
Denmark	94	80
United Kingdom	79	78
European Union	82	78
United States	100	100

Source: Bourlès and Cette (2005).

pushing up average productivity (see the discussion later in this section on the debate about the job deficit in low-wage activities). Eventually, the high rate of unemployment among low-skilled workers probably plays a role. It generates another selection effect owing to the fact that the least-productive workers are not employed.

Work Intensification and Poor Working Conditions High hourly productivity may also partly result from high work intensity. Work intensification may be a strategy for firms to lower the cost per efficiency unit of labor, and there is some evidence that it has been used in France in recent years, especially in low-wage jobs. Along with new information and communication technologies, firms have introduced new forms of work organization. Just-in-time has been developed, as well as teamwork and job rotation. The organization of work has become less hierarchical, and horizontal communication among workers has become generalized. Total quality management has also been widely adopted. Such organizational devices developed quickly in the United States in the early 1990s (see Osterman 2000) but were not introduced in France until the end of the 1990s (see Askenazy 1998); the country finally caught up at the beginning of the 2000s.

In many countries the development of these new organizational devices has generated some form of work intensification (see Green and MacIntosh 2001; Askenazy, Caroli, and Marcus 2002). This has been the case in France, where work has become more stressful since the mid-1990s. Evidence of such changes can be found in the Surveillance Médicale des Risques (SUMER) surveys, which were conducted in 1994 and 2003 by 1,200 occupational practitioners through face-to-face interviews with 48,000 workers at their workplaces (in the private sector and in public hospitals). They provide quantitative information on working conditions, but unfortunately the SUMER surveys do not include information on wages.

The results of both waves suggest that employees are working under increasingly stringent working time and organizational constraints (see table 2.13).

Between 1994 and 2003, the proportion of workers working on Sundays or at night increased. Similarly, electronic control of work rapidly expanded, as did unexpected changes in tasks. In contrast, physical constraints decreased, except for noise. As shown in figure 2.3, work intensification has been particularly widespread in France compared to other European Union countries.

Several factors may have contributed to these changes: changes in the organization of production, particularly those linked to the development of just-in-time or lean production systems; changes in work organization in relation to increasing task flexibility and multi-skilling; and technological changes—more specifically, computerization.

These changes affect both skilled and unskilled workers, but inequality in working conditions is still very strong (see table 2.13). Inequality in physical working conditions has increased: though physical demands remain marginal in skilled occupations, they are very widespread in clerk and blue-collar jobs, in which low-wage workers are concentrated.

The thirty-five-hour working week laws have played a role in maintaining working condition inequality across occupations. Following the 1999 and 2000 Aubry laws, the actual reduction in working time has reached 7 to 8 percent (rather than the official 10 percent) of the former number of hours worked, with half of it being compensated for by increases in productivity. In exchange for this substantial reduction in hours worked, the laws introduced a lot of flexibility in working time, especially because working time can now be computed on an annual basis: firms can have employees work up to forty-four hours per week at some times, provided that the weekly average is not more than thirty-five hours over the whole year. The estimated impact of the thirty-five-hour law on the frequency of irregular work schedules is particularly significant for blue- and white-collar workers in manufacturing firms with fifty workers or less—irregular work schedules have increased by more than fifteen and

Table 2.13 Working Conditions, by Occupation

Percentage of Workers Affected By ...	Managers	Supervisors and Foremen	Clerks[a]	Skilled Blue-Collar Workers	Unskilled Blue-Collar Workers	All Workers
Constraints on working time						
Working on Sundays even occasionally						
1994	24.3%	20.6%	33.6%	16.1%	11.2%	18.9%
2002[b]	24.7	22.1	33.3	16.4	11.5	20.0
Working at night even occasionally						
1994	9.4	11.3	9.3	18.6	10.9	11.7
2002[b]	9.2	11.5	8.7	21.2	14.2	12.7
Organizational constraints						
Permanent control by hierarchy						
1994	12.5	22.9	30.3	33.0	41.0	28.4
2003	11.5	21.9	27.3	32.3	36.7	25.5
Electronic control						
1994	13.6	19.0	9.2	11.5	8.7	14.5
2003	25.9	33.3	15.8	26.9	20.3	27.0
Frequently changing tasks to carry out unexpected tasks						
1994	66.0	56.2	43.4	35.8	25.5	46.2
2003	75.6	67.9	52.6	45.5	39.5	58.4

	1994/2003				
Physical constraints					
Noise (greater than eighty-five decibels) for more than twenty hours per week					
1994	0.6	2.5	0.3	13.1	14.1	5.8
2003	0.5	2.6	0.4	15.0	14.6	6.0
Carrying around heavy weights for more than ten hours per week					
1994	1.4	5.5	17.2	20.7	25.0	12.5
2003	0.7	4.9	16.8	21.2	26.6	11.8
Standing for more than twenty hours per week					
1994	6.5	19.1	49.1	40.6	44.8	28.3
2003	3.5	16.3	46.8	43.1	46.8	26.7
Repeating the same movement for more than ten hours per week					
1994	1.6	3.5	14.4	15.6	31.9	12.5
2003	1.5	2.8	12.2	14.0	26.0	9.5

Source: Arnaudo et al. (2004).

[a] Trade and service sectors.

[b] Enquête Emploi data. The question was not asked in the 2003 Surveillance Médicale des Risques (SUMER) survey. So we used the Labour Force Survey (LFS) and computed the relevant information for the same scope as the one used for SUMER 1994.

Figure 2.3 Percentage Change in the Proportion of Workers Declaring that They Work at High Speed at Least 50 Percent of the Time

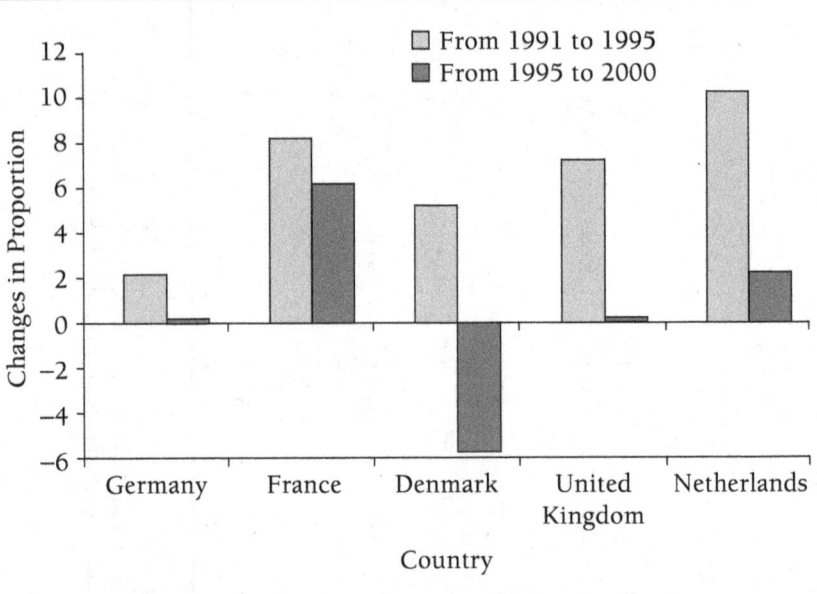

Source: European Surveys on Working Conditions, various years.

thirty-six percentage points, respectively (see Afsa and Biscourp 2004). The changes introduced by the Fillon law (2003) increased the legal maximum of overtime. This could lead, in the coming years, to an increase in the number of hours worked while working time flexibility remains. Fifty-nine percent of workers report an improvement in the quality of everyday life following the reduction in working time (see Cette, Dromel, and Méda 2004). An improvement in working conditions, however, is reported by only 26 percent of workers. Life has been made more complicated and stressful for unskilled, blue-collar women: for 20 percent of them the quality of everyday life has worsened (compared to an average of 13 percent in the working population), and for 35 percent of them working conditions have worsened, compared to an average of 28 percent in the population.

In addition to working conditions, statistics on occupational health and safety at work highlight the poor performance of France

Figure 2.4 Change in the Number of Work Accidents (with Three Days or More Off Work) for 100,000 Persons Employed, 1995 to 2003

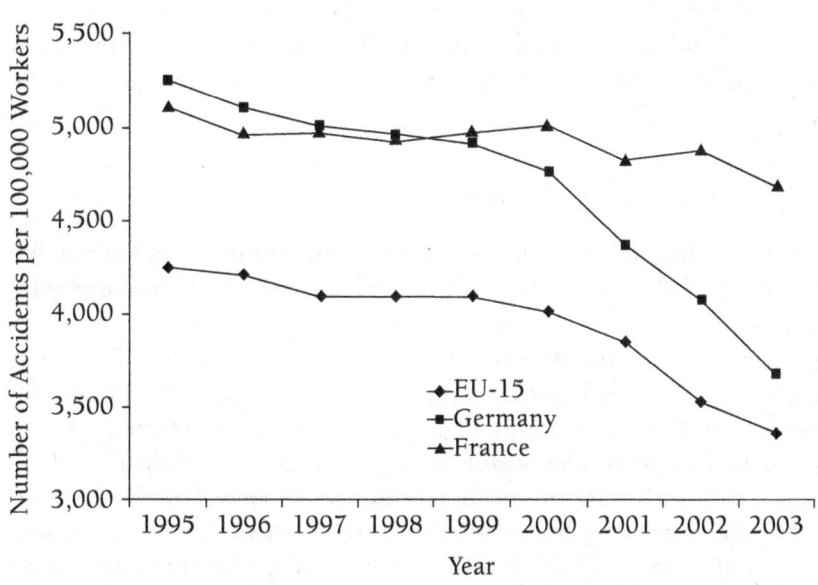

Source: Eurostat.

compared to other European countries. The number of (nonfatal) accidents per worker decreased much less in France than in the rest of the European Union over the past decade and was much higher than average in 2003 (see figure 2.4).

The number of occupational illnesses (musculoskeletal disorders, cancers, and so on) is also growing fast. According to the National Institute of Health Supervision, about 16 percent of female workers suffer from musculoskeletal disorders, as do 13 percent of males. Epidemiologic work using data on cancers that have an occupational origin suggests that the incidence of such cancers in France is far above the European average (Banaei et al. 2000), and workers who have worked in low-skilled occupations are the main victims. More generally, one of the explanations for the low employment rate of older low-skilled workers in France lies in this structural health problem (Coutrot and Waltisperger 2005).

Overall, the French "equilibrium" relies on a mixture of a "high" minimum wage (by American standards) and flat wage profiles (at the bottom of the distribution), as well as high labor productivity made possible by a high capital-to-labor ratio and by strong and increasing work intensity. Of course, we must be very cautious when interpreting the causal links between these elements. A plausible assumption is that this equilibrium results, at least partly, from firms' strategies to cope with the cost of labor.

A Low-Wage Job Deficit?

Another potential consequence of a high minimum wage (in relative terms) is a deficit in the number of jobs in low-skilled, potentially labor-intensive activities. There is some evidence of such a deficit in France. In 1970 the global employment rate was only 1.2 percent higher in the United States than in France. This gap went up to 17.1 percent in 2000, with about 95 percent of it being accounted for by a job deficit in the service sector, mainly in trade (wholesale and retail) and hotels and restaurants. According to Andrew Glyn (2005), in 1999 the number of hours worked in the distribution sector (trade, hotels, and catering) per head of population age fifteen to sixty-four was 304 in the United States, 239 in the United Kingdom, 217 in Germany, and only 175 to 180 in France and the Netherlands. So the gap in the employment rate in this sector between France and the other countries was as high as 70 percent with the United States, 33 percent with the United Kingdom, and 21 percent with Germany.

There is a wide debate as to the causes of this job deficit. One reason often put forward is that the labor intensity of French services is low due to the high cost of low-skilled work. Thomas Piketty (1999), for example, stresses that the deceleration of the trend of employment growth in the service sector is highly correlated to the large increase in the SMIC in the 1970s (see figure 2.1). As a matter of fact, in some sectors firms have specialized in high-value-added activities, where their comparative cost disadvantage is lower. This is the case, for example, in call centers.

This view is challenged by Glyn (2005). According to him, the lack of jobs in the distribution sector is mainly due to differences in consumption levels across countries. The level of consumption being much higher in the United States than in Europe, the demand for distribution goods is higher there. In France, an additional (although secondary) explanatory factor would be that labor productivity in the distribution sector is higher than in the United States.

However, the high cost of labor may also help explain the deficit in the consumption of labor-intensive services—and more specifically, the reason why Europe in general and France in particular have not "marketized" household-type services (caring, catering, and all domestic services) as much as has occurred in the United States. If the cost of household services is higher in France than in the United States, consumers will tend to work more within the household, producing by themselves services that Americans usually buy on the market (see Freeman and Shettkat 2002). This would also be consistent with the rather high labor productivity in French services: if firms withdraw from labor-intensive activities and focus on high-value-added businesses, productivity is likely to be higher on average, as already mentioned. Nevertheless, the relative cost of labor is probably not the only explanation: it may be noted that in Denmark, where the bottom end of the wage distribution is even more compressed than in France (the D5/D1 ratio is 1.5 compared to 1.6 in France), the employment rate in service activities is substantially higher.[12]

Recent analyses have also pointed to product market regulations as a major source of the shortage of jobs in some activities (Cahuc and Kramarz 2004). According to the OECD (2005a), productivity and employment growth in the French service sector have been impaired by the lack of liberalization of network industries (such as telecom, electricity, postal services, railways) and by strict restrictions on entry and business operation in retail and business services. Especially in retailing, where low-wage work is widespread, the Royer and Raffarin laws limit the development of supermarkets and hypermarkets (see chapter 7). Preliminary evidence suggests that these regulations substantially reduced employment growth in this sector: according to some econometric estimates, employment could be up to 15 percent higher without them (see Bertrand and Kramarz 2002). Conversely, deregulation of the road freight haulage industry in 1986 seems to have boosted business and job creation in this sector.

Moreover, France is characterized by numerous barriers to entry in a number of occupations. These may reduce employment or mobility (and also push prices up or hamper innovation). For example, the quota system in operation for taxi drivers gives important power to the "insiders" (the owners of the permanent licenses) and at the same time dramatically reduces the supply of taxis: at the end of the 1990s, for the same number of inhabitants, there were 50 percent more taxis in the United Kingdom—where the taxi market is much less regulated—than in France. High formal qualifications are also required for numerous jobs. For example, an individual can be employed as a hairdresser without any qualification but cannot set up his or her own business without an upper secondary vocational diploma. This type of regulation mechanically reduces not only earnings mobility in the affected occupations but also firm creation (Cahuc and Kramarz 2004).

Overall, the minimum wage plays an important role in France in reducing the incidence of low-wage work. The other side of the coin, however, is that *the high relative cost of low-skilled labor may also account for the small number of jobs in potentially low-wage, labor-intensive services, even if product market regulation also plays a role.*

LABOR MARKET REGULATIONS AND INDUSTRIAL RELATIONS

Cross-country comparisons of national labor markets usually show that French jobs are more protected than those in the United States. This statement should be qualified, however, at least for workers and jobs at the bottom of the skill distribution: nonpermanent contracts are very numerous, and employment protection regulations are not always implemented. Contributing to the impression that French jobs are more protected are the characteristics of French industrial relations: if unions appear rather powerful at the national and branch levels, they are much weaker at the firm level.

EMPLOYMENT PROTECTION LEGISLATION IN THEORY AND PRACTICE

From a global perspective, French workers may appear to benefit from secure jobs. As mentioned earlier, almost one worker in four is employed in the public sector, and most public employees have civil servant status, meaning that they are at no risk of being fired unless they engage in serious misconduct. Public employment has played an important role in the building of the French postwar employment model: it served as a model for the internal labor markets of big firms,

Table 2.14 Indices of Strictness of Employment Protection Legislation, 2003

	Denmark	France	Germany	Netherlands	United Kingdom	United States
Protection of regular workers against (individual) dismissal	0.61	1.03	1.12	1.27	0.46	0.07
Specific requirements for collective dismissal	0.65	0.35	0.63	0.50	0.48	0.48
Regulation on temporary forms of employment	0.57	1.51	0.73	0.49	0.16	0.10
Summary (0 to 6 scale)	1.83	2.89	2.48	2.26	1.10	0.65

Source: OECD (2004).

and workers are on average very attached to job security and seniority rules. Average tenure is quite high in France (about eleven years in the beginning of the 2000s, compared to about six years in the United States and eight years in the United Kingdom).

Job stability is promoted by employment protection legislation. According to the OECD indicator, French EPL is rather strict (see table 2.14).

Protection of regular (permanent) workers is actually close to the OECD average—and is even lower than in some other European Union countries (such as Germany and the Netherlands)—even if it is clearly much higher than in the United States. Although permanent contracts still characterize a wide majority of jobs, temporary forms of employment have increased in the past years in response to the need for labor flexibility expressed by firms.[13] In 2005, 87.7 percent of all workers were on open-ended contracts, and among the 12.3 percent on temporary contracts, 7.0 percent were on a fixed-term contract, 2.2 percent were on a temporary agency work contract, 1.3 percent were apprentices, and 1.7 percent were on a labor market policy scheme.

The incidence of temporary employment is quite high among low-skilled, low-paid workers: in 2002, 27.9 percent of unskilled blue-collar workers and 13.8 percent of clerks were on nonpermanent contracts, compared to an average of 10.7 percent in the whole population (Amira and De Stefano 2005). Young workers are also widely affected: 45.9 percent of workers age fifteen to twenty-four years are on nonpermanent contracts. This is largely due to the fact that, for instance, in 2005 more than 70 percent of newly hired workers were on temporary forms of employment.

Nonpermanent employment in France is apparently much more protected than in other OECD countries: according to the OECD index (table 2.14), EPL on temporary forms of employment is twice as strict in France as in Germany and ten times as strict as in the United States. However, aside from "standard" open-ended, fixed-term contracts and temporary agency work, which are fairly well regulated, there exists a wide range of derogatory contracts.[14]

Derogatory contracts show that there actually is a lot of flexibility at the margins of the EPL system. Most of these contracts are not taken into account in the building of the OECD index, but they are widely used by firms in a number of sectors. This creates zones of the labor market that are extremely flexible and, to a large extent, uncontrolled. These zones are, of course, particularly numerous at the lower end of the labor market, where derogatory contracts are used for low-skilled, potentially low-paid jobs. All the sectors covered in this study, including public hospitals, use a wide variety of nonpermanent contracts.

The gap between the formal regulatory framework of "standard" nonpermanent contracts and the reality at the firm level also results from illegal practices (witnessed even in the public hospitals). One reason for this lies in the lack of controls. In 2004 there were about 1,300 labor inspectors for 1.5 million firms and about 15 million employees in the private sector—in other words, far too few to ensure that the law was enforced, particularly in small and very small firms. A reform adopted in 2006 should increase the number of labor inspectors in France in the coming years. Another reason for illegal practices derives from the weakness of unions at the firm level, which prevents them from ensuring that the law is enforced.

THE ROLE OF INDUSTRIAL RELATIONS

In many European countries—Denmark and Germany, for instance—unions and collective agreements play a crucial role in the regulation of the labor market. This is also the case in France, but the French industrial relation system is characterized by one peculiarity: unions seem to be strong at the national and branch levels but are very weak at the firm level. One consequence of this is that low-paid, low-skilled workers are poorly covered and defended.

The Strength of Unions at the National Level Employee organizations in France are dominated by five trade unions that are officially recognized by the law as "representative," that is, they can participate in negotiations and sign collective agreements at the branch or firm level.[15] The two main unions are the Confédération Générale du Travail (CGT, which had very close ties to the French Communist Party until the 1990s) and the Confédération Française Démocratique du Travail (CFDT, a more reformist union, closer to the Socialist Party). Turning to employers' associations, the most important one is the Movement of French Enterprises (MEDEF), which represents employers for most national bargaining rounds. The Confédération Générale du Patronat des Petites et Moyennes Entreprises (CGPME), the second main employer organization, represents small and medium-sized firms.

At the national level, labor unions are apparently quite powerful. One reason is that they are key actors in collective bargaining in a country where about 90 percent of workers in private firms are covered by collective agreements (95.8 percent when we include the publicly owned companies). Traditionally, collective bargaining in France has been quite centralized at the branch or national level. At the national level, several important agreements have been signed during the past ten years (on reductions in working time, retirement, and continuous training). At the branch level, agreements usually cover topics such as wages, working time, continuous training, complementary health insurance, and equal opportunity. In general, most branch agreements are "extended" by the government, that is, they are included as part of the labor law that applies to all firms in the branch. The extension is independent of the effective representativeness of the organizations that signed the agreement. The only condition is that the agreement be signed by one of the five recognized labor unions and one employers' organization.

The national and branch-level collective agreements are thus also binding upon employers that did not take part in any collective bargaining or were not members of any employers' representative grouping that was party to the negotiations. Given that most firms have an activity linked to one of the 220 organized branches in France, the rate of coverage of collective agreements is very high. This, of course, gives a great deal of power to the labor unions that negotiate these agreements, but this power is heavily dependent on the "extension mechanism"—hence, on state intervention.

The central role of the state and the law in the French industrial relation system is taken for granted by all actors. Both unions and employers' associations spend a lot of their time and energy lobbying to influence the content of the law. This is particularly the case for employment protection legislation. Even if the five labor unions are often quite divided, they actively lobby in favor of the preservation of the existing system. As for employers' associations, although branch-level organizations may have different views on this issue, the traditional position of the MEDEF is in favor of massive labor market deregulation. So far unions have been successful in maintaining the general architecture of the system, but as mentioned earlier, the use of derogatory contracts has increased under the pressure of employers' associations. Beyond EPL, the role of the law is also central to industrial relations on a large number of topics, such as working time, health, and safety.

The Weakness of Unions at the Firm Level and the Low Effective Coverage of Low-Wage Workers   Although state and legal intervention play a major role in industrial relations, unions are actually quite weak at the local level. Part of this weakness is due to the very low level of unionization. As in many other countries, unionization has sharply declined in France since the 1980s, but it started from a much lower level than in the rest of the OECD: from about 25 percent in 1950, the rate of unionization fell to 18 percent in the 1970s and is currently around 8 percent. At the beginning of 2005, about 1.9 million workers are members of a union, the unionization rate being higher in managerial occupations (it is about 5 percent for clerks, 6 percent for blue-collar workers, but more than 14 percent for managers) and in the public sector (15 percent compared to only 5 percent in private firms and even less in small ones).[16]

One consequence is that, although unions are still very strong in some segments of the public and manufacturing sectors (particularly in the automotive and chemical industries), they are on average very weak at the local firm level in the private sector. In particular, in small enterprises their members are few, and their representatives end up being very isolated and thus powerless. Moreover, harassment of union members and representatives is still quite common in various sectors, particularly in low-wage sectors, such as retail trade (see chapter 6). According to a comparative survey (see Blanchard and Philippon 2004), the quality of labor relations is particularly bad in France, and even the worst among twenty-one OECD countries.[17] Moreover, unions are often divided at the workplace level (reflecting divisions at the national level), and in recent years they have been overtaken by spontaneous workers' committees (so-called "coordinations") in a number of social conflicts.

Overall, these features have important consequences owing to the development of more decentralized forms of bargaining since the 1980s. The 1982 law was a first step in that direction, and the trend toward decentralization was reinforced by the implementation of laws on working time reduction at the end of the 1990s.

The weakness of unions at the firm level particularly affects unskilled, potentially low-wage workers, who were traditionally defended by unions, especially the CGT. Nevertheless, as in other industrialized countries, union militants historically have been male breadwinners employed in the manufacturing sectors, while immigrants, women, and youth have been underrepresented. The picture has not changed much in recent years and is probably even more dualistic now owing to the decline in unionization. As already mentioned, unions remain powerful in some segments of the public and manufacturing sectors. But these are not low-wage sectors, and they are male-dominated. Unskilled women are overrepresented in service sectors—like hotels and catering and retail trade—where unionization is very low. Low-skilled, low-paid youth are concentrated in a peripheral labor market—labor market policy schemes or temporary agency work—or in small firms.

The poor representation of low-skilled, low-paid workers by unions may negatively affect their earnings. However, this is mitigated by the major role played by the national minimum wage in the determination of earnings at low-wage levels. The weakness of unions is more likely to be particularly damaging in terms of employment and working conditions. In particular, it may be a permissive cause of high work intensity and bad working conditions. One more consequence of the weakness of unions at the firm level is that rules and laws are not always thoroughly implemented. This is the case for work contracts, and thus employment protection legislation (as illustrated in the food-processing and hotel sectors; see chapters 3 and 5), but also for health and safety regulations (for example, in the retail sector; see chapter 6).

Overall, *the French labor market appears to be highly segmented.* A substantial share of low-skilled, low-paid workers are on nonpermanent contracts, and therefore job insecurity is a big issue for workers and unions. Moreover, effective employment protection is substantially weaker at the local firm level than seems to be the case when looking at the macro level. This is partly due to the industrial relations system, which is characterized by rather strong unions at the national level and in the state-owned sector and by weak union representation at the firm level in the private sector. The resulting balance of power at the firm level is not in favor of low-wage workers, so that the labor market is much more flexible than might be expected, in particular at the bottom end of the skill and wage distribution. Beyond the issue of effective employment protection, the weakness of unions at the firm level also has damaging effects on working conditions.

THE STABILITY OF THE FRENCH MODEL

Given the high rate of unemployment in France, one key question is raised by the French model: what has made it so long-lasting? The answer is twofold: the French labor market so far has been well preserved from the potential pressure that arises from immigration, and the unemployed benefit from a number of income support schemes. Although this equilibrium is now being strongly questioned, until now the political economy of the French model has not been deeply undermined.

Coping with High Unemployment

Surprisingly, French society has tolerated a rate of unemployment as high as about 10 percent for more than twenty years. Public policy has played a key role—by implementing a very strict immigration policy and, above all, by developing income maintenance schemes for the unemployed.

Keeping Immigration to a Minimum   The global impact of immigration on the lower end of the labor market is much debated—especially in the United States (see, for instance, Borjas and Katz 2005; Card 2005). In the French context, which is characterized by high and persistent unemployment, immigration has been clearly considered a threat. Since 1974, French borders have been officially closed to immigration. The decision was taken following the first oil crisis, and it has been maintained by all governments since then. For the past thirty years, the official immigration policy has been based on two principles: improve the integration of immigrants who are legal residents in France and fight against illegal immigration—even though, in practice, left-wing governments have fought this battle less intensely than right-wing ones.

Despite this unfriendly policy, immigration has not stopped in France. But the number of immigrants has grown very slowly in the past thirty years. While the number of immigrants doubled between 1946 and 1975, it increased by only 26 percent between 1975 and 2004. In 2004 there were 4.9 million immigrants in France, representing 8.1 percent of the population (see Borrel 2006).[18] Correspondingly, the inflow of immigrants is small, and even very small (about 10 percent of the total inflow) when considering immigrant *workers* (see Haut Conseil à l'Intégration 2004).[19] Immigrants represent only 8 percent of the workforce, and even in sectors where they are numerous (such as domestic services or hotels) few of them have recently arrived (data from Institut National de la Statistique et des Études Économiques [INSEE]). One issue is, of course, that of illegal immigration. By definition, this is difficult to quantify and estimates vary a great deal: according to a report commissioned by the French Senate (2006), between 400,000 and 800,000 foreigners live illegally in France, and between 30,000 and 80,000 illegal immigrants get in every year. These seem to be concentrated in a small number of sectors, including construction, domestic services, and agriculture (seasonal work). In the hotel sector, there is some evidence that illegal immigration contributes to maintaining rather low wages and bad working conditions (see chapter 5). However, this is more the exception than the rule; on average, the pressure of illegal immigration on wages and working conditions is still quite limited.

However, things may change in the near future. First of all, the number of foreign "posted" workers is rapidly increasing. It has been possible since 1996 to outsource abroad some services. However, the European Union directive setting up the rules of international outsourcing was properly translated into French law only in August

2005. Since then, the number of workers coming from abroad for short periods of time has been increasing. These workers must be paid at least the minimum wage and are subject to French labor law, but for those coming from European Union countries, employers' social contributions can be paid in the home country. This is a potential source of social dumping, at least for workers coming from Eastern Europe, where social security is much less generous than in Western Europe. A second source of changes lies in a law adopted in July 2006 that opens up limited (but real) opportunities for working immigration for the first time since 1974. For a number of highly skilled occupations (such as in science, culture, or sports) or for occupations for which labor is in short supply in France (for example, jobs in the construction, hotel, and agriculture sectors), working permits may be issued for a limited period of time. The effects of this change in policy will have to be evaluated in the future, but it may increase wage and job competition in the short run in some of the lowest-skilled, lowest-paid jobs.

Social Benefits and Labor Market Policy Schemes   Despite the variety of policy measures aimed at boosting low-skilled employment, a substantial proportion of potentially low-wage workers are unemployed in France. However, the social consequences of this high rate of unemployment are mitigated by a number of income support measures and labor market policy schemes.

Some income support measures are *general*, in the sense that they are not targeted to a specific group of workers. This is the case with unemployment compensation. The French unemployment compensation system relies on two key mechanisms: in the insurance system, the unemployment benefit is proportional to the previous wage (the replacement rate varying from about 75 percent for the lowest wages to 57.4 percent for the average wage), and its duration is linked to that of previous contributions; in the assistance system—for those who are no longer entitled to the insurance benefit—the benefit relies on a means-tested allowance.

Compared to other OECD countries, the French unemployment benefit may appear rather generous in terms of the eligibility criteria, the replacement rate (59 percent of the gross wage on average in 2004), and the duration—up to three years for those with the highest employment record. But the reality of coverage and effective benefits yields a more mixed picture. In 2004 the coverage rate amounted to

62.3 percent of all the job-seekers registered at the public employment service, and only 43.3 percent of the unemployed under twenty-five years old were covered (Monneraye and Jugnot 2006). Nevertheless, the limited generosity of unemployment compensation may be compensated for (in terms of incentives) by the fact that control over job-seekers is quite loose in France. This is the case despite the reform passed in 2001 promoting the "activation" of unemployment compensation (the plan d'aide au retour à l'emploi). In particular, the "rate of sanctions" for not searching enough or for cheating the unemployment compensation system appears to be much lower in France than in other OECD countries like Germany, the United Kingdom, and Denmark (see Cahuc and Kramarz 2004).[20] But overall, empirical evidence shows that while job-seekers with previously high earnings (hence high benefits when unemployed) tend to choose when to return to work, this is much less the case for low-wage earners (see Dormont, Fougère, and Prieto 2001).

People who are unemployed may also benefit from several means-tested allowances in France. Some correspond to special needs (such as housing benefits or some family benefits), and others are more general income support schemes. Among the latter, the main one is the minimum (or basic) income benefit (revenu minimum d'insertion, or RMI), which is restricted to people age twenty-five or older and amounts to about 40 percent of a full-time monthly minimum wage for a single person (see chapter 1).[21] At the end of 2006 there were about 1.26 million beneficiaries. RMI has become de facto the third pillar of the unemployment compensation system.

In contrast to general income support schemes, a wide range of *targeted* active labor market policy schemes have been implemented in France during the last three decades: subsidies to employment in the private sector (mainly through reductions in employers' social contributions), the creation of temporary jobs in the public and nonprofit sector, and subsidized training contracts. These measures are targeted at youth and "hard-to-place" workers, such as older workers and long-term unemployed.

Active labor market policy schemes represent an important segment of the low-wage labor market in France, especially for youth.[22] These schemes significantly impinge on the low-wage labor market because in most of them the beneficiaries are paid at the hourly minimum wage (and even less in the training schemes) or slightly above. Because of the global job shortage, many skilled youth (that is, high school graduates or young people with even higher school attainment) are hired on such schemes. This has contributed to the increase in the educational level of low-wage workers over time, as pointed out earlier.

France has a long tradition in the field of publicly funded early retirement schemes, and that is a key factor in the low employment rate of workers above age fifty-five. Moreover, since 1997 unemployed workers older than fifty-five can benefit, under certain conditions, from a specific unemployment allowance without having to search actively for a new job.[23] In this case, they disappear from the official unemployment statistics (based on the ILO unemployment definition). At the end of 2004 about 6 percent of all fifty-five- to sixty-four-year-olds were benefiting from this unemployment benefit (among them, 80 percent were former blue-collar workers or clerks). Overall, these schemes may help explain the relatively small share of older workers among low-wage earners in France, and notably, compared to the United States, the small incidence of low-paid, low-skilled "stop-gap jobs" to (full) retirement—the so-called bridge jobs. People who are over fifty-five years old are often outside the labor market, either as compensated unemployed (not job-seekers), as early retired, or as pensioners—the legal retirement age being sixty.

Finally, the child care system has an ambiguous impact on the labor supply of low-skilled women. Its general impact on the labor supply of women is usually considered positive: France reconciles a high participation rate of women, especially among the younger generations, with the highest fertility rate in Europe (overtaking Ireland in the mid-2000s). This is mainly due to the high availability of kindergartens and nursery schools. But the effect of child care benefits is quite ambiguous in terms of work incentive. On the one hand, several schemes are based on income tax and social contribution reductions to help workers hire a nanny to be at home. This has a positive effect on women's participation, but essentially only for high-income households. On the other hand, as Thomas Piketty (1998) shows, the "child-raising allowance" introduced in the late 1990s had a strong disincentive effect on the supply of low-skilled women's labor.[24]

Reforming the Social Benefit System   The issue of the financial sustainability of the social benefit system is raised at the macro level: there are threats to the balance of the state budget and to that of the social security system. As a consequence, a number of reforms have been introduced to cut costs. For instance, from the end of the 1990s the various governments have tried to curb the number of beneficiaries of early retirement because this policy contradicted the aim of raising the employment rate of older workers and lengthening the contribution period for the pension system. Various schemes were suppressed, and as a consequence the number of beneficiaries was divided by nearly three between 2000 and 2003.

At the micro level there have been concerns that unemployment compensation and income support schemes might have raised the reservation wage too much. In particular, the "making work pay" issue has been a growing concern since the 1990s. Aside from budgetary reasons, this may explain why the minimum income benefit has increased much less than the minimum wage since the end of the 1980s: the RMI level was about 50 percent of the net, monthly, full-time minimum wage when it was created in 1988, but had fallen to about 40 percent by 2005. Various reforms of the RMI and the related allowances were also adopted between 2000 and 2004. During the same period, a sort of negative income tax (the prime pour l'emploi, or premium for employment) was introduced.[25] But its impact on incentives—as well as on poverty reduction—appears to be limited so far: the maximum potential benefit, depending on earnings and on the composition of the household, amounts to 5 percent of income (compared to a potential maximum of 40 percent for the Earned Income Tax Credit [EITC] in the United States and 160 percent for the Working Families' Tax Credit [WFTC] in the United Kingdom; see Cahuc and Zylberberg 2004). As a result, the intention of a reform adopted in 2006 is to increase the level of the negative income tax.

These reforms have tended to raise the incentive to return to employment. The difference between paid work and the minimum income (all other national social benefits and negative income tax being taken into account) has increased overall during the last ten years, but it remains not very large for households with only one employed person (see table 2.15). Moreover, at the local level many municipalities offer additional social benefits (usually connected to the RMI) that help reduce the gap with paid work; these are not taken into account in table 2.15 (Anne and L'Horty 2002).

Overall, to maintain the social sustainability of its employment model, France has implemented a restrictive immigration policy and

Table 2.15 Differences Between the Household Incomes of Minimum-Wage Earners and Unemployed Persons Collecting the RMI and Other Social Benefits

	1993	2003
Single		
Part-time worker (50 percent)	−1%	+10%
Full-time worker	+50	+53
Lone parent with two children		
Part-time worker (50 percent)	+7	+11
Full-time worker	+45	+36
Couple with two children		
Part-time worker (50 percent)	−2	+3
Full-time worker	+13	+16
Couple with four children		
Part-time worker (50 percent)	−1	+2
Full-time worker	+25	+18

Source: Observatoire National de la Pauvretè, *Rapport 2003–2004*.
Note: These figures are calculated for households with only one person working or receiving the minimum income benefit (revenu minimum d'insertion, or RMI), the amount of which depends on the composition of the household. A single person working part-time (that is, half time) and earning the minimum hourly wage rate, in 1993, earned 1 percent less than if he or she were receiving RMI benefit (including other social allowances). In 2003, the difference was positive and amounted to 10 percent. In 2003, a full-time minimum wage earner, with an inactive partner and two children would earn 16 percent more than if he or she were on the RMI.

provided substantial social support to the unemployed. *But this equilibrium is under pressure.* On the one hand, immigrant flows may increase in the near future with the entry of Eastern European countries into the European Union. At the same time, questions have arisen about the budgetary cost of social policies, and their potential negative impact on individual incentives to work are increasingly denounced.

THE POLITICAL ECONOMY OF THE FRENCH EMPLOYMENT MODEL: OR WHY HAVEN'T THE FRENCH BECOME AMERICANS OR DANES?

Even if the current equilibrium appears to be fragile, and despite the persistently high level of unemployment, no large-scale reform of the labor market has taken place in France so far. Nonetheless, there are debates about the opportunity to move toward an American or Danish type of employment model, both of which have yielded better labor market performances in terms of unemployment. The American model is characterized by a very high flexibility in both labor and product markets. In contrast, in the Danish model the relatively high flexibility of the labor market is compensated for by the fact that workers benefit from strong guarantees of unemployment benefits and from very active labor market policies (the "flexicurity model"). Any move toward either the American or Danish model would have to account for the fact that the French working population still has a rather low level of education; as a result, many people are not prepared to accept higher flexibility, which would increase the risk of losing their job. Any change would also have to factor in the deep distrust at the root of French industrial and social relations.

The Low Skill Level of the French Workforce The education level of the French population is not very high compared to international standards. The proportion of people age twenty-five to sixty-four in 2003 who had left school with an educational attainment below upper secondary education was 36 percent, compared to 31 percent in the OECD as a whole (OECD 2004). Forty-one percent had reached upper secondary education (44 percent in the OECD), and only 24 percent had reached tertiary education (23 percent in the OECD). This relatively low level of education is mirrored in the average years of schooling in the adult population—10.9 years in 2002, compared to 11.8 in the OECD.

This situation is largely due to the low educational level of elderly generations. Among people age fifty-five to sixty-four, only 48 percent had reached at least an upper secondary education. This proportion is much lower than in other European countries and even lower than in the OECD as a whole (see table 2.16). This lag in educational attainment holds for the younger generations down to the age of thirty-five.

Younger generations (below thirty-five years old) are clearly catching up; their secondary educational attainment is well above the OECD average. Over the past twenty years, the proportion of people leaving school with a high school diploma increased from 15.6 percent in 1980 to 23.6 percent in 2002. Similarly, the share of workers entering the labor market with a university diploma increased from

Table 2.16 Population That Has Attained at Least Upper Secondary Education, 2003

	Twenty-five to Sixty-four Years Old	Twenty-five to Thirty-four Years Old	Thirty-five to Forty-four Years Old	Forty-five to Fifty-four Years Old	Fifty-five to Sixty-four Years Old
France	65%	80%	69%	59%	48%
Germany	83	85	86	84	78
Denmark	81	86	82	80	74
Netherlands	66	76	71	62	53
United Kingdom	65	71	65	64	57
United States	88	87	88	89	85
OECD mean	66	75	70	62	51

Source: OECD, *Education at a Glance* (2005b).

15.2 percent to 38.1 percent. In 2002, however, 20.3 percent of young people still left school with no diploma (that is, either no diploma at all or a lower secondary education diploma, or brevet), and some 18 percent left school with no more than a lower secondary vocational diploma (CAP or BEP).

So educational attainment remains low among a substantial proportion of the French workforce. For these workers, the only way to improve their labor market opportunities is to rely on continuous training. Despite the increasing skill requirements of the labor market, investment in training has decreased in France over the past ten years (DARES 2005).[26] Moreover, only 59 percent of the €22 billion (US$31 billion) spent on continuous training in 2002 were devoted to employed workers. The rest funded active labor market policies targeted to low-educated young people and the unemployed. For employed workers, participation in training sessions reached 46 percent in 2002 (OECD 2004)—less than in Denmark (54 percent) or the United Kingdom (50 percent), but more than in the Netherlands (36 percent) or Germany (25 percent).

Because firms give priority to training workers for whom the expected return is higher, access rates are extremely variable, both across employers and across workers. Large firms invest more than small ones in training, and older workers have fewer training opportunities than younger ones. But the most impressive type of inequality has to do with occupations. The proportion of blue-collar workers participating in training in 2000 (Ministry of Education 2003) was 20 percent, compared to 29 percent for clerks, 45 percent for technicians and supervisors, and 54 percent for managers. So the French training system offers relatively few training opportunities to workers at the bottom of the skill/wage distribution. Strong guarantees of lifelong learning, which could be traded against more flexibility, do not exist. However, a law passed in 2004 created an "individual right" to training so that access to training might improve for low-skilled workers in the coming years.

In the meantime, the proportion of low-educated workers with limited training opportunities is still quite high. Their low skill levels make these workers ill equipped to adapt to changes in their work environment. They feel threatened by technological changes as well as changes in work organization. The feeling of job insecurity is indeed very high in France: out of eighteen OECD countries, France ranks among the worst on this measure in international subjective surveys (see also OECD 2004). There may be several reasons for relatively high feelings of job insecurity among French workers, but one of them is the greater pressure in recent years from firms to make the labor market more flexible. As noted earlier, the share of nonpermanent contracts has been increasing in the last twenty years. But even permanent workers—who theoretically have a low probability of losing their job—feel insecure. They know that if they lose their job, their risk of long-term unemployment is high, particularly if they are older and low-skilled.

Distrust in Industrial Relations and the Lack of Structural Reform According to the standard political economy approach, the persistence of the (bad) French equilibrium stems from a classical "insiders/outsiders" configuration: workers on permanent contracts manage to maintain high wages and strong EPL, at the expense of nonpermanent and unemployed workers. But in reality, if unions have been strongly opposed to reforming the minimum wage and employment protection, they are not quite strong enough to prevent *any* change, especially in the EPL system. Overall, unions have succeeded in maintaining the general architecture of the EPL system, but they have not been able to prevent the increase in the share of temporary and derogatory work contracts. On the other hand, employers' associations are not much stronger: they have some difficulties in coming up with consistent positions on which a wide majority of their members would agree. Differences between large and small enterprises, and also across sectors, account for this lack of common views. Overall, the French tradition of professional negotiations is very limited, partly because of distrust between labor unions and employers' associations (distrust fueled by the lack of successful negotiations), but also because of the incapacity of both parties to arrive at the negotiation table with viable suggestions. This logjam, of course, reinforces the role of the state in industrial relations, and the state's enhanced role, in turn, reduces the scope for fruitful negotiations.

Another problem with the standard "insiders/outsiders" view is that the "outsiders" are supposed to have different views than the insiders—that is, they are supposed to be in favor of reforms. But in reality, beyond the weakness of industrial relations, the lack of structural reform of the labor market is also due to the fact that most unemployed people (or parents of young unemployed workers) are not in favor of more flexibility on the labor market. A vast majority hope that at some point the doors of employment will open for them so that they will be able to get a secure job. Hence, they are not pushing for any deregulation. One reason for this reluctance to seek reform lies in the general lack of trust at the root of social relations in France (see Algan and Cahuc 2006) and, notably, in the bad labor relations already mentioned (Blanchard and Philippon 2004). In this context, more flexibility on the labor market is expected to generate more precariousness, while the potential gains in terms of employment are not clear. This view is shared by people with jobs, but also by most of the unemployed. It is supported by the everyday experience of workers who are confronted with the gap between the formal employment protection legislation and the local reality of firms' practices with respect to work contracts. "Precarious" contracts are used to put pressure on workers in terms of wages, work intensity, and so on, as evidenced by the following chapters. This may be another key difference with Denmark, for instance: Danish workers accept a lesser role for the state and the law because the countervailing power of their unions is much stronger at the firm level than in France.

This helps explain why any structural reform of the labor market is very difficult to propose and implement in France. This was made very clear by the "CPE episode" in early 2006. The government attempted to introduce a new, more flexible work contract—the contrat première embauche (CPE), or first hiring contract—for youth entering the labor market. This was seen as a first step toward a general deregulation of the labor market. It brought hundreds of thousands of people onto the street to protest for several weeks; eventually the government had to withdraw the reform. This is one of many examples of how difficult it is to make any significant reforms in the French labor market.

CONCLUSION

Overall, the French model relies on an equilibrium that combines a relatively small share of low-wage workers and a high rate of unemployment. Low-wage work does exist, but not on a large scale, except in some specific sectors. It has been decreasing in recent years, mainly because of the increase in the hourly legal minimum wage, which plays a crucial role here. Some empirical evidence suggests that most French firms do not directly compete on the cost of labor but rather rely on a high capital-to-labor ratio and a high and increasing work intensity—with negative effects on working conditions. The unemployment rate is high, in particular for low-skilled workers. Aside from the minimum wage, the rather strict EPL is often cited as a reason for the high unemployment rate. Indeed, permanent workers are relatively well protected, but there are many temporary and derogatory contracts, and their impact is felt primarily by low-paid workers. Although unions play an important role at the national and branch levels, they are weak and divided at the firm level, with strong consequences for the low-paid, low-skilled segment of the labor market.

Until now, a restrictive immigration policy and a strong social support system for the unemployed have limited both the external and internal pressures, but this equilibrium may be increasingly fragile. On the one hand, the entry into the European Union of much less developed Eastern European countries may induce a large increase in the number of immigrant workers, as already witnessed in Germany and the United Kingdom in the mid-2000s. On the other hand, persisting high unemployment and the aging of the population challenge the financial sustainability of the France's welfare state. Many timely reforms have been passed over the past twenty years concerning such issues as unemployment compensation, work contracts, and flexibility in working time. But any general reform is hampered by the very deep distrust underlying social and political relations in France. A widely shared view is that any large-scale change in the functioning of the labor market would surely eliminate the existing guarantees without providing any new opportunity, in particular for low-skilled, low-paid workers.

Research assistance by Jean-Baptiste Berry, Marie-Cecile Cazenave, Elise Coudin, and Anna Okatenko is gratefully acknowledged. We are very grateful to Annette Bernhardt and Tom Cook for the extensive comments and suggestions they offered on an earlier version of this chapter. They have been extremely helpful in improving and sharpening our analysis. We also thank all of the co-authors of the following chapters, as well as Christine Erhel, David Howell, Gilbert Lefèvre, François Michon, Gerhard Bosch, Aixa Cintron-Valdez, Geoff Mason, Ken Mayhew, Niels Westergaard-Nielsen, Wiemer Salverda, Christopher Tilly, and Eric Wanner for useful comments. The usual disclaimer applies.

NOTES

1. The policy constraints imposed by the European Union monetary integration are often mentioned in relation to this point.
2. The corresponding figures are 25.9 percent for Denmark, 40.1 percent for the Netherlands, and 54 percent for Germany.
3. Hourly wages are computed as the ratio of monthly wages to the number of hours worked during one month.
4. The Enquête Emploi has information on monthly wages, bonuses, and premiums and on hours worked. People are asked how long they usually work every week, and if they have not worked "normal" hours, they are asked how long they were working during the week before the interview. The main advantage of the Enquête Emploi is that it provides a lot of details on workers' characteristics and jobs and covers both the public and private sectors. The main drawback of this dataset is that measurement error is likely to be non-negligible, given that the information on wages and hours worked relies on workers' declarations. An alternative data source would be the DADS. This database is built using compulsory employers' claims, which cover all workers in the private sector and in state-owned companies belonging to the competitive sector. It provides good-quality, exhaustive information on wages, bonuses, and premiums as well as on hours worked. Unfortunately, the DADS data cover neither the public noncompetitive sector nor household services. Given that this partial coverage of salaried workers is likely to induce major biases when estimating the proportion of low-wage workers, we choose to rely on the Enquête Emploi to describe low-wage work in France. We did not go beyond the year 2002 because the structure of the Labor Force Survey was greatly modified in 2003, and wage data in particular are not easily comparable.
5. Euro-dollar purchasing power parity is the rate of currency conversion that eliminates the differences in consumption price levels between France and the United States. It is computed using the exchange rate provided by the Bank of France and the comparative price levels computed by the OECD. The "Big Mac" purchasing power parity is the exchange rate that would leave a burger in any country costing the same as in the United States. It is computed for the Euro zone as a whole by *The Economist* using McDonald's data.
6. The purchasing power parity used here is the same as the one used earlier for the low-wage cutoff—in other words, it is the rate of currency conversion that eliminated the differences in consumption price levels between France and the United States in August 2006.

7. Apprentices and temporary agency workers are not included in these statistics. The basic wage does not include seniority premiums, compensating premiums for "working conditions" (cold, heat, night), or earnings from profit-sharing schemes.
8. The D5/D1 ratio of monthly wages (net of social contributions) of full-time workers in the private sector fell to 1.49 in 2004, and the D9/D1 ratio to 2.97, the lowest level since 1951 (Bignon 2007).
9. Employers' social contributions complement employees' social contributions. They include mainly payments to the social security system covering health insurance, pensions, work accidents, family allowances, and compulsory unemployment insurance.
10. Wage mobility is measured as the probability of transition from a lower to a higher wage decile.
11. Hourly productivity is measured by the average value-added per person-hour; capital intensity is measured by the relative physical capital per hour worked in 2002.
12. In 2001 the employment rate (defined as the number of workers in all service activities divided by the total working-age population) was more than 12 percent higher in Denmark than in France (Cahuc and Debonneuil 2004, from OECD data). Nevertheless, part of this gap may be due to the shorter average working time in these activities in Denmark.
13. The most common employment contracts in France are permanent, open-ended contracts and temporary forms of employment. Permanent open-ended contracts come in two types:
    - Under *"standard" open-ended contracts* (contrat à durée indéterminée, or CDI), workers are employed for an open-ended period and any layoff, dismissal, or collective redundancy must be properly justified by the employing firm.
    - Under the *"new hiring" open-ended contract* (contrat nouvelle embauche, or CNE)—a type created in 2005 that is restricted to firms employing twenty people or less—employment protection is reduced during the first two years of the contract.

    Temporary forms of employment include four types:
    - A *"standard" fixed-term contract* (contrat à durée déterminée, or CDD) can only be used to substitute for absent permanent workers or to hire workers on specific occasions (for specific missions, during seasonal activity, or during an unusual peak in activity). The length of the work period is specified in the contract, the contract cannot be renewed more than once, and its total length cannot exceed eighteen months. At the end of the contract, the worker is entitled to a "precariousness" bonus amounting to 10 percent of the

total wage (if not recruited by his employer on an open-ended contract), plus paid holidays accumulated during the contract.
- Contracts for *temporary agency work* can be used on the same conditions as the CDD. At the end of the contract, workers are also granted a "precariousness" bonus amounting to 10 percent of the total wage, plus paid holidays accumulated during the contract.
- *Apprenticeship* contracts are offered under initial vocational training programs.
- *Labor market policy schemes* cover publicly subsidized contracts in the profit and nonprofit sectors and workers on vocational training schemes.

14. There are three main types of derogatory fixed-term employment contracts:
    - Under a fixed-term *seasonal contract*, the length of the work period does not have to be indicated and firms do not have to pay the 10 percent wage bonus at the end of the contract. This contract can be renewed from one season to the next without any limit of time. But the length cannot exceed eight or nine months within a year. It can be used in all sectors that are officially recognized as having a strongly seasonal activity.
    - A fixed-term *contract of constant use* can be used for unlimited periods of time in a number of sectors where these contracts are recognized by law as being "of constant use." The *extra* work contract, used in the hotel and restaurant sector, is a special case of this type of contract.
    - The *student seasonal contract* can only be used for students working during school holidays. It lasts for two months at the most. No wage bonus is owed at the end of the contract.

    There are several other types of derogatory contracts:
    - The *sporadic permanent contract* can be used when the activity is recognized to be irregular owing to tourism, school rhythm, seasons, or arts performances. Workers are employed on an open-ended contract and work on call with a minimum number of paid hours guaranteed in the contract.
    - Under *Tâcheron contracts*, posted (national) workers are employed for specific tasks, mainly in food processing, and paid at piece rates.
    - *Office des Migrations Internationales (OMI) contracts* allow employers to hire foreign workers from Morocco, Tunisia, and Poland for up to eight months. These contracts must be authorized by the local administration, which guarantees that the workers will return to their home country as soon as the contract ends.

15. This recognition was awarded to the trade unions after World War II

(and legalized in 1966) because they actively participated in the Resistance and the liberation of France.

16. According to the 2003 INSEE Survey on Living Conditions of Households, unionization is as low as 3.5 percent in establishments with fifty or fewer workers, compared to 8.7 percent in establishments with five hundred or more employees.

17. Blanchard and Philippon's (2004) measure of the quality of labor relations relates to the year 1999 and is based on the answers given by a sample of executives to this question: "Do you agree with the following statement: labor/employer relations are generally cooperative." Responses varied from 1 (strong disagreement) to 7 (strong agreement). Actual mean responses varied from 3.3 in France to 6.4 in Switzerland; the United States and the United Kingdom scored around 5, and the Netherlands, Denmark, and Sweden around 6.

18. Thirty-nine percent of immigrants came from European countries (with 34.5 percent coming from the EU-15), 31 percent from North Africa, and 30 percent from the rest of the world (essentially Turkey and southern Africa).

19. For instance, in 2003, 173,100 persons immigrated permanently into France—21 percent coming from the European Economic Area and 79 percent from outside. On average, only 10 percent were workers, the rest being family members of people living in France, refugees, sick people, and so on.

20. The rate of sanction is measured by the ratio of the number of unemployed who were sanctioned during the year to the total number of unemployed.

21. There are specific minimum incomes for lone parents and for disabled and handicapped persons.

22. At the beginning of the 2000s, more than 10 percent of school leavers benefited from such a scheme in the three years following their entry into the labor market.

23. Workers who are younger than sixty and have contributed to their pension fund for at least forty years can benefit from this allowance until they reach the legal age of retirement (sixty); if they are older than fifty-five, they may be permitted not to search for a new job actively. The same holds for all unemployed over the age of fifty-seven and a half, with no condition concerning their pension contributions.

24. The aide parentale d'education was replaced at the beginning of the 2000s by a similar allowance, the prestation d'acccueil du jeune enfant.

25. It is an employment-conditional benefit; the earnings derived from work initially had to be higher than 0.3 times the full-time annual SMIC (and less than 1.4 times the full-time, annual SMIC). The tax-

able income of the household to which the person belongs must not exceed a threshold that varies according to the size of the household. The benefit increases with the annual working time, and, for a given working time, it is greatest for an hourly wage at the SMIC level.

26. After reaching a peak of 1.9 percent of GDP in 1992, investment in training fell to 1.43 percent of GDP in 2002. Most of it is paid for by private firms (44.2 percent), followed by the state (35.4 percent), the regions (9.6 percent), and households (3 percent).

REFERENCES

Afsa, Cédric, and Pierre Biscourp. 2004. "L'Évolution des rythmes de travail entre 1995 et 2001: Quel impact des 35 heures?" ["The Evolution of Work Hours Between 1995 and 2001: What Is the Impact of the 35-Hour Week?"]. *Économie et Statistique* 376–77: 173–213.

Aghion, Philippe, and Peter Howitt. 2006. "Appropriate Growth Policy: A Unifying Framework." Joseph Schumpeter Lecture delivered at the twentieth annual congress of the European Economic Association. August 24–28, 2006, Amsterdam.

Algan, Yann, and Pierre Cahuc. 2006. "Why Is the Minimum Wage So High in Low-Trust Countries?" Working paper. University of Marne la Vallée. Accessed at http://www.cepremap.cnrs.fr/algan/trust_union.

Amira, Selma, and Gilbert De Stefano. 2005. "Contrats à durée déterminée, intérim, apprentissage, contrats aidés: Les emplois à statut particulier ont progressé entre 1982 et 2002" ["Fixed-term Contracts, Agency Work, Apprenticeship and Subsidized Employment: The Number of Non-standard Work Contracts Has Increased Between 1982 and 2002"]. *Première Synthèses* (DARES) 14(2).

Anne, Denis, and Yannick L'Horty. 2002. "Transferts sociaux locaux et retour à l'emploi" ["Local Welfare Transfers and Returning to Work"]. *Économie et Statistique* 357–58: 49–78.

Arnaudo, Bernard, Isabelle Magaud-Camus, Nicolas Sandret, Thomas Coutrot, Nicole Guignon, Sylvie Hamon-Cholet, Dominique Waltisperger, and Marie-C. Floury. 2004. "L'exposition aux risques et aux pénibilités du travail de 1994 à 2003" ["Exposure to Risks and the Pains of Work from 1994 to 2003"]. *Premières Synthèses* (DARES) 52(1, December).

Artus, Patrick, and Gilbert Cette. 2004. *Productivité et croissance*. Paris: Rapport au Conseil d'Analyse Economique.

Askenazy, Philippe. 1998. "Le développement des pratiques flexibles de travail." In *Nouvelle économie*, edited by Daniel Cohen and Michèle Debonneuil. Paris: Rapport au Conseil d'Analyse Économique.

Askenazy, Philippe, Ève Caroli, and Vincent Marcus. 2002. "New Organizational Practices and Working Conditions: Evidence from France in the 1990s." *Louvain Economic Review* 68(1/2): 91–110.

Banaei, Alireza, Bertran Auvert, Marcel Goldberg, Alice Gueguen, Danièle Luce, and Stephen Goldberg. 2000. "Future Trends in Mortality of French Men from Mesothelioma." *Occupational and Environmental Medicine* 57(7, July): 488–94.,

Berry, Jean-Baptiste. 2007. "Les bénéficiaires d'une revalorisation du SMIC au 1er juillet 2006" ["People Impacted by the Increase in the Minimum Wage on July 1st, 2006"]. *Premières Synthèses* (DARES) 13(1).

Bertrand, Marianne, and Francis Kramarz. 2002. "Does Entry Regulation Hinder Job Creation? Evidence from the French Retail Industry." *Quarterly Journal of Economics* 117(4): 1369–414.

Bignon, Nicolas. 2007. "L'éventail des salaires se resserre légèrement entre 1996 et 2004 pour les salariés à temps complet du secteur privé" ["Salaries Between 1996 and 2004: The Wage Dispersion Among Full-Time Employees Decreases Slightly in the Private Sector"]. *Premières Synthèses* 39(1, September).

Blanchard, Olivier, and Thomas Philippon. 2004. "The Quality of Labor Relations and Unemployment." Working paper W10590. Cambridge, Mass.: National Bureau of Economic Research (June).

Borjas, George J., and Lawrence F. Katz. 2005. "The Evolution of the Mexican Workforce in the United States." Working paper W11281. Cambridge, Mass.: National Bureau of Economic Research (April).

Borrel, Catherine. 2006. "Enquêtes annuelles de recensement 2004 et 2005: Près de 5 millions d'immigrés à la mi-2004" ["Annual Census Sruvey of 2004 and 2005: Almost 5 Million Immigrants at the Halfway Point of 2004"]. *INSEE Première* 1098.

Bourlès, Renaud, and Gilbert Cette. 2005. "A Comparison of Structural Productivity Levels in the Major Industrialized Countries." *OECD Economic Studies* 41(2): 75–108.

Cahuc, Pierre, and Michèle Debonneuil. 2004. *Productivité et emploi dans le tertiaire* [*Productivity and Employment in the Tertiary Sector*]. Rapport au Conseil d'Analyse Économique 49. Paris: La Documentation Française.

Cahuc, Pierre, and Francis Kramarz. 2004. "De la précarité à la mobilité: Vers une sécurité sociale professionnelle" ["From Precariousness to Mobility: Towards a Professional Social Security"]. Report to the French minister of finance and the French minister of labor and social affairs.

Cahuc, Pierre, and André Zylberberg. 2004. *Le Chômage, nécessité ou fatalité?* [*Unemployment: Necessity or Fatality?*]. Paris: Flammarion.

Carcillo, Stéphane, and Benjamin Delozier. 2004. "Le SMIC en France: Pouvoir d'achat et coût du travail sur longue période" ["The SMIC in France: Purchasing Power and the Cost of Work over a Long Period"]. *DP Analyses Économiques* 39.

Card, David. 2005. "Is the New Immigration Really So Bad?" Working paper

W11547. Cambridge, Mass.: National Bureau of Economic Research (August).
Cette, Gilbert, Nicolas Dromel, and Dominique Méda. 2004. "Les déterminants du jugement des salariés sur la RTT" ["The Explaining Factors of Workers' Judgments About Education in Working Time"]. *Économie et Statistique* (376–77): 117–51.
Conseil Supérieur de l'Emploi, des revenus et de la Cohésion Sociale (CSERC). 1999. *Le SMIC (salaire minimum interprofessionnel de croissance)*. Paris: La Documentation Française.
Coutrot, Thomas, and Dominique Waltisperger. 2005. "L'emploi des seniors souvent fragilisé par des problèmes de santé" ["The Employment of Seniors Often Weakened by Health Problems"]. *Premières Synthèses* (DARES) 8(1).
Direction de l'Animation de la Recherche, des Études et des Statistiques (DARES). 2005. "Une légère baisse des dépenses de formation professionnelle en 2002" ["Vocational Educational Spending Falls Slightly in 2002"]. *Premières Synthèses* 9(1).
Dormont, Brigitte Simone, Denis Fougère, and Ana Prieto. 2001. "L'effet de l'allocation unique dégressive sur la reprise d'emploi" ["The Impact of the Flat Time-Decreasing Benefit on the Probability to Go Back to Employment"]. *Économie et Statistique* 343(September): 3-28.
European Commission. 2004. "Labor Market Transitions and Advancement: Temporary Employment and Low Pay in Europe." In *Employment in Europe*. Luxembourg: Department for Employment and Social Affairs.
Fougère, Denis, and Francis Kramarz. 2001. "La Mobilité en France de 1967 à 1999" ["Mobility in France from 1967 to 1999"]. In *Inégalités économiques* [*Economic Inequalities*], edited by Anthony Atkinson, Michel Glaude, Lucile Olier, and Thomas Piketty. Rapport pour le Conseil d'Analyse Économique. Paris: La Documentation Française.
Freeman, Richard, and Ronald Shettkat. 2002. "Marketization of Production and the U.S.-Europe Employment Gap." Working paper 8797. Cambridge, Mass.: National Bureau of Economic Research (February).
French Senate. 2006. "Immigration clandestine: Une réalité inacceptable, une réponse ferme, juste et humaine" ["Illegal Immigration: An Unacceptable Reality, a Firm, Fair, and Humane Response"]. Rapport de la Commission d'Enquête sur l'Immigration Clandestine. Accessed at http://www.senat.fr/rap/r05-300-1/r05-300-1.html.
Glyn, Andrew. 2005. "Employment in Distribution, Productivity, and the Growth of Consumption." In *Low Wage Employment in Europe*, edited by Ive Marx and Wiemer Salverda. Leuven, Belgium: Acco.
Green, Francis, and Steven MacIntosh. 2001. "The Intensification of Work in Europe." *Labor Economics* 8(2): 291–308.
Haut Conseil à l'Intégration. 2004. "Rapport 2002–2003: Observatoire statistique de l'immigration et de l'intégration" ["2002-2003 Report: Statistical Observation on Immigration and Integration"]. Accessed at http://

www.ladocumentationfrancaise.fr/rapports-publics/044000610/index.shtml.

Lhommeau, Bertrand. 2005. "Des perspectives salariales un peu moins avantageuses pour les bas salaires dans les années quatre-vingt-dix" ["Wage Prospects Slightly Less Favorable for Low-Wage Workers in the 1990s"]. In *Les Salaires en France* [*Wages in France*], edited by INSEE. Paris: INSEE.

Mason, Geoff, Ken Mayhew, and Matthew Osborne. 2008. "Low-Paid Work in the United Kingdom: An Overview." In *Low-Wage Work in the United Kingdom*, edited by Caroline Lloyd, Geoff Mason, and Ken Mayhew. New York: Russell Sage Foundation.

Mason, Geoff, Brigid O'Leary, Mary O'Mahony, and Kate Robinson. 2007. *Cross-Country Performance at the Sector Level: The U.K. Compared with the U.S., France, and Germany*. London: National Institute of Economic and Social Research.

Ministry of Education. 2003. "From Continuous to Life-long Training?" *Education et Formation* 66: 201-7.

Ministry of Labor. 2005. *An Assessment of Collective Bargaining in France in 2005*. Paris: Ministry of Labor.

Monneraye, Olivier, and Stéphane Jugnot. 2006. "En 2004, le nombre de demandeurs d'emploi indemnisés cesse de croître pour la première fois depuis quatre ans" ["In 2004, the Number of Job Applicants Benefitting from Unemployment Compensation Did Not Increase for the First Time in Four Years"]. *Premières Synthèses* (DARES) 47(1, November).

Organization for Economic Cooperation and Development (OECD). 2004. "Employment Protection Regulation and Labor Market Performance." In *Employment Outlook*, ch. 2. Paris: OECD.

———. 2005a. *Economic Surveys: France*. Paris: OECD.

———. 2005b. *Education at a Glance*. Paris: OECD.

———. 2006. *Employment Outlook*. Paris: OECD.

Osterman, Paul. 2000. "Work Reorganization in an Era of Restructuring: Trends in Diffusion and Effects on Employee Welfare." *Industrial and Labor Relations Review* 53(2): 179-95.

Piketty, Thomas. 1998. "L'Impact des incitations financières au travail sur les comportements individuels: Une estimation pour le cas français" ["The Impact of Financial Incentives to Work on Individual Behavior: An Estimate on the French Case"]. *Économie et Prévision* 132-33: 1-35.

———. 1999. "L'Emploi dans les services en France et aux États-Unis: Une analyse structurelle sur longue période" ["Service Sector Work in France and the United States: A Structural Analysis Over a Long Period"]. *Économie et Statistique* 318: 73-99.

Regnard, Pierre. 2006. "Minimum Wages 2006: Variations from 82 to 1503

Euro Gross per Month." *Statistics in Focus* (September). Brussels: Eurostat.

Seguin, Sébastien. 2006. "Les Salariés au SMIC en 2002: Un sur deux travaille dans une petite entreprise, un sur quatre gagne plus que 1,3 SMIC horaire grâce aux compléments de salaire" ["Workers Earning the Minimum Wage in 2002: One Out of Two Works in a Small Firm; One Out of Four Earns More than 1.3 Times the Hourly Minimum Wage Thanks to Bonuses and Premiums"]. *Premières Synthèses* (DARES) 27(2, July).

Sraer, David. 2007. "Allègements des cotisations patronales et dynamique salariale" ["Employers' Social Contributions Exemptions and Wage Dynamics"]. Working paper G 2007/01. Paris: INSEE, Direction des Études et des Synthèses Économiques.

CHAPTER 3

Operators in Food-Processing Industries: Coping with Increasing Pressures

Ève Caroli, Jérôme Gautié, and Annie Lamanthe

France's food-processing sector is particularly interesting to study because it has many employees and is representative of the French employment model described in the previous chapter. Indeed, the sector is characterized by large numbers of low-skilled workers and difficult working conditions, both of which would make it a low-wage industry in other countries, especially the United States. Yet, while wages may be lower than in most industries, the share of low-wage workers is small. This sector is also marked by strong dualism: permanent staff are generally not low-paid, and poor wages affect mainly temporary workers, who are a structural feature of labor in this sector, given its specific nature (significant seasonal fluctuations, but also weekly and even daily ones for some products).

Given the strong rise in competition in recent years, it is actually remarkable that the share of low-wage workers has remained so limited. This raises questions about the strategies that companies have used to meet competitive pressures and about the impact of these strategies on workers. Is it possible to identify good practices and the factors that may cause or favor them?

We have had to make some methodological choices to answer these questions. Given the heterogeneity of the sector overall, our work has concentrated on two, contrasting subsectors: meat processing and confectionery. In both cases, our study looks at all operators, in production as well as in packaging. Various sources have been used. To provide an overview of the sector and put the representativeness of the case studies in context, we used statistical data and conducted interviews with various actors in the branch (unions and employers' associations at the branch and regional levels, as well as occupational physicians). Moreover, we conducted detailed surveys in seven companies (three in confectionery and four in [pork] meat processing). The companies were chosen so as to represent both "small-batch" as well as "mass-production" firms. It should be stressed that getting access to companies was difficult (many of the companies we contacted refused to participate), so that the representativeness of the sample is limited. We interviewed members of top management, employees, and workers' representatives in each firm. In some cases, we also interviewed staff from the temporary employment agencies working with the companies we studied. We conducted about one hundred interviews overall, including those with branch-level representatives.

Our study shows that companies have indeed had to meet rising competitive pressures. These stem from changing consumer habits and tougher hygiene and safety requirements, stronger international competition, and, above all, the spread of super- and hypermarket retailing, which now distributes nearly 70 percent of the sector's products. These changes have raised constraints in terms of cost, quality, adaptability, and responsiveness to demand. Although none of the companies studied have adopted "social dumping" strategies, many have put pressure on compensation, challenging certain aspects of the traditional French employment model. They have also resorted to greater use of automation and new forms of work organization, especially multitasking. These changes have had contradictory effects on workers: there is not as much hard physical labor, but the intensity of work has increased without higher wages to compensate. This has led to much frustration among the employees we interviewed. Some companies have nevertheless tried to adopt good practices, especially those relating to training and multiskilling for permanent workers and improving job security and compensation for temporary workers.

In the first section, we describe the food-processing sector and present the two subsectors in detail, stressing their contrasting features. The next section analyzes the competitive pressures that companies have faced in recent years and presents the case studies, linking them to the different positions in the supply chain and to business strategies. Finally, we set out the impacts on different operators, distinguishing between permanent and temporary workers.

THE FRENCH FOOD-PROCESSING SECTOR

Food manufacturing is the leading manufacturing sector in France in terms of sales (€146 billion [US$208 billion] in 2004) and the third-largest in terms of employment (about 606,000 jobs in 2004). France ranks very high internationally in this industry, being the leading European producer and the second-largest world exporter. Total employment in the industry increased during the 1990s until the beginning of the 2000s, but has decreased slightly since then. Profitability tends to be lower than in the rest of the manufacturing sector. The majority of the sector was traditionally composed of small and medium-sized firms: in 2003 only 6.5 percent of firms in the sector had more than twenty employees. However, concentration has been taking place, and large groups are emerging. Despite this long-run trend, today only one-third of French food manufacturing groups employ more than five hundred workers, and only five of them are among the top European twenty (Ministry of Agriculture 2004).[1]

Another characteristic of the French food industry is its very high proportion of blue-collar workers. In the beginning of the 2000s, these workers amounted to 65 percent of the salaried workforce, compared to an average of 30 percent for the whole manufacturing sector. Correspondingly, the share of managers and supervisors was only 17 percent, compared to 39 percent in the entire French manufacturing sector. Moreover, the proportion of jobs classified as "unskilled" is very high among blue-collar jobs in food manufacturing: 44 percent as opposed to less than 32 percent in all manufacturing sectors. The sector is also more feminized, with women holding about 40 percent of the jobs—compared to 30 percent in all manufacturing sectors—and being employed more often as manual workers. Young workers are also overrepresented: 30 percent of employees are under thirty years old, compared to 20 percent in all manufacturing sectors (Ministry of Agriculture 2006). Indeed, the low-skilled and seasonal nature of the work, together with high labor turnover, provides more opportunities for new entrants to the labor market. In contrast, the sector employs few immigrant workers: in 2004 only 3.3 percent of food-processing employees were foreign nationals, while only 7.5 percent were born abroad.

Food processing is halfway between agricultural production and final consumption. It is subject to strong activity fluctuations: daily variations are more important than in construction and in the tertiary sector (Jourdain et al. 1999). As a result, the sector relies heavily on temporary work contracts (10 percent of all jobs, as opposed to 8 percent in all sectors). On the other hand, part-time work is less important (about 7 percent compared to 16 percent). Labor turnover is comparatively very high: in 2004 it stood at 39.7 percent, compared to 16.4 percent for all manufacturing sectors (for plants with ten or more employees). The use of temp agency workers is twice as prevalent as in all sectors: in 2004, 6.4 percent of employees were employed by temp agencies (Ministry of Agriculture 2006). Young workers are more likely to have temporary contracts; in addition, food-processing companies offer young workers short-term contracts more frequently and tenured contracts less frequently than in all industries (Lamanthe 2003).

Finally, industrial relations in the food-processing sector are quite representative of a large number of sectors in France (see chapter 2): negotiations at the branch level are fairly active, but unions are weak (or even absent) and often divided at the firm level. According to the trade unionists we interviewed at the branch level, it should also be noted that union officials and representatives suffer a certain degree of harassment in many firms (and not just in the smallest ones).

Two Contrasting Subsectors: Meat Processing and Confectionery

Apart from these common characteristics, the branches within the food-processing sector also manifest great diversity. These are well illustrated by the contrasts between meat processing and confectionery, which in 2004 employed 46,000 and 18,000 workers, respectively, in companies with more than twenty employees.[2]

The meat-processing sector is less concentrated than confectionery. In sugar confectionery, for instance, the biggest three groups—Cadbury, Haribo, and Wrigley—control two-thirds of the market, while in meat processing the ten largest firms accounted for only 25 percent of sales in 2004. Both capital intensity and productivity are also higher in confectionery; correspondingly, labor costs represent a smaller share of value-added—58 percent compared to 68 percent (see table 3.1). Finally, the sector appears to be quite open, with imports and exports accounting for as much as 25 percent and 21 percent of sales, respectively (Agreste 2004; Ministry of Agriculture 2004). This is less the case in meat processing.

Meat processing and confectionery are also quite different with respect to the nature of the jobs and the characteristics of the workforce. The former has many more low-skilled occupations than the latter: blue-collar workers amount to 79 percent of the workforce in

Table 3.1 Characteristics of the Meat-Processing and Confectionary Sectors, 2004

	Firms with More than Twenty Workers			All Firms
	Confectionary	Meat Processing	Average Food Processing	Average Food Processing
Value-added per average worker	€75,000	€45,000	€62,000	€50,000
Labor cost/ value-added	55%	68%	58%	—
Capital intensity	€115,000	€71,000	€110,000	€84,000
Imports/turnover	25.2%	8.2%	10.7%	9.9%
Exports/turnover	21.2%	4.1%	15.4%	14.1%

Source: Authors' compilation from Statistiques structurelles d'entreprises, Accès en Ligne aux Statistiques Structurelles d'Entreprises (ALISSE) database, Institut Nationale de la Statistique et des Études Economiques (INSEE).
Note: The data also include firms with fewer than twenty workers, but only with a turnover higher than €100,000.

the meat-processing sector, compared to only 59 percent in confectionary (see table 3.2).

The proportion of women is higher in confectionary than in meat processing (about 49 percent compared to 42 percent). The proportion of workers of foreign origin seems small overall in both sectors,

Table 3.2 Characteristics of Workers in the Meat-Processing and Confectionary Sectors, 2000

	Meat Processing	Confectionary
Occupation[a]		
Managers and engineers	3.4%	10.9%
Technicians and supervisors	5.6	7.9
Clerks	12	22.3
Blue-collar workers	79	58.9
Blue-collar workers working in unskilled jobs	60	45.8
Gender[b]		
Men	58	51.3
Women	42	48.7

[a] Authors' compilation from Déclarations Annuelles des Données Sociales (DADS) (2000).
[b] Authors' compilation from DADS (2002).

Table 3.3 Working Conditions in Meat Processing and Confectionary, 2003

	Meat Processing	Confectionary	All Manufacturing Sectors
Constraints on working time			
Working at least ten Sundays per year	3%	19%	11%
Not knowing hours to be worked in following week	34	21	9
Organizational constraints			
Permanent hierarchical supervision	43	45	42
Computerized control	31	37	37
Physical constraints			
Noise greater than eighty-five decibels, for more than twenty hours per week	32	22	29
Standing for more than twenty hours per week	76	66	54
Handling heavy loads for more than twenty hours per week	45	30	23
Repetitive manual operations for more that twenty hours per week	59	39	29

Source: Authors' compilation from Surveillance Médicale des Risques (SUMER) survey, 2003; data provided by Jean-François Chastang, Institut National de la Santé et de la Recherche Médicale (INSERM).

especially in the rural areas where many firms are located.[3] (This was particularly the case in our case study firms.) Although there are some differences between the two branches in terms of working conditions, these are generally more difficult than in the manufacturing industry as a whole, especially with respect to the predictability of hours from one week to the next and physical labor (the number of hours that workers spend on their feet, handling heavy loads, and doing repetitive manual operations; see table 3.3).

Regarding earnings, even if wages tend to be lower than in the rest of the manufacturing sector, both subsectors display a small proportion of low-wage workers: 7.2 percent and 6.2 percent, respectively, in 2003, compared to 10.4 percent on average (for all sectors except the public sector and the domestic services; see table 2.10). Why is this so?

WHY FOOD PROCESSING IS NOT A LOW-WAGE SECTOR

The Role of Collective Bargaining Agreements in Setting Wages The "paradox" of there being few low-wage workers in this sector is partly explained by the role played by the French model (described in chapter 2), at least as far as permanent workers are concerned. As with other manufacturing sectors, food processing appears to be better structured professionally and in terms of its industrial relations than the service sectors studied here (except hospitals; see chapter 4). This is reflected in the collective bargaining agreements that are applied by law to all companies and that provide workers (at least permanent ones) with numerous bonuses.

Table 3.4 presents the branch job evaluation schemes—each job or post being characterized by a coefficient that is determined on the basis of several criteria, including the complexity of the tasks to be carried out, the competencies required, in particular the education level, the degree of autonomy in the post, the duration of on-the-job training required to become fully productive, and the level of technical expertise. Pay coefficients corresponding to operators and clerks range from 120 to 190. The minimum wage corresponding to each coefficient is negotiated at the branch level. The wages presented in table 3.4 are basic wages as set out in collective agreements; "effective" basic wages at the firm level may be higher.

In both sectors, branch-level collective agreements define various bonuses awarded on top of basic wages: an annual premium (the so-called thirteenth month, which indeed amounts to a full monthly wage, as set out in the agreement), a seniority premium, and various other bonuses for factors such as hot or cold working conditions, night work, contributions to lunch expenses, and dressing and undressing time.[4] Large firms also have profit-sharing schemes[5] and very often other fringe benefits (such as complementary health insurance).

Annual, branch-level collective agreements also fix yearly recommendations for across-the-board wage increases. Following the implementation of the law on the thirty-five-hour week at the end of the 1990s, wage moderation has been the norm. As a result, increases in the legal minimum wage (the SMIC) have been the driving force behind hourly pay rises, but monthly wages have risen much less than hourly wages, because of the reduction in the working week. In the

Table 3.4 Wage Levels in Branch-Level Collective Agreements, Beginning of 2006 (Full-Time Operators, Thirty-Five Hours a Week, 151.67 Hours a Month)

	Meat Processing[a]			Confectionary[b]	
	Gross Minimum Wages			Gross Minimum Wages	
Coefficient in the Job Classification	Monthly	Hourly	Coefficient in the Job Classification	Monthly	Hourly
120	€1,231.35	€8.12	120	€1,221.03	€8.05
130	€1,235.65	€8.15	130	€1,228.68	€8.10
140	€1,240.85	€8.18	140	€1,236.49	€8.15
150	€1,265.70	€8.35	150	€1,260.24	€8.31
160	€1,302.27	€8.59	160	€1,284.70	€8.47
170	€1,341.46	€8.84	170	€1,312.82	€8.66
180	€1,389.44	€9.16	180	€1,344.92	€8.87
190	€1,437.57	€9.48	190	€1,377.84	€9.08

Source: Author's compilation from the collective agreements of the two subsectors.
[a] Main collective agreement of the activity (signed by the FICT (Fédération française des industriels charcutiers, traiteurs, et transformateurs de viands), employers' organization); the majority of slaughterhouses are covered by other collective agreements.
[b] Collective agreement (signed by the Alliance 7 employers' organization) covering, among others, sugar confectionary and chocolate confectionary.

meat-processing sector, for instance, the real hourly wage for a job coefficient of 120 rose by 19.6 percent between the beginning of 1998 (before the implementation of the thirty-five-hour week) and the beginning of 2006. But at the same time, the real monthly wage rose only by 6.9 percent. In addition, the wage distribution was slightly compressed during this period: for example, the monthly wage for the 190 coefficient was 17.6 percent higher than for 120 in 1998, but only 16.7 percent higher in 2006.

Moreover, up until the early 1980s in the confectionery sector and the start of the 2000s in meat processing, annual agreements on wage increases concerned effective wages: a firm had to increase its wages according to the rate decided at the branch level, even if those wages were above the basic branch wage. This is no longer the case. Consequently, effective wages at the bottom of the wage distribution tend to converge on collective branch wages in many firms, and hence on the legal minimum wage. (The SMIC amounted to €1,217.91 gross per month (US$1733.65) for a thirty-five-hour week, at the beginning of 2006.)

Because the low-wage threshold defined here (two-thirds of the median hourly wage; see chapter 2) is very close to the SMIC (the gap was less than 6 percent at the beginning of the 2000s), the "thirteenth month" salary and other bonuses may bring average hourly compensation in both sectors above this threshold, even for the lowest-paid workers. This is the case for almost all permanent workers, who, moreover, are usually not indexed at the lowest coefficients in the job classification, except in the first month of their contract. Most of them have a coefficient rating of at least 140. Overall, at the beginning of 2006, just to take an example, the gross hourly compensation of full-time workers who had five years of tenure in the meat-processing sector and were classified with a coefficient of 150 in the job evaluation scheme might have amounted to at least €9.50 (US$13.52) (taking into account only the thirteenth month and the seniority premium). If these workers worked night shifts and in a cold environment, their pay rose by about 25 percent more. The net wage of employees' social contribution (but before income tax) was about 22 percent lower (see chapter 2), but they would have benefited from the social security system (covering health, pensions, work accidents, family allowances, three months' maternity leave, and so on).

The situation is often quite different for nonpermanent workers. Temp agency work pays relatively well, owing to the 10 percent "precariousness" or job insecurity bonus awarded by law at the end of the contract (plus another 10 percent corresponding to paid holidays). In contrast, seasonal workers are often allocated the lowest coefficients in the classification (120 or 130) and do not benefit from most bonuses. They are the employees mainly affected by low-wage work—even those who regularly come back every year— because of the lack of any recognition of seniority (until recently, as discussed in a later section).

It should be mentioned that there is a gender dimension to wage inequalities because of segregation in employment: women are found more often in some occupations (such as packaging operators) or are more likely to have certain employment statuses (such as seasonal workers) for which wages are lower. But differences in pay between jobs may also reflect the monopsony power of firms (especially in rural areas, where women's opportunities for mobility are reduced) and more generally the lower bargaining power of women. As acknowledged by trade unionists, certain jobs have a lower coefficient in job evaluation schemes because they are feminized.

To summarize, as a result of numerous bonuses, average wages in the sector are not very low in relative terms. However, quite significant inequalities exist, both between men and women (owing to unequal access to different types of jobs) and between permanent and temporary workers (with low-wage work being especially concentrated among the latter).

Beyond Wages: The Lesser Role of Institutions Beyond wage determination, institutions also play a role in shaping local working time arrangements and offering some expertise in the area of continuous training. However, their impact is less direct in this area than it is on wages.

In recent years, negotiations at the branch level have been focused on reducing working time in both sectors, in order to implement France's laws introducing the thirty-five-hour working week. Firms could choose to annualize working time on the basis of an average of thirty-five hours worked per week, allowing for greater flexibility.[6] Firms that decided to maintain the level of monthly wages while reducing working time were allowed to suppress seniority premiums for new entrants and premiums were frozen for incumbents; this option was adopted by many firms in the confectionery sector. They were also allowed not to raise wages for two years provided that the inflation rate remained below 2 percent over the period. Negotiations have also taken place concerning training, at the level of the food-processing sector overall. A new system for certifying competencies acquired during training spells was adopted (via the certificats de qualification professionnelle, or CQP).[7] In the mid-2000s, health and safety at work has become another important subject of negotiation (especially in the meat sector), with the aim of reducing work accidents and illnesses (especially cumulative trauma disorders, which have increased a lot in recent years).

Aside from branch-level collective negotiations and agreements, other institutions have to be taken into account. The food manufacturing sector in France has a specific institution in charge of continuous training, called Agefaforia, which collects funds from member firms to finance workers' training. It also provides firms in the sector with advice regarding their specific training programs and is responsible for implementing the branch-level training policy—especially through the CQP. The Mutuelle Sociale Agricole (MSA), a health insurance fund that covers the agricultural sector as well as some parts of the food-processing sector, and the Caisses Régionales d'Assurance Maladie (CRAMs), the regional health insurance funds of the social security system that cover almost all sectors in the economy, run surveys on these issues and can provide expertise as well as subsidies to help implement improvements in working conditions. So do the regional agencies for the improvement of working conditions (Agence Régionale pour l'Amélioration des Conditions de Travail, or ARACTs), often with the encouragement and support of the Ministry of Labor's regional and departmental branches. Finally, the regional presence of professional trade associations and unions, which are active to varying degrees, may be noted, as well as that of employers' organizations, some of which try to contribute to employers' collective analysis of human resource management in the sector.

Overall, the institutional framework affects not just wages but also, notably, training, hours worked, and working conditions. This latter impact, however, is less direct and uniform. On the one hand, collective agreements at the branch level do no more than set out general frameworks, and progress in certain areas has only been recent and often quite modest. On the other hand, other existing institutions constitute a sort of "toolbox" that companies are free to use or not. Training practices and working conditions in particular are potentially much more variable than salaries.

COMPETITIVE PRESSURES, TENSIONS, AND STRATEGIES

Companies in food processing have faced increasing competitive pressures since the second half of the 1990s, due to the tightening of various constraints, both national and international. A widespread strategy has been to try to produce higher value added products, but differentiated strategies still exist, the position in the supply chain being an important factor, as illustrated by the companies in our sample.

THE TIGHTENING OF CONSTRAINTS AND RISING COMPETITIVE PRESSURES

Traditionally, food processing firms have been very dependent on fluctuations in the prices of raw materials, which have tended to rise in recent years. But structural pressures have also increased with changing consumer habits, tighter hygiene and sanitation requirements, the expansion of international competition, and, above all, the rise of super- and hypermarket chains.

Changing Consumer Habits and Tougher Hygiene Rules The performance of the meat-processing and confectionery sectors is very sensitive to the ongoing changes in domestic demand. Consumption of (pork) meat products in the home has declined during the last decade, though there has been a small recovery in recent years, mainly owing to the sharp increase in sales of "self-service" products in supermarkets. These have developed considerably and now account for nearly 60 percent of sales. Such changes are closely related to changes in consumer habits in favor of convenience foods and products that are easy to consume. As for confectionery, despite the recent increases in consumption, producers are quite pessimistic about demand prospects in the near future, owing to rising concerns about obesity.

In addition, hygiene and quality control requirements have become much more stringent, partly because consumers are increasingly concerned about health issues, and partly because legal regulations have been passed at the European level (like the regulation on quality traceability passed at the beginning of the 2000s). Accordingly, food manufacturers have been forced to introduce quality control procedures and sometimes to reorganize their production in order to meet new hygiene requirements.

The Rise of International Competition The international openness of the meat-processing sector has been relatively limited so far in France (see table 3.1), but there is a growing concern about increasing competition from Eastern European countries in the years ahead. As for confectionery, firms that produce niche and regional products are so far still protected from foreign competition. But since the beginning of the 2000s, large multinationals, which play a major role in this sector, have tended to reorganize their production, at least at the European level, and this restructuring has led to some plant closures. More generally, restructuring puts pressure on labor costs and work productivity.

Rising Pressure from Super- and Hypermarket Retailers In recent years, the most important source of competitive pressure has come from large-scale retail chains. They have become the main clients for almost all noncraft producers: in the food-processing sector as a whole, nearly 70 percent of sales turnover in 2005 was recorded by supermarkets and hypermarkets. One major problem arises from the fact that retail chains are much more concentrated than suppliers, which allows them to exert strong downward pressure on producers' prices (Canivet 2004). This pressure usually takes the form of "commercial cooperation contracts": in exchange for alleged merchandising services offered by retailers, producers pay them back part of their margins (see chapter 6 for details). Pressure from large-scale retailers has also led to organizational changes, owing to these retailers' just-in-time requirements and their practice of cutting their stocks to a minimum by passing on demand fluctuations to suppliers. Such fluctuations, which may also result from product promotion campaigns, come on top of the seasonal nature of certain products. Pressure from large retailers is greatest for the "first price products" (the lowest-priced products) and for products sold under own-brand names (so-called retail chain brand products, or RCBs).[8] At the start of the 2000s, retail chains introduced Internet auctions for first price products. As for their own-brand products, retailers check the production process thoroughly and impose production standards on subcontractors. Generally, large retailers seek to raise the share of RCBs in their sales, while producers complain that retailers are eating up their productivity gains.

Overall, the rise of large-scale retailing affects all the constraints weighing on companies: cost reductions, increased quality, and greater responsiveness and adaptability to demand (in terms of quality and quantity). From this point of view, it should be noted that super- and hypermarket retailing not only amplifies changes in consumer habits but tightens hygiene and sanitation requirements.

Companies' Differentiated Positioning Strategies

Business Strategies to Cope with Increasing Pressures Changes in business strategy in response to competitive pressure vary across both subsectors and according to market segments within them. However, because the low-quality, high-volume segment of the market is subject to very strong price competition, owning a brand is a key element in resisting the pressure of large retailers. It must be stressed that almost no producer nowadays can afford not to work with mass retailers. Almost all firms, even big multinationals, have to produce at least some RCB products, and occasionally some find themselves competing with their own branded products.

Some independence can be gained through improvements in product quality, and this goal is at the heart of all single producers' business strategies. Improved quality can be achieved through the vertical integration of the production process, which permits better control of the quality of inputs, and through long-term relationships with raw material providers (for example, pork breeders in the meat-processing sector). Quality controls are also a key element to this strategy and had been introduced in all the firms we visited. Most often, a quality function has been created and skilled employees have been hired to fill it. In addition to quality controls, most producers try to increase the share of high-value-added products in their output. This was the case with all the firms we visited except one. To ensure quality recognition, a number of high-value-added producers rely on geographical labeling. In particular, European labels protect them from the product competition that could arise outside their region. However, such labels impose very strict constraints on production processes and may increase producers' dependence on local suppliers of raw materials.

Along with increasing the share of high-value-added products, product diversification is another important source of increased autonomy. One way to achieve diversification is through buying out other firms. The most common strategy, however, is to climb the ladder in the supply chain: in the meat-processing sector, for instance, slaughterhouse firms (the first stage in the chain) develop meat-processing activities (the second stage), whereas many meat processors now produce increasingly transformed products and convenience foods (the third stage).

Positions in the Supply Chain and Business Strategies in Our Sample
Overall, it is possible to distinguish between four categories of producers in the market. This classification can be linked to our case studies (see table 3.5).

The first group is composed of big firms that produce their own brands. They are usually quite large. Some of them are multinationals, especially in the confectionery sector, and as mentioned earlier, their business strategy involves relocating production at the international level and/or outsourcing. This is particularly true in the con-

Table 3.5 The Case Study Food-Processing Companies

Name of Firm	Type and Size of Firm	Product	Local Labor Market
Meat processing			
Canpat	Independent, mainly family-owned firm; 190 permanent workers	Medium- and high-quality products (mainly canned paté and sausage) own-brand and RCB products	Rural labor market
Hambac	Owned by an American group; 560 permanent workers	Mass production of RCB and first price products (mainly ham and bacon)	Quasi-rural labor market, but in an area where other food factories operate
Multiprod	Independent, mainly family-owned firm; two establishments, with 80/250 permanent workers	Medium- and high-quality products (ham, paté, convenience food); own-brand and RCB products	Urban labor market in a rural region
Regsaus	Independent firm; 90 permanent workers	High-quality products (regional labeled sausage); own-brand and RCB products	Rural labor market
Confectionary			
Chochris	Owned by a French group; 250 permanent workers	Medium- and high-quality products (Christmas and Easter chocolates); own-brand and RCB products	Urban labor market in a depressed area
Chocind	Owned by a French group; 120 permanent workers	Mass production of industrial chocolate with no brand	Urban labor market
Regsweet	Independent firm; 62 permanent workers	High-quality, regional labeled sweets; own-brand and RCB products	Urban labor market

Source: Authors' compilation.
Note: RCB products are medium-quality products sold by retail chains under their own brand. First price products are low-quality products sold by retail chains under no brand label.

fectionery sector, where some multinational firms have almost stopped direct production to concentrate on brand management—their production units being transformed in subcontractor firms. Unfortunately, none of the companies we contacted agreed to take part in our study, which explains the absence of multinational confectionery firms in our sample.[9]

The second group of producers specializes in high-volume, low-quality mass production. Such firms often try to become subcontractors for large groups in order to escape from total dependence on large-scale retailers. Their strategy also involves industrial restructuring with their concentration (for example, Chocind in our sample); this strategy sometimes allows them to buy existing brands (such as Hambac).

A third group is made up of medium-sized companies that have their own brand follow a mixed strategy based on diversification of products and distribution channels (for example, Chochris, Multiprod, and, to a lesser extent, Canpat). The strategy is to generate economies of scale by producing for large retailers (including own-brand or RCB products) and economies of scope by selling high-value-added products in small batches, under the producer's own name; these products are sometimes distributed through other channels. (For example, Multiprod also distributes its products through pork butchers and delicatessen shops and is trying to set up a shop network under its own name.)

A last group of producers comprises small businesses that produce niche products. Two firms in our sample produce geographically protected, labeled products: Regsweet for regional almond sweets and Regsaus for local sausages. In general, producers of niche products are not of interest to large groups. Firms in this group are very heterogeneous: some are very successful, whereas others have invested very little and their production techniques are antiquated. The risk is very high that this type of firm will close down when the owner retires if he or she has not properly organized his or her succession.

THE EFFECTS OF COMPANY STRATEGIES ON LOW-SKILLED, LOW-WAGE WORKERS

Our case studies make it possible to analyze the consequences of companies' adaptation strategies on the working conditions of low-skilled, low-wage workers. These consequences vary according to whether employees are permanent or temporary (temp agency workers, seasonal workers, or fixed-term contract workers). Overall, permanent workers operate under a traditional employment model. Our observations show that this model is under pressure from company adaptation strategies. Although the nature of certain activities (notably seasonality) induces food-processing firms to make structural use of temporary labor, we observed that practices have diversified and become more complex, given the need for greater flexibility. Since low-wage workers are mainly temporary workers of one kind or another, it is important to study how they too have been affected by the changes under way.

PERMANENT WORKERS: TENSIONS IN THE TRADITIONAL MODEL

Company Reactions to Rising Constraints None of the companies in our sample had resorted to "social dumping" strategies—that is, aggressive policies to cut labor costs. It is interesting to note that none of the employers interviewed complained spontaneously about excessive labor costs, and none complained about the legal minimum wage (SMIC). Apart from problems related to sample bias (we did not manage to get access to companies experiencing the greatest competitive pressures), the firms studied were still little affected by international competition. Their main competitors were national and therefore faced the same constraints—the minimum wage applied by law to all. This limited individual social dumping strategies and marked an important difference with, for example, Germany, where there is no legal minimum wage. It might also be stressed that the local labor markets in which the companies studied here operated had been relatively protected, up until the present, by legislation limiting the influx of immigrants who would accept worse employment conditions (on the impact of immigration on labor markets, see chapter 2).

That said, company strategies do aim at cutting costs in various ways. It is interesting to note that, according to some unionists we interviewed at the branch level, the major multinational companies in confectionery (which were not in our sample) used to provide the best salaries in the sector but are increasingly adopting minimum pay rates set out in collective agreements at the branch level. However, in our sample labor cost reduction strategies seemed generally to be defensive—ways of dealing with cuts in the working week and rises in the minimum wage imposed by law—rather than offensive.[10]

The ending of seniority premiums in the confectionery companies is without doubt the strongest illustration of cost cutting, as it directly touches on one of the pillars of the traditional French employment model, based on internal labor markets. This measure was accepted within the collective agreement applying the thirty-five-hour working week, and it has been implemented by the three confectionery companies in our study (Chocind, Chochris, and Regsweet).

The application of the thirty-five-hour working week led to calculating working time on an annual rather than weekly basis in nearly all of our case study companies. As a result, overtime hours—which are paid at a higher hourly rate than regular hours—were strongly limited and sometimes scrapped. This has had a particularly strong impact at Regsaus, where some middle-aged male workers have been induced to quit the company and look for a job across the Swiss border.

Generally speaking, the unions remain very attached to traditional ways of setting salaries on a monthly basis, including wage negotiations on the basis of job evaluation schemes and annual, across-the-board pay increases and the maintenance of traditional bonuses. Employers, on the other hand, tend increasingly to want to negotiate the whole remuneration package (basic pay and supplements) on an annual basis, with the aim of limiting wage increases. At the same time, the growing importance of individualized pay and profit-sharing (intéressement) are leading to changes in the traditional model for setting wages, especially in larger companies. This is the case, for example, at Hambac and Multiprod, as well as at Chocind, which is part of a large group. Profit-sharing is also a management tool, as it is often dependent on performance indicators relating to safety and quality.

Companies may also resort to particular types of outsourcing to try to limit labor costs. Some firms subcontract certain activities, such as the cleaning of the premises and the machinery, which is important work. Others, like the large confectionery multinationals, subcontract production activities entirely or make their subsidiary producers compete against each other—which more or less amounts to the same thing—while they concentrate on marketing.

To keep wages low or to limit pay rises due to labor shortages, some companies try to attract "peripheral" labor (compared to intermediate-aged, male breadwinners): young mothers and other young workers. Thus, Hambac, for example, faced with a shortage of de-boners, started to employ and train women for what is traditionally a male job. At Regsaus, male workers left the company in the wake of the application of the thirty-five-hour working week and the fall in monthly wages resulting from the suppression of overtime work. Many of their jobs were taken by women workers and younger workers.

Finally, strategies to save on labor costs may also rely on automation and increasing capital intensity in order to reduce the unit labor cost of permanent workers.

In both confectiona
ry and meat processing, automation has developed quite rapidly in recent years. The extent of computerization of production and packaging processes varies across products and firms.[11] It is quite limited for very high-value-added products, for which manual packaging and sometimes shaping is the rule, as at Chochris, for instance, where some specially decorated sweets are partly handmade. When interviewed, managers did not explicitly mention the cost of labor as a major reason for automation. However, it was quite clear that capital-labor substitution was taking place. At Regsweet, it was explicitly mentioned that computerized equipment had been introduced in order to reduce the need of seasonal workers, who were in short supply. This case is unique, however, given that the firm is located in a highly urban area (on the periphery of a town with more than 130,000 inhabitants), where a number of other sectors compete strongly for low-skilled workers.

In all cases, the main reason mentioned for increased automation was the need to increase labor productivity in order to meet competitive pressure. Automation suppresses jobs in the production line and is often accompanied by the implementation of "lean" production processes. The resulting rise of productivity is due not only to higher capital intensity but also to work intensification: the same amount of work is allocated to fewer workers. To take one example, some segments of the production lines at Canpat were modernized at the beginning of the 2000s, and the number of workers on these lines was cut from five to three. As one of the remaining operators noted, "The speed of the machine did not increase, but as there are fewer of us than before on the line, our work is more tiring."

Another reason often mentioned for automating production processes was the improvement of working conditions, and it is a fact that after automation a number of very painful tasks (especially those involving heavy loads) are carried out by machines. However, the overall impact on working conditions is quite uncertain.

Along with automation, firms have usually introduced important reorganizations of work at the shop-floor level. Shift systems—to optimize the use of capital—had been introduced in almost all of our case study firms since the 1990s. Moreover, the "annualization" of working time increases the flexibility in working time schedules; because this is a form of internal flexibility, the need for external flexibility is thus reduced.

Along the same lines, job rotation has been developed to reduce slack times. Permanent operators are often required to be able to perform a variety of tasks, corresponding to different posts, according to the needs of the production process. However, the use of job rotation may be limited by hygiene norms, in particular in the production and packaging of fresh products for which the various stages of the production process have to be clearly separated, as illustrated by Hambac. Wherever implemented, job rotation requires some multiskilling. In our sample, Canpat, Chochris, and Multiprod (in one of its plants) had been very active in developing multiskilling—also in order to promote functional flexibility and to reduce external, numerical flexibility.

There have been a number of other changes in work organization. The adoption of quality norms and the subsequent need for permanent quality controls have forced many firms to reorganize production processes. Here again, new competencies are required from the operators who pick up product samples and sometimes carry out the first quality tests (as was the case at Chochris, for example). The need for them to be extremely careful and precise is sometimes seen as an additional constraint raising the workload. More responsibility is also awarded to workers in relation to computerization. Operators are sometimes asked to record inputs and outputs on computers, and that was never the case in traditional production processes. Moreover, those trained as line or machine conductors have to control highly sophisticated equipment on which the rate of breakdowns is sometimes very high.

Lastly, it may be noted that in some small companies, such as Regsaus and Regsweet, automation was accompanied by organizational restructuring that resulted in the creation of line- and machine-conductor positions.

Overall, the introduction of computerized technologies on the shop floor has been accompanied by a number of changes in work organization. As we will see in the next section, this has important consequences not only for human resource management but also for the working conditions of low-skilled operators.

Workers' Reactions to Increasing Pressures Permanent workers in our case study firms were more often men, especially in production jobs, which are more often skilled jobs; (low-skilled) packaging jobs are dominated by women. The overwhelming majority of employees were of French origin and from the area in which the firm was situated. Strong rooting in the local community was especially marked, since most of the companies were located in rural areas, where unemployment rates tend to be high. Such local entrenchment played a strong role in supporting family solidarity, especially with respect to child care arrangements when both members of a couple worked. (Indeed, it was not unusual for both partners to work in the same company.) Many workers had held several jobs before entering the company, and these had often been precarious or had offered little job security. (This was particularly the case for women who had been obliged to stop work to bring up their children.)

Two examples—Eric and Jocelyne—can be taken from Hambac. Eric was thirty-four and worked as an operator receiving incoming meat. He had nine years' seniority. He was trained as a general mechanic and then as an apprentice roofer, but he failed his apprenticeship certificate. After turning eighteen, he took a lot of training courses (including as a road-haulage driver) and held numerous temp jobs (including in a slaughterhouse and a cement factory). In 1996, at the age of twenty-five, he was recruited as a temp by Hambac for eight months, first for de-boning meat (at night), then for receiving meat. He subsequently received a permanent contract, with a coefficient of 140, and his level now was 150. His wife worked in the same company, temping at nights.

Jocelyne was fifty-six and worked as a molding operator. She had fifteen years' seniority. She held a brevet d'études professionnelles (BEP, a middle school vocational diploma) in accounting. From the age of seventeen onward, she had worked in accounting. She quit paid work between 1972 and 1980 to bring up her children. After that, she went back to look for a job. She received some training to update her accounting skills, but then worked in a café; later she was fired from that job. In 1988 the National Employment Service (ANPE) offered her training in the food-processing sector, during which she had to undertake an internship. She chose Hambac because she knew the company was recruiting. She did not finish the internship because Hambac offered her a six-month, fixed-term contract. The contract was renewed three times (first in conditioning and then in molding). After eighteen months, she got a permanent contract. Her job coefficient was 150, and she was now a union member.

Once on a permanent contract, most operators demonstrate strong job stability. Turnover rates are very low for permanent workers—around 2 percent or less. A low turnover rate can actually create a problem for companies, which have to be very selective in recruitment when workers are likely to stay for a long time and flexibility margins are limited. The low mobility of workers is often accompanied by paternalist management practices, which may even persist when a small family business becomes a much bigger firm (for example, Multiprod) or a subsidiary of a large group (such as Chochris). Operators in rural areas, especially older ones, very often come from the agricultural sector. It must also be stressed that educational levels are generally very low. Very few workers age thirty or older have passed the baccalaureate, France's high school–leaving exam. All of these points are important in understanding the expectations and opinions expressed by workers about their jobs.

As has already been noted, numerous bonuses allow nearly all permanent workers to earn more—and sometimes substantially more—than the hourly low-wage threshold as defined in this study (two-thirds of the hourly median wage). But the purchasing power of monthly wages (that is, income after social contributions and taxes have been deducted) is not so high, and it takes two full-time incomes in the household for a family to gain access to the basic "French way of life" (owning one's home, going away for annual holidays). The ability to raise monthly earnings by working overtime—which used to be quite common—has been reduced or even totally scrapped with the implementation of the thirty-five-hour week. Very few workers seem to do regular paid work outside their main job: only at Regsaus did we meet some who did. Many interviewees (especially women) told us that because of the high work intensity they were too exhausted after a day's work. Young men often use their leisure time to do major construction work on their own homes—a good example of self-sufficient production, that is, using time not sold on the labor market.

Overall, even if hourly wages do not appear to be so low for many permanent workers, poor pay was nearly always cited when interviewees were asked about work satisfaction.

"The main problem is with the wages. It's hard to get by," commented Eric of Hambac. Monique, who worked at Canpat, was fifty-four years old, and had seventeen years of tenure, said: "I live alone, and the money is short. My wages don't allow me to make ends meet." Monique had had a wage coefficient of 150 since almost the beginning of her career.

The feeling of being stuck at low pay levels is indeed an important source of frustration. Even if permanent workers are usually not low-wage earners, they have very few prospects of wage promotion. The wage gap between coefficients 190 (line supervisor) and 120 (entry level in the least-skilled jobs) in the operators' wage scale (see table 3.4) is not even 20 percent. Furthermore, given that most workers start above 120 and will never reach 190, "wage careers" end up being very short. The seniority premium therefore plays a crucial role, but as we have seen, it has been suppressed in many firms in the confectionery sector. Flat wage profiles are consistent with the "low-wage trap," which may be partly induced by a high legal minimum wage in relative terms. To try to tackle such pay limits, some companies, like Chocind (with its "progress bonus") or Multiprod, have introduced individual wage increases, which are granted following assessment interviews. But staff do not always appreciate such bonuses. According to one female operator at Chocind, "The progress bonus is just smoke and mirrors and actually led to a lot of ill feeling among the workers." A colleague of hers confirmed this impression, noting that the "atmosphere had got bad." An operator at Multiprod remarked critically that "the assessment interviews are phony."

Also, there has tended to be less upward mobility to jobs above the operator level, a progression that was common in the past as a pillar of the traditional internal labor market. As technology gets more complex, the higher levels of the production hierarchy tend to be filled by skilled workers hired on the external labor market.

Discontent arises too from recent changes. As detailed earlier, increases in monthly wages have been quite small in the past years. A common complaint in our interviews was: "We're always asked to do more, but pay does not keep pace." This brings us back to new forms of work organization and to working conditions more generally.

The working conditions at the companies in our sample were quite representative of the branch as a whole, even if they were far from being among the worst. Working conditions used to be very hard in food manufacturing until a few years ago. Work accidents and illnesses are still frequent in both subsectors, and many operators in their fifties or even forties are "physical wrecks." Companies used early retirement schemes extensively in the past, and they still use the dismissal procedure for "incapacity," which is allowed by French labor law. We met employees in a number of companies who were over fifty, physically worn out, and anxious about losing their jobs.

Until recently, tolerance of bad working conditions has been rather high among workers, and this is sometimes still the case. During our visit to Chochris, for example, we met a worker who was near retirement and had never wanted to change jobs despite the fact that in his workshop, where cocoa beans were melted in cauldrons, temperatures ran between 40°C and 50°C (105°F to 120°F) and the work still involved handling heavy loads. Such tolerance partly arises from the fact that most food-processing firms are located in rural areas, where workers are used to hard physical labor. Moreover, blue-collar workers, especially those from a rural background, are traditionally reluctant, for cultural reasons, to complain about working conditions and their resulting health problems. As a result, trade union claims typically used to focus on wages and bonuses—in other words, on the compensation for bad working conditions rather than on their improvement. Another reason why workers tolerate bad working conditions is that trade unions have lacked expertise on the subject and have also feared that automation would decrease employment.

Younger workers, however, are much more reluctant to accept bad working conditions and are more conscious of the difficulty of their work and its potential long-term health consequences. Whereas older workers used to show "loyalty" on the issue, younger workers are more prone to "exit" and to "voice" attitudes. Their "exit" behavior could make turnover high among young workers, especially those on nonpermanent contracts, and generally a labor shortage is lamented in the whole food-processing sector. Their "voice" is less of a factor, but trade unions have become increasingly concerned about working conditions. Indeed, the role of unions and workers' representatives may be very important for the improvement of working conditions. At Hambac, the only firm we visited in which unionization was important, the local union had launched an information campaign about occupational diseases and cumulative trauma disorders. The objective was not only to put pressure on management but also to make workers more conscious of the risks they were facing. It should be noted that the union was led in this firm by a young operator, who was also a university graduate.

Automation has improved the working conditions of operators in some respects. A large number of the most "physical" tasks have been automated during the last decade: most of the handling and storing is now carried out by machines, so that the occupational risks related to these operations have been substantially reduced. As mentioned earlier, the improvement of working conditions is often cited by managers as one of the reasons for the introduction of new production technologies. However, the impact of new technologies on working conditions is somewhat ambiguous. In the short run, the adaptation period may be very hard: "As they've automated practically everything, there are machines everywhere now," remarked a Regsweet operator. "Work space is small, there's no room, [and] it's not adapted. . . . There was a time after everything was automated when there were a lot of accidents, cuts, fingers cut . . . just to make us work faster."

Indeed, a number of workers, especially women, reported strong work intensification, particularly at Regsweet, Hambac, and Chochris. A female operator in the packaging sector at Chochris told us that "the management has gone mad" (concerning the workload). But it was also true for Multiprod, Chocind, and Canpat, where an operator complained, "We're always asked to do more. . . . We're fed up. . . . They're taking us for a ride, there's always more to learn, we've really had it." Beyond the pace of work, the sense of intensification seems to arise from a number of other factors as well: systematic attempts to raise productivity by reducing staff, eliminating slack times, reducing breaks, and chasing production failures; a greater need for attention and cautiousness due to the tightening of hygiene and quality controls and the introduction of fragile computerized equipment; and product diversification (with changing small-batch series) and functional flexibility, which are often perceived as stressful because unskilled blue-collar workers are not well prepared to cope with multiskilling requirements. (This demand is, of course, particularly onerous for many older workers but may also be a source of mental strain for younger ones.)

Under these circumstances, the extra time off provided by the thirty-five-hour week is generally appreciated, since it allows workers to unwind from the heavy intensity of work. In some companies, average hours worked per week have not fallen, but the number of days off has risen. Nevertheless, because hours worked are now calculated on an annual basis, some companies impose very strong constraints on when workers may take days off. Furthermore, some workers link the intensification of work to the thirty-five-hour week: "The thirty-five-hour week [and] extra days off are quite pleasant, remarked a female Canpat operator. "We've got used to them in a certain way, but we get these days off in winter, and work more in summer. Personally, I feel that the pace of work has risen strongly as a result."

Looking for Good Practices It is not easy to correlate wage levels with companies' characteristics and the various types of strategies identified here. Of course, size and own brands (along with high-value-added products) play a role. Traditionally in the confectionery sector, wages (and working conditions) were much better in large firms that produced their own brands than in niche producers and producers located in the lower segment of the market (mass production). Wage negotiations in the former group used to be largely independent from branch-level negotiations, and the wages paid were systematically much higher. Firms were also more likely to offer fringe benefits, such as complementary pension schemes. However, as underlined by various trade union representatives at the branch level, this is no longer the case owing to competitive pressure to reduce production costs. In contrast, mass-production firms traditionally offered lower wages and worse working conditions, partly because of pressure from large-scale retailers. In the niche production group, wages and working conditions were heterogeneous and very dependent on the owner, given that management often appeared to be paternalistic. In some cases, such as Canpat, pay conditions were not bad. But Regsweet offered a counterexample: despite its high-value-added strategy, it paid low wages that were recognized as such, both by management and by workers' representatives.

The complexity of the pay systems (that is, the numerous varieties of bonuses and the increasing individualization of wages) that goes with the development of multiskilling and performance-based wage increases makes it very difficult to compare average wage levels across firms. Even if differences between the firms in our sample seem to be limited (on the basis of the data we were able to obtain), some firms appear to pay higher wages. The high unionization rate (and big strikes in the recent past) seemed to play an important role in the case of Hambac. For Multiprod, on the other hand, both its position in the supply chain (higher-value-added products, a lower dependency on retail chains) and the (relative) tightness of the labor market were important factors.

It is worth noting that some firms, such as Multiprod and Hambac, were concerned about the issue of male-female wage differentials; Hambac, in fact, had participated in an "equal opportunity" program (named EQUAL) funded by the European Community. But attempts to attract women into some traditionally male-dominated occupations (such as meat de-boning) may also be seen as a strategy to avoid wage pressure, induced by the labor shortage of male workers in some areas, as mentioned earlier.

We also pointed out earlier that no company in our sample had used "social dumping" strategies. Some companies even seemed to have adopted the opposite strategy, which we might call the "high road" to raising productivity through training, "high" wages, and "good" working conditions. In some firms, like Canpat and Multiprod, automation had been accompanied by an active training policy, based in particular on the branch's vocational qualification certificate (CQP). These two companies had also introduced more participative management methods in the form of regular consultation meetings on work organization and working conditions—within a "method groups" framework at Canpat and through the recent introduction of "semi-autonomous" teams at Multiprod. They had also collaborated with labor market institutions such as ARACTs and CRAMs to improve working conditions. Finally, both companies (and nearly all the firms in the sample) were trying to take into account the competencies acquired as part of the multiskilling process in fixing wages. The aim was also to favor wage mobility, which used to be very limited.

There are a number of reasons why these companies would choose such high-road strategies. First, a firm's position in the supply chain (own brands and a larger diversity in distribution outlets, especially in the case of Multiprod) and its form of ownership (family companies with a certain tradition of paternalism) seem to play a role. But a company's insertion into the local labor market also counts. Canpat, the main employer in its area, strove to adapt and motivate employees to spend their working lives with the firm. Multiprod, located in an urban labor market (even if the region, Brittany, is rural), sought to foster loyalty among its young employees, who are known to be more demanding. As a result, in the words of the human resource director, "all our policies are geared toward younger workers." From this point of view, the contrast between this company's two plants, which are only five kilometers apart, is striking. In one plant, which mainly produced cold cuts and delicatessen products, employees' average age was high, production techniques were older, and working conditions remained very tough. Nearly all of the firm's young workers were to be found in the second plant, which produced mainly salads and cooked dishes. Automation there was also more advanced and the organization of work much more innovative.

Temporary Workers: A Crucial Source of Labor That Raises Problems

Varying Employment Situations for Multiple Uses Temporary work actually involves various types of work contracts. While French labor law is generally quite restrictive, it also allows for a large variety of contracts that provide much de facto flexibility (see chapter 2). Companies choose among these according to two criteria:

1. *Cost*: Temp agency work contracts and fixed-term contracts provide workers with a "precariousness" or job insecurity bonus amounting to 10 percent of the basic wage
2. *The rules of use*: These are the conditions that set out which particular type of contract may be used, the maximum length of the contract, and so on

All of the companies in our sample used temporary labor, for several reasons. Some companies had a structural need for such labor, linked to the strong seasonality of their activities. In our sample, Regsweet and Chochris, for instance, generated 60 to 70 percent of their turnover in the Christmas period. Their activity was legally recognized as seasonal, so they were allowed to use seasonal contracts. This was not the case for Regsaus, though its activity was also highly seasonal: because the consumption of sausages is much higher in winter, output increased fivefold. Staff levels in the three companies rose by 30 to 50 percent in the high season. For these companies, then, the availability of a sufficient number of reliable seasonal and temporary workers was vital. It is interesting to note that expanded sales through supermarkets and hypermarkets have increased the seasonal nature of production. Moreover, short-term variations in production, brought on by promotion campaigns, have also increased. These variations could lead to a 30 percent rise in output at Regsaus from one week to the next. The companies used temp agency workers to deal with short-term fluctuations and used workers on seasonal contracts or "standard" fixed-term contracts to handle seasonal fluctuations.

In other firms where activity rates were more constant over the year, temporary workers were mainly used as temporary replacements for permanent workers. Such use is generally rising. On the one hand, companies tend more and more to manufacture year-round, with no interruptions (for example, Canpat had stopped closing down completely for one month in the summer). On the other hand, the introduction of the thirty-five-hour working week has led to a significant increase in the number of days off (up to twenty-three days on top of the normal five weeks of annual vacation at Hambac, for instance). Furthermore, absenteeism and sick leave have led to an additional and increasing need for occasional manpower. And finally, the constraints of working with large-scale distributors (just-in-time production, promotion campaigns) have increased demands in terms of flexibility. Overall at Hambac, for example, where the absenteeism rate was especially high (15 percent among operators), temp agency workers made up 15 to 20 percent of all workers. While standard fixed-term contracts are used mainly to replace workers on summer holiday, temp agency work is used predominantly throughout the year.

There are other reasons as well for using temporary contracts, such as launching a new product, entering a new market, or easing the transition to the automation of certain jobs for which permanent workers, who have gone into retirement or are assigned elsewhere, are not replaced. It should also be stressed that companies use temporary workers as a way of selecting permanent staff. Multiprod, for example, implemented what the human resource director called a real "obstacle race" for recruiting workers, who had to spend up to eighteen months working on temporary or fixed-term contracts.

Finally, a particular type of nonpermanent worker needs to be mentioned, namely, tâcherons, or pieceworkers, who are only to be found in meat processing. Tâcherons are used to cope with the lack of labor supply for very specific tasks, such as de-boning, in which working conditions are very hard and workers are worn out very rapidly. Tâcherons are officially "posted" workers, that is, they are employed by another firm. In fact, they are de facto independent workers who work with their own tools within the establishment. They are paid according to piece rates (which is normally forbidden by French law), even if they officially receive a monthly wage.

Temporary Workers: The Core of Low-Paid, Low-Skilled Work Temporary workers are largely employed in production and packaging jobs, the simplest, least-skilled occupations (goods handling, manual packaging, and so on). Their pay rates thus tend to carry low wage coefficients (120 or 125 in the job evaluation schemes). They generally remain at these levels, even if they complete several successive contracts for the same company. They normally do not benefit from bonuses and other advantages accorded to permanent staff,[12] which explains why low pay is concentrated in this category of workers. Since 2005, seasonal workers have been entitled to seniority premiums in the firms that use them, subject to certain conditions and proportionally to the time spent in the company. This eligibility was introduced by a change in the law regulating seasonal contracts. Workers hired on standard, fixed-term contracts and as temps nevertheless benefit from job insecurity bonuses, but workers on seasonal contracts or student contracts have no right to them.

Only very few staff have access to training. Generally, workers receive basic training in hygiene and safety on entering the company. (For example, such training for young recruits on short-term contracts and for students lasts four hours at Hambac.) For temp agency workers, training is minimal, and it is often carried out by the agencies. Indeed, temporary workers are used for the simplest jobs precisely to avoid the need to train them and to have them operational as quickly as possible. Similarly, promotion prospects for this group of workers are virtually nonexistent, apart from those who are eventually employed permanently. The temporary workers we spoke to also felt that work rates have intensified. In addition, temp workers are less protected than permanent employees against health problems, even though they suffer from a disproportionately high rate of accidents. Moreover, given the insecurity of their positions, they played down their health problems in interviews. Finally, temporary workers believe that they are only poorly represented by the unions, or not at all, and that impression was confirmed by the employee representatives we interviewed. For example, the personnel representative at Regsaus admitted that "we don't know the temporary workers—we have little contact with them." The feeling of being "second-class" workers is particularly widespread among seasonal workers.

Marie-Georges, a forty-eight-year-old seasonal worker at Chochris, is a good example. She had already once been a seasonal worker at Chochris for five years, from 1973 to 1978. She stopped work to bring up her three children, then started working again in 1994. She was still a seasonal worker, even though she would have liked a permanent job. Her wage had been capped at the 125 coefficient since she started working—about the level of the minimum wage. She was given four hours of on-the-job training when she first started working in the company, but had had no training since. She had a lot of pain in her arms as well as back problems and had to see a physiotherapist. She had calculated that she probably lifted one ton per day of five-kilogram (eleven-pound) boxes. Many of her seasonal colleagues had become discouraged and quit or had stopped work because of back problems. Doctors had certified that she was partly incapacitated, but she hadn't mentioned this to the company for fear of not being hired anymore. "We're nothing," she told us. "We don't get any of the benefits offered by the works council, we're not represented by the unions, we do the same work as the permanent employees, but we get paid less."

This depiction of "minimal" personnel management, however, needs to be qualified. In practice, nonpermanent workers are treated in different ways, depending on the company they work for, and variations sometimes even exist within a company. In several cases, temporary employment was part of a company's strategy to encourage loyalty and filter recruits for permanent jobs. At Hambac some temporary workers had come back several years running, after being contacted by foremen, because they knew the job. These were workers who were felt to be potential recruits as permanent staff.

Temporary work corresponds to particular phases in workers' personal and professional lives and does not therefore have the same meaning for all the workers concerned. Temporary workers are largely young people, women, and older men forced to change jobs. For young people, these jobs (especially temp agency work) may be taken up immediately after leaving school while they are searching for more stable employment or for work more connected to their studies. In rural areas, young workers may also take temporary jobs while learning to drive; once they can drive, they are more mobile. On the other hand, an increasing share of temp agency workers are men over age forty who have run out of unemployment benefits or who are changing jobs after being laid off. Temps may also be women who have moved to follow their partners and so lost their previous jobs. Women account for a majority of seasonal workers (nearly two-thirds at Regsaus and Chochris, for example). Older women workers hold almost all of these "stabilized" forms of temporary jobs: some may be seasonal workers for the same company for very many years (for example, up to ten years or more at Chochris, as with Marie-George). Generally speaking, temporary women workers tend to be married women who are earning a supplementary family income, single mothers, or women who, having gone back to work after raising their children, find that their skills and qualifications have become obsolete after spending many years out of the labor market.

These workers' situations and incomes vary widely. As already noted, temp agency work is more rewarding financially—owing to the "precariousness" bonus and paid holidays—than other types of temporary contracts, especially seasonal contracts. It may even be better paid than some permanent jobs at a certain wage coefficient. (The pay difference may run to €300 (US$427) per month, according to some interviewees.) So some workers prefer to be temps.

Françoise was forty-four and had three years of seniority with Hambac. She held a baccalaureate in sciences and had studied medicine for three years. When she married, she stopped studying and had two children. She took over a horse stud and went into debt (loans, a mortgage, and so on). She started looking for a salaried job in 2000 and signed on as a temp. She worked in various jobs in a slaughterhouse for two and a half years. The company offered her a permanent job, but she refused, preferring to earn more as a temp. She was therefore fired. As of June 2002, she was working as a temp agency worker at Hambac on a meat-cutting production line, a job she held for one and a half years. When Hambac offered her a permanent job, she had to accept it. She worked in the same meat-cutting job, though her coefficient rose from 140 to 145. In early 2005 she took a two-month training course in meat de-boning offered to her by the company. Françoise became the first woman in the company to work as a de-boner.

The same is true for the tâcherons, who are mainly young or intermediate-aged men: their monthly wages may be significantly higher than what is earned by permanent staff in the same positions, given piecework pay and certain bonuses (transport, and so on). Some workers may thus choose these types of employment at particular moments in their lives as a strategy to increase their wages. But such work is not seen as a long-term strategy, especially by tâcherons, whose efforts to do piecework quickly leads to physical deterioration. For others, temporary work is seen as a stepping-stone to a stable job within the company and is accepted as such.

Increasing Tensions and Emerging Good Practices We have stressed that using temporary labor is central to companies' strategies to cope with production, organizational, and commercial constraints. The hardening of these constraints, the increases in competitive pressures, and the resulting changes in production organization also affect the ways in which temporary labor is used. These changes have led to rising tensions between the growing demands of flexibility, on the one hand, and increasing problems with labor reliability and quality, on the other hand.

Most of the companies we surveyed had faced recruitment problems for the temporary personnel they needed: such jobs are not considered attractive, working conditions are tough, they are poorly paid, and there is competition from other jobs, especially in urban or border areas. Companies thus face increasing difficulties in finding enough personnel with the right behavior. Turnover rates for recruited staff are very high: in some of the companies in our sample, turnover ran to 200 percent for temporary contract workers in the summer holidays. Permanent staff are generally responsible for supervising and training temporary workers on the job, and this task is increasingly burdensome as the volume of temporary workers continues to rise. The high turnover rates for temporary workers was seen by our case study firms as a cause of worsening working conditions, since their supervision required extra work that was usually not remunerated.

Several practices had emerged to handle problems with temporary workers, some being used in combination. Some companies had tried to limit the use of temporary labor through automation and the development of internal flexibility. (At Regsweet and Chochris, for example, seasonal workers had been cut back by nearly 30 percent.) Some companies were also trying to improve working conditions: improving temporary workers' access to benefits normally reserved for permanent workers, for example, or paying higher wages. Chochris, which took on seasonal workers as line supervisors, had recently decided to pay them a compensatory wage at the end of their contracts. This extra compensation was equivalent to the coefficient differential between seasonal workers and permanent staff with the same skills doing the same job. Furthermore, seasonal workers received a thirteenth-month salary proportional to the length of their contracts. The Regsaus management also had a policy of training and building the loyalty of their seasonal staff: stable, seasonal women workers had been trained to run machinery and were paid at the corresponding coefficient, which they carried over from one season to another. These workers also benefited from the profit-sharing plan usually reserved for permanent staff (the intéressement scheme). Overall, there was some upward pressure on compensation because of the shortage of reliable workers in some areas.

Another strategy to stabilize temporary workers and therefore reduce precariousness or job insecurity is to participate in multi-employer groups; in our sample, Multiprod and, more recently, Regsweet had adopted this strategy. These groups of employers offer permanent contracts to the workers, and member firms then "share" workers according to their needs. The employees work in several companies during the year, usually in firms with opposing high seasons—for example, in the autumn and winter for one company and in the spring and summer for another, depending on the nature of the products. But these workers share the benefits of permanent employees (especially seniority premiums and intéressement) and become skilled. Multi-employer groups tend to develop where local labor markets are particularly tight, but they require effective coordination between employers, local authorities, and labor market institutions.[13] Such groups are rare, however, because they are constraining and complicated to set up. Two companies in our sample that had tried to use such a scheme, Regsaus and Chochris, dropped out of it because of the constraints involved and because the group's resources were a poor match with their needs.

CONCLUDING REMARKS

From numerous points of view, the food-processing sector is quite representative of the French model and provides a good illustration of the pressures exerted on this model in recent years. Branch-level institutions may seem quite significant when compared to other countries, and they do indeed have an important impact on wage determination. But the effect in other areas is less important, and unions are weak and often divided at the company level, which limits their countervailing power. As for permanent workers, most operators' wages are above the low-wage threshold once all bonuses and benefits are taken into account. But wage profiles are relatively flat, and wage increases have been low in past years. As in food manufacturing in the United States (Lane et al. 2003), internal labor markets are still a reality in France, but opportunities for promotion (especially to management positions) have generally decreased, and the traditional wage model has been put under pressure as some firms scrap seniority premiums, increasingly individualize wage increases, and so on. Working conditions are still hard, even though increasing automation has eased some of the more arduous physical tasks. However, this has been partly offset by greater work intensity, which is not compensated for by wage increases. The overall dissatisfaction of the workers on this issue appears to be high. In addition, temporary workers (mainly temp agency workers and workers on seasonal or standard fixed-term contracts), who represent a notable share of the workforce, are often treated as "second-class" workers and do not benefit from the same compensation and benefits as permanent workers.

The sector has gone through substantial transformation in recent years. From many points of view, food processing is today at a crossroads. International competition, which has so far been limited to certain segments (standardized confectionery produced by multinational companies, for example, or the poultry sector), will expand, especially with the increasing competition from Eastern Europe. This increased competition is likely to coincide with reforms of the European Common Agricultural Policy and risks destabilizing the fragile equilibrium of the sector.[14] But there are internal challenges too.

Younger workers are more demanding, especially in terms of working conditions, and firms must take that into account. At the other extreme, business practices that consisted of shedding older workers on the basis of incapacity and using early retirement schemes are less and less viable given the raising of the retirement age and the priority attached to increasing the labor force participation rates of older workers. Overall, the traditional model may no longer be sustainable. Improving working conditions is a key challenge for the future of the sector, to make jobs both more attractive for young workers and more sustainable for older ones.

Given these challenges, our research contributes to a better understanding of the adoption of good practices. From a comparative, international perspective, the crucial role of the national, institutional context must be kept in mind, and notably the legal minimum wage, which limits the monopsony power of firms, as well as other institutions that contribute to the determination of the reservation wage and, more widely, the outside options of workers (see chapter 2). Even if the French unemployment rate is high overall, many firms in the food-processing sector face a shortage of labor because of the unattractiveness of the available jobs. This is particularly true with respect to temporary workers, who fill the least attractive jobs. Tension is generated as workers, especially young people, grow more reluctant to accept these jobs at the same time as firms increasingly need a flexible, reliable, and high-quality workforce. So far the temptation to hire foreign labor has been limited by law, in contrast to the United Kingdom and Germany.

Improvements must also be sought in companies' functioning. Apart from labor shortages, what factors are associated with the adoption of good practices? It is revealing that the two most innovative companies in our sample—Canpat and Multiprod, two mainly family-owned enterprises—are characterized by management that is both paternalistic (the firms have a sense of social responsibility) and modern (they are opening up to new management practices and new forms of work organization). Their position in the market also gives them a certain room for maneuver because so far they have been less dependent on large retailers, which is not the case for other companies. Such good practices may draw on various branch or local institutions. Finally, it must be stressed that the unions can also play a key role, but this assumes that they are united and have a legitimate position within firms. Unfortunately, this is rarely the case.

We are grateful to Christine Erhel, Gilbert Lefèvre, François Michon, and Bertrand Réau for research assistance. We are also grateful to Nicholas Sowels for translation assistance.

NOTES

1. These five manufacturers are Danone, Lactalis, Pernod-Ricard, Bongrain, and Sodiaal.
2. Strictly speaking, meat processing here covers mainly pork meat processing, whereas beef meat and poultry production are classified in other branches.
3. Data are available only for meat processing. In 2006, 3.3 percent of employees were foreigners, and 6.6 percent were born abroad.
4. The seniority premium usually amounts to an extra 3 percent for every three years of tenure, with a maximum of 15 percent. The cold-work bonus in meat processing amounts to 8 percent of the basic wage for temperatures between −5°C and +3°C (23°F and 37°F), and 4 percent for temperatures between 3°C and 10°C (37°F and 50°F). The hourly wage rate during night shifts (between 9:00 PM and 6:00 AM) is 20 percent higher than the normal rate.
5. There are two kinds of profit-sharing schemes: intéressement is a voluntary form of profit-sharing, based on company agreements, whereas "participation" in profits is obligatory for companies with more than fifty employees. The income received via "participation" is locked into an account for five years (often the company's savings account); this makes it a form of forced savings.
6. "Annualization" means that working time is computed on a yearly rather than a weekly basis. For instance, workers can work thirty hours some weeks and forty-two hours other weeks without being paid at the hourly overtime rate (which is higher than the normal rate) for the time worked each week exceeding thirty-five hours.
7. Certificats de qualification professionnelle (or vocational qualification certificates) are defined at the branch level. A CQP ensures that a worker has mastered the skills required for a specific job. His or her competencies are validated, and he or she receives complementary training in order to obtain the certificate.
8. First price products are the lowest-quality products, usually sold with no brand; the retail chains' own-brand products (RCBs) are rather medium-quality products.
9. Ongoing restructuring may also explain why we could not get access to any multinational firm in the confectionery sector; for example,

Nestlé explicitly cited restructuring as the reason for its refusal to meet us.
10. "Social dumping" strategies are more common in other subsectors, such as the poultry sector.
11. In some cases, automation may fail. This was partly the case at Regsweet, where computerizing the production process was a real challenge. The production process for making almond sweets is very specific, and no standard equipment could be adapted. Prototypes were constructed, but some of them did not work properly and eventually had to be removed.
12. Except for bonuses compensating for specific working conditions: cold/heat, night work, etc.
13. The multi-employer group in which Multiprod participated was initially subsidized by an association of employers and the local authorities of the area.
14. To give but one example, the export subsidies attributed to the poultry sector are to be phased out by 2010. More generally, France's food-processing industry is very much linked to French agriculture, so that shocks to the latter cannot but affect the former (Butault 2004).

REFERENCES

Agreste. 2004. *Industries agricoles et alimentaires: Entreprises de 20 salariés et plus [Agricultural and Food Industries: Business of 20 or More Employees]*. coll. Chiffres et données – Agroalimentaire 121. Paris: Ministry of Agriculture

Butault, Jean-Pierre, editor. 2004. *Les Soutiens à l'agriculture: Théorie, histoire, mesure [Supports for Agriculture: Theory, History, Measurement]*. Paris: Inra Editions.

Canivet, Guy. 2004. *Equilibre entre le grand commerce et les fournisseurs [Balance Between Big Retail Chains and Suppliers]*. Report to the Ministry of Economics.

Jourdain, Colette, Claude Minni, Alice Tanay, and Agnès Topiol-Bensaïde. 1999. "Dans les industries alimentaires, l'emploi résiste mieux que dans le reste de l'industrie" ["In Food Industries, Employment Resists Better than in Rest of the Industry"]. *Premières Synthèses* (DARES) 28(2, July): 8.

Lamanthe, Annie. 2003. "Pratiques de branches et voies d'accès à l'emploi stable dans les IAA" ["Practices of Branches and Access to Stable Employment in the Food Processing Industries"]. In *Entreprises et jeunes debutants [Businesses and Young Workers]*, edited by J. F. Lochet. Paris: L'Harmattan.

Lane, Julia, Philip Moss, Harold Salzman, and Chris Tilly. 2003. "Too Many Cooks? Tracking Internal Labor Market Dynamics in Food Service with Case Studies and Quantitative Data." In *Low-Wage America*, edited by

Eileen Appelbaum, Annette Bernhardt, and Richard J. Murnane. New York: Russell Sage Foundation.

Ministry of Agriculture. 2004. *Panorama des industries agro-alimentaires* [*Overview of Agricultural and Food Industries*], 132.

———. 2006. *Panorama des industries agro-alimentaires* [*Overview of Agricultural and Food Industries*], 132.

CHAPTER 4

Good Jobs, Hard Work? Employment Models for Nurse's Aides and Hospital Housekeepers

Philippe Méhaut, Anne Marie Arborio, Jacques Bouteiller, Philippe Mossé, and Lise Causse

Of the five sectors studied in this book, the hospital sector may display the largest number of distinctive features. It combines characteristics of both industry and the service sector. On the "industrial" side, its activities depend on major investments in equipment and rapid technical progress. It is subject to the classic production constraints of a twenty-four-hour-a-day, 365-day-a-year operation, the quest for "error-proof" work, and rising demands for full accountability. But caregiving is also a service that mobilizes a vast workforce and rests in part on coproduction between the patient and the staff, whether through discussions of diagnosis between the patient and the medical and nursing staff or through the patient's necessary participation in basic nursing tasks such as washing and moving from one place to another. It is also a sector largely dominated by public organizations: the majority of workers in public hospitals are in civil service jobs. The hospital sector expanded greatly in the 1960s and 1970s, at a time when the internal labor market model was being constructed. It displays most of the characteristics of the French model described in chapter 2, sometimes in the extreme.

Although the hospital sector employs primarily skilled and highly skilled workers, it also provides a large percentage of semiskilled or unskilled jobs, especially housekeeping and basic nursing jobs, on which this chapter focuses. In the United States the vast majority of these jobs are performed by unskilled workers and the turnover rate for housecleaning staff is high (Appelbaum et al. 2003). We have chosen these tasks as the basis for the international comparison. In France, the organization and structure of work and the skill level of the workforce differ significantly from the American model. Nurse's aides and housecleaning staff are better trained and have more stable jobs (at least those who form the core of permanent employees) and do not belong to the category of low-wage workers. In fact, the hospital sector has the lowest rate of such workers in France (see chapter 2). This is also true for Holland and Denmark but not for Germany, the United Kingdom, or the United States.

The first section explains the high level of regulation in the French hospital sector, both of the labor market and of the conditions for providing care. Regulation accounts for the negligible incidence of low wages and for a greater homogeneity between the public and private sectors than might be expected. In both subsectors, nursing and housekeeping tasks are job categories that are well defined in collective bargaining agreements, though the actual work organization may vary from one hospital to another. Both jobs can be considered more highly skilled than in the United States. Housekeepers also have higher skills than their counterparts in French hotels. This factor is another reason for the negligible incidence of low wages. The next section analyzes another important characteristic of the French hospital employment model: its high level of segmentation. On the one hand, there are a great many workers in the sector with very stable jobs—civil service employment in the public sector, open-ended contracts in the private—and a low turnover rate. The model of "employment for life" persists, even for nurse's aides and housekeepers. These jobs are more attractive than elsewhere because of their stability, the wage progression based on seniority, and a work schedule that, despite the "unsocial" hours, allows for a better balance of family life and work life than in other sectors. That attractiveness explains why there are almost no problems finding qualified job applicants, either in the public or the private sectors. In addition, the model allows hospitals to use a large peripheral reserve labor force working under unstable conditions. Organized on the model of a waiting line, that pool is a powerful instrument of flexibility. Here again, we find some of the exemplary characteristics of the French model as set out in chapter 2.

In the following section, we examine the changes under way in relation to that standard model. As in other countries, French hospitals are subject to strong pressures related to the demand for care and the financing system. There have been major restructurings, but they came about later than in the United States or the United Kingdom. That delay explains why the consequences for managing the workforce are not always very significant, especially since institutional resilience leads to a certain uniformity. Of course, both public and private hospitals have reacted with efforts to increase work productivity by requiring higher skills and a faster pace of work. The organization of work is in transition, especially for housekeepers. But there is also some reluctance to implement organizational changes. In the end, though the impact is perceptible, especially in the deterioration of working conditions, the classic model of hospital employment seems to be holding fast.

This chapter relies on the general methodology identified for research on low-wage work. It uses a set of national statistical data, primarily from the Ministry of Health (in particular, annual statistics on health institutions and the 2003 survey on working conditions in hospitals).[1] Eight case studies were done in 2005 and 2006 on mid-sized hospitals and clinics (100 to 800 beds, excluding university hospitals). Four are public hospitals, four are private for-profit clinics. Four are located in labor markets with a high rate of unemployment and four in tighter markets (see the appendix for the chief characteristics of the sample).[2] In each case study, we conducted between twelve and fifteen in-depth interviews with hospital management (executive director, human resource manager, nursing care manager), union leaders, nurse's aides, and hospital service workers, primarily in medical units. In one case, a hospital that subcontracts some of its work, the interviews also dealt with the subcontractor's business and workers.

A VERY REGULATED SECTOR WITH FEW LOW-WAGE WORKERS

Of the five sectors studied in this work, the hospital sector has the lowest incidence of low wages. It is also the most regulated, with significant intervention from the state, in terms of both health policy and the general rules governing public employment.

THE ORGANIZATION OF THE FRENCH HOSPITAL SYSTEM

Public Versus Private   To understand the structure of French hospitals, we must look to the past. Originally, hospitals provided assistance and care to the poor. They depended primarily on churches or municipalities. After the French Revolution, a number of hospitals were placed under state control, but throughout the nineteenth and early twentieth centuries a "voluntary" sector developed under the influence of large paternalistic ventures and charity organizations. In the twentieth century, private physicians established clinics, often small and specialized, and combined their office practices with work at the clinics (Imbert 1982; Maillard 1986). Hence, a public hospital sector whose vocation was to care for the poor gradually came to coexist with a voluntary and for-profit private sector intended primarily for well-off patients. That for-profit sector, overhauled in the late 1950s, grew significantly until the 1990s, while granting access to less fortunate members of society. For its part, the public hospital underwent a transformation, becoming more attractive and less restricted to the working class. As a result, and within a context of intense budget constraints, the private sector has lost ground in the last ten years.

For medical, surgical, and obstetric (MSO) services alone, with which this chapter deals more specifically, the for-profit private sector represents 26 percent of beds, the public 65 percent, and the nonprofit sector 9 percent. The for-profit private sector is undergoing a strong trend toward concentration, with a drop in the number of establishments and a rise in their size. In medicine, the average number of beds per establishment has risen from 70 to 84 from 1995 to 2005. The public sector is also experiencing a reduction in the number of establishments, but the average number of beds per establishment has fallen as well (from 220 to 210) (DREES 2005).

Specialization is high in the for-profit private sector, particularly in surgery (where its share is rising), obstetrics (where its share has recently dropped), and certain other medical disciplines, but also in medium-term care (primarily follow-up and convalescent care). That specialization is part of a quest for profitable "niches": costly medical procedures (fitting prostheses, for example) and predictable care services that ensure a high use rate for technical equipment and beds. Within our sample, all the private clinics were 100 percent specialized in MSO services. Nevertheless, they belonged to groups with other operations, such as retirement or convalescent homes. Public hospitals are more diversified and more integrated, with a mix of MSO and psychiatric services and sometimes an integrated retirement home.

The distinction between public hospitals and for-profit private hospitals constitutes the chief variable in the sample. In particular, the opposition between the public and the for-profit private sector makes it possible to contrast labor market institutions: the regulations concerning civil service jobs in the public sector and the private-law collective agreements in the for-profit private sector.

A High Percentage of Civil Servants   Unlike the United States and European countries other than France, the majority of workers in public hospitals are civil servants (about 80 percent). Because of the scope of these public hospitals, civil servants hold more than half of all jobs in the hospital sector as a whole (public and private). In 1955 wage regulations were applied uniformly in all public hospitals. These regulations were renewed in 1986, becoming totally integrated into civil service regulations generally. They govern all questions relating to hiring, mobility, wages, bonuses, and leaves. They are subject to negotiations and adjustments between the state, the unions, and public hospital representatives and can be compared to a collective bargaining agreement. But the state plays a determining role. For example, annual wage increases are decided by the central government for the entire public sector, hospitals included. A "licensed" hospital worker is recruited "for life."[3] But the unions play a major role through a set of structures of representation, both at the individual hospital level and at the national level. The force of the civil service regulations characteristic of the French model explains the homogeneity in the public hospitals.

Is the Public-Private Dichotomy More Apparent Than Real?   All the same, as we will see throughout this chapter, the differences between the public and private sectors are less sharp than might be expected. Three major factors come into play to reduce the gap between the two subsectors.

Regulations governing the health system have a major impact in that they are common to both public and private hospitals. The two subsectors depend on the same major source of financing (the national social security system) and on similar financing rules. Private clinics and public hospitals are subject to a set of norms that play a role in standardizing job descriptions and working conditions and setting the conditions for operating a hospital: for example, there is a minimum requirement for the number of nurses and nurse's aides on the job. These norms are also increasingly applied to a certain number of procedures that must be respected, and these have a direct influence on the nature and volume of work performed by the staff: respect for the patient, codified in the charter of patients' rights and duties, rules for pain management, and hygiene regulations designed to fight nosocomial infections. These rules, which are similar to the quality control practiced in industry, influence job descriptions (the definitions of protocols and procedures), accountability (the records kept in patients' files), and the skill level and structure of the labor force.

Public and private hospitals are in competition, especially when hiring skilled staff (nurses and nurse's aides). That competition can sometimes be felt for housekeepers as well, because of the attractiveness of civil service jobs. It is a factor tending to homogenize the private and public sectors, and union organizations also play a role in that trend. As in the public sector as a whole, unionization in public hospitals is appreciably higher than the national average. We do not have any data on the private sector, but in all the case studies unions were present and active, especially in wage disputes. At the national level, the fact that the same union federations often attract employees from both the public and private sectors facilitates the coordination of demands. Public sector regulations and collective bargaining in the private sector develop in tandem, sometimes with clauses and structural rules (seniority, job classifications) that are functionally very similar. The difference is essentially one of level (wages, bonuses, the length of the workday). Hence, in 2002, the new collective agreement signed in the private sector stated that "the parties intend to improve the working conditions of employees by promoting a convergence of salary levels between the private and public sectors."

NURSE'S AIDES AND HOSPITAL SERVICE WORKERS: TWO WELL-IDENTIFIED CATEGORIES OF THE LABOR FORCE

In the French hospital system, housekeeping and basic nursing tasks correspond to two categories of staff, clearly demarcated by their educational backgrounds, job titles, and hiring conditions: hospital service workers and nurse's aides.[4] Along with nurses, they constitute the family of caregivers (Chevandier 1997).

Hiring   Although no particular degree is required for hospital service workers, the percentage of hospital service workers with a vocational training degree has risen, partly because of the general rise in the training level of young people in the last twenty years and partly in response to the increasing demands of hospitals.

For nurse's aides, a vocational degree as a nurse's aide is obligatory. It entails twelve months of vocational training composed of theoretical and practical courses and internships. It can also be awarded by equivalency—to student nurses after their first year of training, for example. A common career path among the nurse's aides we interviewed was compulsory education until the age of sixteen, followed by two years of vocational training in health and social welfare, then a one-year specialization at a school for nurse's aides. In addition, the proportion of high school graduates among nurse's aide trainees is growing (about 25 percent in 2003). Unlike in the United States and Germany, a nurse's aide in France must have a specific degree. This is a quasi-professional labor market (governed by rules of access, though these rules, and especially the number of degrees awarded, are not controlled by employers and trade unions), which reinforces the similarity between the private and public sectors.

Clear Job Descriptions Corresponding to these well-identified job categories is a traditional work organization, which we found with few variations in all eight case studies for nurse's aides and in four (public and private) cases for hospital service workers. As we shall see later, this organization is undergoing a change in the other four hospitals, which are restructuring the hospital service workers' tasks.

Better trained than their German, English, or American counterparts, French nurse's aides perform tasks that place them between the nurse and the hospital service worker. These tasks, distinguished from those that only a nurse may perform, are codified at the national level by the Ministry of Health.

In all our cases, the nurse's aides were assigned to a particular hospital unit. They performed basic nursing tasks (washing and dressing the patient, helping with meals, helping to move the patient), hygiene (cleaning the area near the patient, making up occupied beds, disinfecting beds and supplies), and managing the unit (providing linen, keeping supplies in stock). As a general rule, they had access to patients' files, to which they could contribute information. Under the nurse's authority and supervision, they also performed tasks on the borderline between nursing and care: helping patients take their medications, taking their temperature, administering glucose, and helping to change dressings. They had frequent interactions with patients (often more than nurses) and with patients' families. The scope of these tasks varied depending on how the unit was organized but also depending on the time of day. In the morning, the nurse's aide would frequently work alongside the nurse (cleaning and dressing patients and changing bandages, for example). In the afternoon, when it is more common for patients to be released, she might work with the hospital service worker cleaning and disinfecting rooms.

The unit supervisor's personality, the stability of the teams, and the quality of relations among coworkers often prevailed over any other prescriptive or organizational logic (see also Sainsaulieu 2005). All the same, several of the interviewees in our case studies mentioned a trend toward less cooperation with nurses, attributed to nurses' lack of availability as a result of increasing technology and bureaucracy. In France, nurse's aides do a portion of the tasks that in Germany, Denmark, and Holland fall under the nurse's job description (see also Vassy 1997, 1999). And their tasks are even broader than those of the English or American nurse's aide (Appelbaum et al. 2003; Carroll et al. 2006). This is truly a skilled staff. A private hospital nurse's aide described her job:

> Our hospital service worker serves the meal. Anything that's housekeeping, warming up the trays, she's the one who does all that! I don't interfere at all. So when she's finished warming up the meals, she puts them on the trays, and then I help her get people set up [and] seat them. It's very rare that we have to spoon-feed people . . . but sometimes we help them eat! It's our job to do that. Here it's the nurse's aide who helps them eat; giving medications is for the nurse. I won't conceal the fact that sometimes we overstep . . . sometimes we check glycemia levels, the nurse's aides do that, but that's where it ends. Okay, I have changed perfusions. . . . Especially when there's resuscitations, everyone joins in, we go beyond our usual jobs.

In the traditional organization of a hospital, the hospital service worker is also an integral part of the unit. The hospital service worker's main job is to clean the rooms (empty or occupied) and common areas. Theoretically, the area around the patient is cleaned by the nurse's aide. The two may work together, in making up empty beds, for example. In addition, depending on the hospital's organizational choices but also on the staff arrangements within the units, the hospital service worker may distribute pitchers of water to patients, do the dishes, and distribute or help in distributing meal trays. Hospital service workers may also help to get patients into chairs, reply when patients buzz for help, and run errands. In hospitals where hospital service workers are most thoroughly integrated into the unit, they also attend change-of-shift meetings and are familiar with pathologies, that is, with the particular cases. They often have contact with patients and their families. Although all workers wear distinctive, differently colored smocks or badges signifying their job category, it is sometimes difficult for patients and families to know whether they are dealing with a hospital service worker or a nurse's aide. In the past, a hospital service worker sometimes filled in as a nurse's aide. That practice is now disappearing with stricter requirements for hospitals regarding the number of licensed nurse's aides, but it persisted in some of our cases.

In our sample, two private hospitals and two public hospitals had the type of organization in which the hospital service worker is part of the unit (or straddles two units), is relatively versatile, and has a personal relationship with patients. Most of the hospital service workers we met greatly valued this type of organization. They expressed their professional identity in terms of their relationships with patients. The value they placed on those relationships was also part of their positive assessment of the job and contributed to the attractiveness of hospitals compared to other sectors, especially the hotel industry. One private hospital hospital service worker explained:

> I really like to listen to patients, they talk about their troubles sometimes. Sometimes it does them good if you listen to them talk, and anyway, I really like to have contact. I'm not someone who won't listen and just turns her back and leaves! I'll never do that, I really like contact with patients, with people.... And then, when I prepare the meal, if they can't cut—some of them have cancer sometimes and aren't strong enough to cut—then we do the cutting. I cut up their meat for them, I fix up everything for them, I open the yogurt, I dress the salad, all that, all they have to do is eat! It seems like, in the beginning—now I think we can, though—we weren't allowed to get the patient set up in a chair, it was the nurse's aide who did that, but they're not always available, that's the problem.

This type of traditional work organization is similar to the experiments with enhanced jobs that Eileen Appelbaum and her colleagues (2003) ran across in American hospitals and to the new "service assistant" model being developed in Holland and Denmark. It clearly differentiates the hospital service worker from the hotel housekeeper, especially in terms of contact with the person occupying the room.

All the same, this organization model is in transition, as we shall see later in the chapter. On the one hand, some hospitals believe that versatility works to the detriment of cleaning quality, which is also more strictly monitored than before through protocols on, for instance, the use of products, frequency of cleaning, and the fight against nosocomial infections. On the other hand, economic and Taylorist rationalization is promoting other forms of organization.

Women's Work and the Presence of Immigrants   As in the hotel industry sector, these hospital occupations are highly feminized. Nearly 90 percent of nurse's aides and 74 percent of hospital service workers are women. Seventy percent live with a partner, and 56 percent have at least one child at home. Ten percent are single parents with at least one child (Institut National de la Statistique et des Études Économiques [INSEE] employment survey, 2002). By contrast—and this is a fundamental difference from the hotel industry—the percentage of immigrants is very low. In public hospitals, foreign nationals represent 0.6 percent of the caregiving staff—nurse's aides, hospital service workers, and nurses (Direction de l'Hospitalisation et de l'Organisation des Soins [DHOS] 2004)—and 8 percent of the medical staff. Until recently, French citizenship was a necessary condition for obtaining a government job, which accounts for this very low rate of employment by immigrants. We do not have national figures for the private sector. But in the case studies, nurse's aides and hospital service workers were also usually French natives. A demand for higher-skilled workers and the importance of contact with patients have also led to hiring requirements and practices that differ from those of hotels.

A Near Absence of Low Wages

As mentioned in chapter 2, French hospitals are scarcely affected by low wages. With the legal minimum wage, the system of promotions based on seniority, and bonuses (overtime pay for nights and Sundays and the year-end bonus), even a starting hospital service worker earns slightly above the low-wage threshold.

Table 4.1 Hourly Wages and Incidence of Low Wages

	Public				Private For-Profit			
	Nurse	Nurse's Aide	Hospital Service Worker	All	Nurse	Nurse's Aide	Hospital Service Worker	All
Mean net hourly wage	€12	€10	€9	€11	€11	€8	€7	€9
Median net hourly wage	€13	€10	€8	€10	€11	€8	€7	€8
Low wage	1.9%[a]	0.9%	3.2%	1.4%	0.3%	4.6%	4.4%	2.9%

Source: Direction de la Recherche des Études de l'Evaluation et des Statistiques (DREES) working conditions survey, 2003, calculations by the authors.
Note: The data for this table are different from those provided in chapter 2. They concern a sample of employees working in private and public hospitals in 2001. For technical reasons, we have considered only full-time employees.
[a] Trainees only.

The Role of Low-Wage Work Table 4.1 shows the incidence of low-wage work for both nurse's aides and hospital service workers. The differences between the public and private sectors are insignificant.

We must qualify that assessment, however. On the one hand, these data do not include government work programs (i.e., active labor market policy schemes; see chapter 2) in public hospitals. These are usually half-time, fixed-term contracts set aside for the chronically unemployed, whose wages are paid by government subsidies and cost the hospitals almost nothing. These jobs, intended to reintegrate recipients into the workforce, are restricted to the public sector and nonprofit organizations (see chapter 2). For these contracts, workers receive the legal minimum wage (SMIC) with no possibility of increases. In our cases, they represented between 3 and 10 percent of staff (3.2 percent was the national average in 2003), which would have to be factored in. On the other hand, we shall later note the scope of the "reserve army" of workers in temporary jobs, on primarily fixed-term contracts. The severance pay that temporary employees receive at the end of their contracts (see chapter 2, note 14) places them slightly above the low-wage threshold. At the same time, however, these employees do not accumulate seniority. Given the time they spend waiting for a permanent contract (a few months to five to seven years), we may consider them on the borderline of low-wage work.

Wage Determinants Variations among our case studies within the same subsector (public or private) were low. The institutions are fulfilling their function. In public hospitals, regulations concerning civil service jobs in hospitals are in force everywhere. Only one hospital deviated from them by granting a special bonus. Placed on notice by the authorities, it was attempting to eliminate the bonus, but was facing union pressure. In private clinics, the collective agreement is also applied universally, but with variations depending on the local context and the union. In one case, wages were 3.8 percent above the agreement, and in another 3 percent above for hospital service workers and nurse's aides but nearly 15 percent above for nurses. The two others abided by the collective agreement. Respect for the minimum wage is the rule everywhere, whatever the category and type of contract. As mentioned in chapter 2, that respect sometimes poses problems. In civil service jobs, the starting wage for hospital service workers stipulated by the agreement was below the legal minimum wage. The wage scale had to be readjusted in 2005. In the private sector, employees begin at an index slightly higher than the bottom of the scale, but remain there longer than stipulated by the collective agreement. As a result, progress toward seniority is frozen for about five years, which leads to a reduction in lifetime wages.

In both subsectors, wage progression based on seniority is significant, more for nurse's aides than for hospital service workers (see table 4.2). Lifetime wages are better for nurse's aides in the public sector than in the private—a cause for complaints about the collective agreement structure in some clinics. For hospital service workers, conversely, the financial benefit of seniority is slightly better in the private sector.

In both subsectors, various fringe benefits supplement the base salary. First, there is a year-end bonus, the equivalent of a month's wages, theoretically adjusted in the public sector to reflect employee absences. In the private hospitals, the year-end bonus took the form of profit-sharing. But in two of the clinics, a conflict arising in the wake of France's compulsory thirty-five-hour working week had turned that profit-sharing benefit into an "automatic" year-end bonus granted to everyone. Second, there are bonuses related to scheduling (overtime pay for night and weekend work) and to working conditions. These benefits, taken together, can amount to 20 percent of base salary. They are all automatic and linked to the particular job. There was no individualization of salary in any of the case studies.

Nevertheless, the wage differential between the public and private sectors remains in force, to the advantage of the public sector. In 2000 (Brahami, Brizard, and Audric 2002) these differences were fairly large. By 2003 (Collet 2005) the gap had narrowed, the result of the universal application of the thirty-five-hour working week and more rapid wage increases in the private sector. But all things being equal, wage scales remain 11 percent lower in the private sector.

That difference is noticeable in the case studies. Workers in the private sector mentioned discrepancies of €200 to €400 (US$282.77 to US$565.54) a month compared to the public sector. Such discrepancies account for the greater labor demands being voiced in the private sector. Hence, in two clinics, wage disputes primarily targeted the methods for granting benefits. In the public sector, conversely, the disputes tend to be national, linked to the general modalities for granting wage increases in civil service jobs. But these discrepancies do not lead to a very high mobility of employees from the private to the public sector. Several reasons for this can be put forward: the cost of such mobility, given that access to the public sector is competitive and waiting lines are already very long; the organization of work time (more regular work schedules were often mentioned as an advantage in the private sector); and the smaller size of private clinics, where the work atmosphere is judged to be more convivial than in public hospitals (which were said to be "like factories").

A few of the employees polled (especially nurse's aides) who had a chance to enter the public sector nonetheless chose the private sector, despite lower wages. A private hospital nurse's aide explained:

> A thousand and forty-seven euros, that's not much, and I even have two years' seniority. But then, you see, what matters to me is the team, the relationship with the team, and I like it here because of that. . . . Hospital [X] doesn't really appeal to me, the working conditions don't really appeal to me. The salary's better! But it doesn't appeal to me as much.

WORK SCHEDULES: ATTRACTIVE BUT SEGMENTED

In addition to the attractiveness of the wages, especially compared to the retail and hotel sectors, hospital workers expressed an appreciation for the organization of work time and employment regulations.

WORK TIME

Days Off Make Up for Shifting Schedules   In French public hospitals, the nurse's aides are generally organized into three shifts: morning (6:30 AM to 1:30 PM), afternoon (1:00 PM to 8:00 PM), and night. Depending on the hospital, the unit, and individual choice, some nurse's aides work only nights or afternoons. But the general rule is to alternate morning and afternoon shifts. This usually also entails working two weekends a month. Hospital service workers often follow the same schedules but do not work nights or weekends.

There were few differences among our four public sector cases. A single private clinic had a fairly similar time organization. In addition to recovery time (especially weekends for the nurse's aides), that type of organization made it possible to have one day off per week. For the three other private clinics, the work schedules tended toward long days (ten to twelve hours) with different start times (6:30 AM or 8:00 AM, depending on the shift) and no morning or afternoon rotation. Over the course of a month, workers alternated between a "short" week (three workdays) and a "long" week (five days, including a weekend). The long-day schedule tended to be valued by the staff: schedules were more predictable, there were more days off, there was no alternating between getting up early and getting home late, and less time had to be spent commuting. These benefits account for some of the appeal of the private sector and partly compensate for the lower wages.

Work schedules are known in advance and are generally decided by the institution, which often takes individual preferences into account. But arrangements among coworkers are also common. These informal arrangements are not merely tolerated but even encouraged. The intensive labor related to scheduling hours (for regulatory staff) culminates in many informal adjustments, introducing a large gap between official and real schedules, particularly as a function of family constraints.

Part-Time Work Is Extensive and Generally Voluntary   Voluntary part-time work is becoming increasingly common. In the public sector, it is the choice of slightly fewer than 20 percent of nurse's aides and hospital service workers. For the most part, however, part-time employees work 80 percent of the normal schedule. In the private sector, part-time work is appreciably less common (10 percent for nurse's aides, 15 percent for hospital service workers). It also consists more often of half-time employment (Direction de la Recherche des Études de l'Évaluation et des Statistiques [DREES], working conditions survey, 2005, calculations by the authors). In both sectors, 80 percent of nurse's aides do not want to work more hours. By contrast, 66 percent of part-time hospital service workers would like to work more.

"Long" part-time work is different from what is found in the Netherlands and Denmark, where a very short work schedule can be considered, in terms of flexibility tools, a functional equivalent of "atypical" (that is, nonpermanent) work contracts in France. In the French case, part-time work is a good example of how work and family life are balanced within a classic form of permanent employment. The choices the hospitals offer also explain part of their attractiveness—compared, for example, to business or the hotel industry, which offer fewer choices, often with "cut" hours. This practice had almost disappeared in our eight hospitals.

In our sample (see appendix), the level of part-time work varied, depending on the category but also on the type of employer. Consistent with national data, private clinics were less open than public hospitals to part-time work. Part-time employment was discouraged by management in that sector. The public hospitals were within the national average for nurse's aides, with two notable exceptions. One hospital required that nurse's aides in home care work part-time, while the other seemed to be responding to local constraints on family organization. It was situated in an area with a high concentration of men doing industrial work in systems shift on a twenty-four-hour schedule. The adjustment variable was the woman's choice of "voluntary" part-time work. As is the case nationally, part-time work among the hospital service workers in our sample was less common. Two public hospitals were the exception, and part-time work in those cases—primarily by staff with fixed-term contracts—was compulsory, justified by the needs for team flexibility and organization.

The Thirty-Five-Hour Working Week Brings Days Off but a Heavier Workload The implementation of the thirty-five-hour working week has tended to reinforce workers' positive evaluation of their work schedules. In most cases, the thirty-five-hour week, negotiated with union organizations, has translated into an increase in days off rather than a reduction in the length of the workday, especially for private clinics. In a very feminized environment, the possibility of having days off (Wednesdays, for example, when children are not in school) is valued. In the case studies of nurse's aides and hospital service workers, we also met some part-time workers who took advantage of the thirty-five-hour week to advance from 70 percent to 80 percent of full-time, thus increasing their wages without losing any days off. Conversely, the establishment of the thirty-five-hour week has not led to the creation of many new jobs, especially in the public sector. The jobs created have tended to be for nurses, to a lesser degree for nurse's aides, and rarely for hospital service workers. The increase in workload, which we discuss further in the next section, is therefore the negative side of the national thirty-five-hour week regulation.

STABLE JOBS AND CAREERS

The prospect of stable employment complements the attractiveness of work schedules.

The Importance of Internal Markets   In the case of nurse's aides and hospital service workers, both public and private hospitals exemplify the internal market in the sense defined by Peter Doeringer and Michael Piore (1971), particularly since seniority is respected when workers move from one institution to another. Wage progression is guaranteed once a worker has entered the internal market, and the turnover rate is very low. This greatly differentiates the French case from the American. Table 4.2 summarizes the major national data.

Civil service regulations, of course, play a major role. But seniority in private clinics is also important, and the turnover rate is also very low. Policies in private hospitals are designed to produce a loyal workforce. In addition to the wage benefits linked to seniority—stipulated by the collective agreement—there are nonwage benefits, sometimes associated with a strongly paternalistic policy (loans to alleviate financial troubles, for example, or housing assistance, as provided in two case study clinics). The internal market model in the private sector is thus similar to that in the public sector.

Prospects for Promotion and Lateral Mobility   In both subsectors, vertical mobility (from hospital service worker to nurse's aide or from nurse's aide to nurse) is possible but not common. In the case studies, we came across one or two such transitions of this type per year, and

Table 4.2 Seniority and Stability

	Public			Private		
	Nurse	Nurse's Aide	Hospital Service Worker	Nurse	Nurse's Aide	Hospital Service Worker
Seniority more than ten years	57%	62%	60%	47%	58%	54%
Change of workplace[a]	6	6	1	2	3	1
Salary increase with seniority[b]	43	39	20	31	30	23

Source: Direction de la Recherche des Études de l'Evaluation et des Statisques (DREES) working conditions survey, 2005, calculations by the authors.
[a] Between 2001 and 2003.
[b] Differential between full-time workers with three to six years of seniority and those with more than twenty years.

these were generally encouraged by the institution (through aid in preparing for the exam and payment of wages and tuition costs, in both the public and private sectors). That prospect plays a strong symbolic role. One public hospital nurse's aide shared her experience:

> I came to the hospital as a hospital service worker, and afterward I took classes, while remaining on the job. After I was licensed, I had my three years of seniority with patients, so I asked to go to nurse's aide school. I took the entrance exam . . . the hospital financed it. During the year of schooling, I was paid normally. We were paid, and we did our training, which didn't last a whole year. We started in September and ended in June, [when] we took the final exam. At the time, there were nine in the hospital and one outside going to school to become a nurse's aide. . . . This year there are only two.

A drop in hospital financing for training has been noted, a result of the higher cost of training, other demands on the budget, and a higher priority given to training specialized nurses, who, at two of the public hospitals and one of the private hospitals, are in shorter supply. But that little door to promotion remains open and contributes, if only symbolically, to the attractiveness of these jobs.

By contrast, internal lateral mobility is high. For the "licensed" staff, it is voluntary, with no differences among our case studies. A job vacancy is posted, applicants respond, and the selection is made based on the applicant's experience. This process gives rise to subtle lateral "careers," in accordance with expectations (variables of age and personal situation) (see also Arborio 2001, 2004). We can identify three principal types:

1. A change of job—from a part-time to a full-time position or vice versa, depending on the age of the children, or from a night shift to a day shift (for nurse's aides)—makes it possible to balance work and family life.
2. A change of job makes it possible to modify working conditions. The workload varies depending on the unit. Some jobs are considered more gratifying than others. Hence, new hires are often assigned to a difficult department and later move to a different one. In this case, especially for hospital service workers, individual preferences play a role—for example, in whether the person values the role of caregiver and contact with patients.
3. A change of job may serve as a preliminary to a vertical career. A hospital service worker who wants to prepare for the nurse's aide exam, for example, may transfer to a medical unit to gain contact with patients, or a nurse's aide planning to take the nursing exam may work in several units with different technical requirements.

These internal lateral markets are very active. At the national level, an index of internal and external mobility (the percentages of those who changed establishment, job, or assignment over three years) has been calculated: 32 percent for nurses, 27 percent for nurse's aides, and 15 percent for hospital service workers, with slightly higher rates in the public sector than in the private. The vast majority of changes (83 percent for nurses, 69 percent for nurse's aides, and 67 percent for hospital service workers) were voluntary (DREES 2005, working conditions survey, calculations by the authors).

Scheduling and employment conditions are attractive enough that hospitals have little difficulty hiring in these job categories and have fairly broad margins for maneuvering, especially in terms of organization and flexibility.

THE PERIPHERAL MARKET AND LABOR RESERVES: WHEN ATTRACTIVENESS ALLOWS FLEXIBILITY

Working alongside the licensed hospital staff is a large contingent of nonpermanent employees, especially hospital service workers. These peripheral jobs are primarily an instrument of flexibility for organizations that need to find replacements for absent employees and deal with industry constraints.

Limited Internal Flexibility   A first set of solutions consists of arrangements for internal flexibility through the permanent core of licensed employees. In all our case studies, hospitals had a replacement pool (primarily for nurses and nurse's aides). Employees in the pool were licensed. In general, the pool was designed to deal with lengthy planned absences (maternity leave, vacations, training leaves). The pool was often small. Another solution was to have employees work extra hours. But that solution was used less and less, since employees increasingly did not want to work overtime, particularly if it would disrupt their work schedules. A third solution (especially for hospital service workers) was to use compulsory part-time employment. Dividing a full-time job in two allows for more flexibility. That solution, rarely used in private clinics, was employed extensively in two of our public hospitals, which imposed it on new hires, though it is theoretically prohibited by civil service regulations.

A Low Use of Subcontracting   These internal solutions, largely unused in the end, are complemented by the use of external flexibility.

The first modality is subcontracting, which is used primarily for food preparation, housekeeping of common areas, laundry, and sometimes a few specialized jobs (such as computers and building maintenance).[5] Nevertheless, we must once more emphasize the importance of labor market institutions. As a rule, when tasks are outsourced, the same staff that had been doing these tasks are hired by the new service provider. As in the United Kingdom, "permanent" hospital staff are then under the authority and management of the service provider (as in one private clinic), or the staff are completely transferred to the employ of the service provider (as in another clinic). But nurse's aides are not affected, and of our eight cases, only one private clinic completely outsourced housekeeping, including the patients' rooms. That outsourcing, which was being implemented at the time of the survey, was justified by management on the basis of greater efficiency, given the small size of the clinic, more than cost savings. The director of that private clinic explained:

Our operations are becoming more and more complex, and we have a lot of trouble being everywhere at once. We've gradually gotten more structured, but in spite of everything, in private establishments the structures we have are pretty loose. There's a director here, but no assistant director, no director of human resources. . . . We deal with the various requests we get with limited means. So in the end we don't manage to be involved everywhere. And we came to realize that there were a number of areas where we were less and less involved, since we were obliged to focus on our core mission—the caregiving part.

No final assessment was possible for this clinic, but there had already been major consequences: the hospital service workers had become the staff of the service provider, fell under its collective agreement, and, symbolically, wore the smock of that new employer and no longer that of the hospital. Theoretically, their current wage levels had been maintained, but enormous confusion reigned at the time of the survey. The staff we met mentioned a loss of benefits and, especially, anxiety about what would happen later on. As for the subcontracting manager, he predicted that future hires would receive the legal minimum wage (that is, the SMIC; see chapter 2). In addition, problems of quality were emerging. That organizational choice to outsource also had a paradoxical consequence: although the clinic was hoping to cut back on nurse's aide positions, the breakdown in cooperation with the hospital service workers had led to overworked nurse's aides and a need to hire in that job category.

National data do not allow us to detect a clear trend. In public hospitals, for example, the share of the budget devoted to purchasing contracted services has tended to drop in recent years (DHOS 2004). One public hospital in the sample, needing to restructure its food services, had negotiated with union organizations to keep them within the hospital in exchange for a cut in the number of staff. Ultimately, the reluctance to outsource is clearly greater in France than in Germany or the United Kingdom. Doubts about the quality of service, a shortage of service providers, union pressures, and a lesser financial interest (given that, theoretically, wages levels must be maintained) are arguments we encountered during the interviews. The SMIC also counteracts subcontracting as it does not allow huge wage cuts.

The Labor Pool and Nonpermanent Contracts   The other solution is to establish an external labor pool under various auspices, such as fixed-term contracts, government work programs, or temp agencies. Because hospital employment is attractive, there are generally many unsolicited applications, and they can be complemented by the use of the National Employment Agency. Names of job applicants are kept on file, usually by the hospitals without any intermediaries.

The purpose of that pool is manifold:

- To fill in for "unplanned" absences due to absenteeism, sick leave, and vacations

- To allow for compulsory part-time work, which is theoretically not permitted for civil servants

- To allow for careful selection of staff members to be "licensed" in open-ended contracts (in the private sector) or civil service jobs (in the public)

- To place temporary hires in the least-skilled categories (hospital service workers), thus freeing up jobs for permanent employees, who are assigned to more-skilled categories

The existence of an external labor pool makes it possible to use a contingent of the workforce at a lower cost and to reduce the payroll by hiring at the legal minimum wage (SMIC) or at the bottom of the pay scale, with no progression toward seniority.

As table 4.3 shows, the hospitals in our study made broad use of the array of nonpermanent contracts mentioned in chapter 2. These contracts covered a significant volume of the labor force, often going far beyond the replacement of absent workers.

The use of government work programs is sensitive to the conditions of the labor market. By government order, public hospitals are required to fill a quota, which varies by region and unemployment rate. This is one of the only areas in which the status of the labor market (tight or soft), chosen as a secondary variable in constituting our sample, is directly at work. Hospitals cannot refuse to meet the quota, nor can they select applicants sent by the local bureau of the Public Employment Service, but they can exceed the quota. Hence, in a budget crisis in the mid-1990s one public hospital used these contracts extensively as substitutes for permanent jobs. Although their numbers were falling at the time of the survey, they still represented nearly 10 percent of all employment contracts.

Table 4.3 Methods for Managing the Reserve Labor Force Using "Atypical" Contracts

Case	Short Fixed-Term Contract	Long Fixed-Term Contract (Three Months or More)	Open-Ended Contract[a]	Government Work Program[b]	Temp Agency	Full-Time Equivalent	Focus
A	Yes	Yes	Yes	Many	No	18%	Hospital service worker
B	Yes	Many	No	Yes, few	No	18	Hospital service worker, 52%
C	Yes	Yes	Yes	Many	No	36	Hospital service worker, nurse's aide
D	Yes	Yes	No	Yes, few	No	24	Hospital service worker, 44%
E	Many	Yes			No	n.a.	Hospital service worker, nurse's aide
F	Many	Many			Yes	14	Hospital service worker, nurse's aide
G	Yes	Yes			Yes	12.5	Hospital service worker, nurse's aide
H	Yes	Yes			Yes	16.5	Nurse, nurse's aide, hospital service worker

Source: Authors' compilation from hospital case studies.
[a] Open-ended contracts are considered atypical in the public sector, where civil service jobs are the rule, but not in the private sector.
[b] Government work programs exist only in the public sector. They are labor market policy schemes, thus special employment statuses: fixed-term part-time jobs, paid usually at the hourly legal minimum wage (SMIC) and leveled mainly by government budget.

"Long" fixed-term contracts are frequently used for medium-term replacements. One public hospital filled nearly half its need for hospital service workers by that means. The contracts were sometimes renewed for five to seven years, with an obligatory period of unemployment—or employment elsewhere—between two contracts. This was both a wage saving policy and a "tradition" of work sharing. Within this employment pool, the primary employer (the hospital) divided the contracts among family members. Under pressure from the union, the practice is declining slightly. Short-term contracts (sometimes for one day) are also widely used, especially for sick days or child care problems.

Only three private clinics used temp agencies to any great extent, usually for skilled staff (nurses, technicians, and, to a lesser degree, nurse's aides).

As table 4.2 shows, all these forms of "atypical" labor contracts can exceed 20 percent of the total volume of labor. Public hospitals use them more widely than private clinics. On the one hand, this is because they cannot control the number of civil service jobs, which is set by the government. They therefore compensate with atypical contracts. On the other hand, as we noted earlier, they use the waiting list thus created to carefully select those who will obtain permanent jobs. And since public hospitals are more attractive than private clinics, they can make the wait longer, particularly since they are not subject to the usual employees' rights regulations governing the private sector and do not fall under the purview of the labor bureau.[6] A care manager at one of the public hospitals explained how atypical contracts work:

> The thing is, we feel that as soon as someone has come on board under contract, she'll do the two or three years she needs to be trained and licensed in civil service.... And it seems to me that for those two or three years she agrees to have maybe a somewhat more lowly position than that of a licensed person, who'll be in a civil service job and who'll have less mobility.... That's sort of the condition for coming on board.

The Waiting Line and Its Consequences   As we have seen, the staff with these various contracts earn lower wages than the permanent staff, especially since they do not progress toward seniority. Those in government work programs are paid strictly the legal minimum wage (SMIC). Most of the compulsory part-time jobs, in which employees start work quickly with little or no training, are also governed by such contracts. In some of the case studies, we found a significantly higher work accident rate for these categories. For example, in one public hospital, employees in government work programs were not issued non-skid shoes. After an unusually high number of falls, a study was conducted, and thereafter these employees were suitably equipped. In another, 25 percent of the work stoppages due to accidents affected staff in government work programs.

The constitution of that "reserve army" is an emblematic case of circumventing the key labor market institutions of regulations and collective agreements, as mentioned in chapter 2. Yet we should not assimilate that peripheral labor market to an "unregulated" market. It is regulated through imitation of the internal market of permanent workers, with which it is closely associated. In fact, for hospital service workers, it is the obligatory point of entry to the internal market. An implicit twofold rule—seniority and availability—is in force. A worker's contract is renewed, and she moves ahead in the waiting line as a function of her seniority and the positive responses she has given to requests for work. Those who know how to navigate that obstacle course will be licensed within a few months or as much as two years in the private sector, closer to three or four years in the public sector.[7] Hence, there is a stormy relationship between the workings of the external labor pool and management of the internal market. A public hospital service worker shared her work history:

> Before, I worked for private individuals, and I didn't get renewed. As soon as I found myself unemployed again, [I was] talking with a friend [and] she told me: "Why don't you make a request at hospital [X]?" At the time I came in, that was called CES,[8] it lasted a year, CES did. My contract ended, I asked to do training, I got training as a seniors' aide, and, um, a year went by. I asked again at hospital [X] for another CES. When the contract ended, the next day they called me back, saying they were giving me an LTC [limited-term contract]. It was a parental leave, so I stayed three years as an LTC. So many hurdles! . . . And then I was accepted as a trainee . . . and I'm waiting for my license.

It must also be said that, though this is a compulsory situation for the most part, especially because of the unemployment rate, some staff prefer this solution. There are people who want to work only in short stints during the week or month and who indicate in advance when they are available and then are called in as needed (especially in two of the private clinics in our study). These individuals may be students, student nurses, or midwives seeking extra income. In addition, some of those hired (as temps or on very short-term contracts) hold concurrent jobs. They may be licensed in one hospital or clinic and, for example, work a few hours or a night in another institution. Theoretically prohibited in the public sector (civil servants must ask for permission) and regulated by rules governing time off (no one can work a night and a day back to back), these concurrent jobs augment relatively low incomes. Three of the sixty-four employees we interviewed mentioned them.

THE CHANGES UNDER WAY

The French hospital system is experiencing the same changes found in most other countries, though some are of much more recent date than in the United States. These changes are having repercussions, particularly on the job descriptions and working conditions of nurse's aides and hospital service workers. Nevertheless, the principal features of the employment system seem to be resisting change, and sometimes they are even gaining strength.

Hospitals Under Great Pressure

Four factors, also found in the United States and European countries other than France, are having an impact on hospitals and prompting changes in the industry (see also Brown, Arnetz, and Petersson 2003).

1. *Technological development is very rapid.* New technologies include new non-invasive diagnostic technologies, new uses for MRIs, new molecular treatments and surgical methods, and automated tools for monitoring patients. Large investment budgets and a growing specialization among technicians and nursing staff are required if hospitals are to remain in the race and offer cutting-edge care. As a result, all the hospitals in our sample were devoting more of their efforts to highly skilled job categories than to nurse's aides and hospital service workers.

2. *Strong pressures to provide care can be felt in emergency units, par-

ticularly in public hospitals, as a result of the reduction in emergency services provided by local doctors. Longer life expectancy brings with it an increasing demand for care of dependent seniors. Demand for higher-quality care and hotel-like comfort is also becoming more acute. For the staff, these demands sometimes lead to more difficult and stressful relationships with patients.

3. *Although kept in check by the hospital charter, competition in France is real.* The patient can choose not only among different public hospitals but also between public and private institutions. That competition is more perceptible in areas with a high density of hospitals. And it is growing as patients gain access to more information such as ratings of hospitals and medical information on Internet websites. For four of the hospitals in our sample (both public and private), patients could easily decamp to urban university hospitals nearby. One public hospital that had scant, poor-quality services almost went out of business when patients fled to other cities; eventually it was restructured in conjunction with local private clinics. The hospital director commented:

> Well, it's true that at one time the hospital was getting old, and in addition, it wasn't attractive, it had a bad reputation. In surgery, there was only one surgeon left. . . . The two clinics were supercompetitive, not only between themselves but also with nearby [A]. And it's true, you could wonder: [C] had twenty thousand residents at the time, now maybe twenty-eight thousand. Was it necessary to have that redundancy, which in my view also led to an unhealthy climate in the population, where you heard comments like: "You get better care in this or that clinic than in the hospital," or, "You get better care at the hospital."

The strong reputation in certain specializations at one private clinic made it competitive with the university hospital in the same city. Conversely, another clinic with no emergency services lost some patients, who were redirected to the public sector. Only one public hospital, located in a mountainous area, had a monopoly—because of transportation difficulties.

4. *New financing rules and growing budgetary pressures are having an impact.* Beginning in the early 1980s, hospitals in France were financed by a global annual budget negotiated with health authorities, with different modalities for the public and private sectors. In recent

years, after oversight designed to limit cost overruns had become stricter, that system was abandoned in favor of a system based on fixed rates for each procedure (similar to the DRG [diagnosis-related group] model in the United States, but with features peculiar to France). The aim was to rationalize and restructure the hospital system under almost market-driven constraints (LeGrand and Bartlett 1993). Monetary pressures and changes in financing methods are now having an impact on the size and structure of hospital budgets. At the time of our survey, the new fixed-rate model was only beginning to be implemented in some of its aspects. But it was leading hospitals to identify areas of profit (and loss), with consequences regarding specialization. Two public hospitals and one private hospital mentioned that they would probably restructure in response to the new fixed-rate system, but they predicted greater consequences for doctors than for other staff.

Strong Restructuring Trends What structural changes have the hospitals made in response?

Within the national context of lower patient capacities (in ten years the number of hospital beds in France dropped from 540,000 to 471,000), all the hospitals in our sample were affected by strong external and internal restructuring trends, their experience being relatively representative of national trends. Mergers and takeovers, accompanied by a restructuring of care options either horizontally (in types of specializations) or vertically (along the entire spectrum of care), were common. One public hospital was taking over psychiatric services from a neighboring hospital, another obstetrics from a private clinic. The aim was to rationalize the delivery of care, avoid duplications within a single territory, and develop public-private partnerships. One director explained the role of his public hospital:

> So there is a serious medical plan under way, getting back on track through modernization. Right now it's a response calibrated to needs, a real role for a public hospital unit, a monopoly situation in obstetrics, with two thousands births . . . in a competitive area, with clinic [X] not far away, and very strong in surgery. We take what others don't want. We're lucky with the new fixed rates, because from now on we'll have a balance. The institution's strategy is to strengthen medical services, cardiology, dialysis. We also need public-private partnerships, for example, for the MRI, which operates at only 75 percent capacity.

... [In] negotiations with clinic [X], when they dropped obstetrics, we could have taken without giving anything back, [but] we traded beds for follow-up care. Now they're building up their clinic and ensuring their profitability.

In 2002 one public hospital in our sample moved closer to two private clinics, creating the first French complex that combined in a single building a private clinic and a public hospital providing services in common. Two private hospitals were taking over several private clinics and retirement homes in their groups. Only the public hospital in a monopoly situation had avoided these trends. Most of our hospitals, then, were in a phase of increasing their size and the number of procedures they offered. In that sense, these "survivors" of the concentration process reflected the national trend toward larger establishments.

Another possibility is to develop alternatives to standard hospitalization in response to economic constraints (shorter stays, a focus on profitable medical procedures) but also to patient demands. Outpatient services are developing, both very specialized (dialysis) and more generalized (home care services for the elderly in public hospitals). These alternative services change the staff's working conditions and job descriptions. On the one hand, they require that the staff be available at different times and in different places: more often during the daytime, in an office or specialized establishment, at the patient's residence. On the other hand, the development of these services is leading to changes in the job structure: more nurses and nurse's aides, fewer hospital service workers. In one of our case studies, home care services for patients (usually provided in the morning) entailed a generalized use of compulsory part-time work.

Finally, hospitals are dealing with shorter hospital stays. The development of outpatient services and the improvement of diagnostic and care techniques allow them to release patients sooner. An occupied bed is more profitable if the patient in it requires intensive care. Beyond that period of acute care, the patient must be directed to other establishments—hence the interest in integrating different institutions into one network, which facilitates rapid patient turnover. Nationally, between 1981 and 2000 hospital stays dropped from 15.5 to 6.5 days for MSO services. The private clinics in our sample were more specialized and had shorter stays (about five days; see the appendix). Public hospitals are less specialized, often providing long-term or geriatric care or psychiatric services, which account for longer stays on average. The general trend toward shortening hospital stays increases the staff's workload. The patient is more dependent in the first days of hospitalization, requiring more monitoring and nursing care. Each departure and arrival involves cleaning and disinfecting the room, opening a new file, and checking in a new patient. Nurse's aides and hospital service workers mentioned that the patient turnover rate was one of the factors contributing to a deterioration in their working conditions.

Changing Jobs

How are we to analyze the consequences of this restructuring of our job categories? First, we need to point out that the consequences have been greater for hospital service workers, the category at the bottom of the scale; they have been less directly perceptible for nurse's aides. We may hypothesize that the most vulnerable workers (those with poor skills and a high unemployment rate) are also those who most easily become the object of "low-road" institutional policies. In addition, we must take into account the pace of change. We have seen, for example, that the new system for financing hospitals was only beginning to be implemented at the time of our survey. We may assume that, given health budget constraints, pressures will increase in the years to come. The developing trends are still far from stable. Contradictory tendencies are becoming visible. That explains why it is difficult to find converging strategies and to correlate one change or another with the variables we initially chose in collecting the sample of case studies. A public hospital may have a strategy close to that of a particular private clinic, but there is no general rule that would allow us, for example, to differentiate public and private institutions. Similarly, the labor market variable (tight or soft) proved to be inoperative. The resilience of institutions may also account for the difficulty in identifying sharply contrasting trends. Three tendencies are emerging, but they are not exempt from contradiction.

A Rise in Skill Level The rise in skill level, a trend not only in France but in most other European countries, is expressed, first, in an increase in the number of nurses and nurse's aides.

Between 1992 and 2002, the number of nurses rose by nearly 15 percent; it rose more quickly in the private sector than in the public.

The number of nurse's aides has also been on the rise (up 19 percent). Of course, part of that growth can be attributed to the increase in part-time work. But the rising number of nurse's aides is a good indication of the rise in skill level since, as we have seen, nurse's aides generally have a vocational degree. By contrast, in the public and private sectors the number of hospital service workers is stagnating (up 3 percent). Two factors play a role in that stagnation: the rise in skill level (the substitution of nurse's aides for hospital service workers) and pressure on the productivity of hospital service workers (an increase in the surfaces to be maintained, increased mechanization).

Our eight cases were representative of national trends. In the period of the survey, all our hospitals were experiencing a rise in numbers because of the introduction of new procedures or the integration of services that had been offered at other institutions. But most new jobs were for skilled staff: nurses, nurse's aides, and executives. One public hospital director predicted that,

> in terms of quality, I personally think there will be fewer and fewer unskilled jobs at the hospital. And it's even possible to foresee that, in extreme cases, these unskilled jobs may be contracted out. That is, something outside the core mission, the hospital's core mission being technology, care, organization . . . and attending to the patient. Skilled jobs have great prospects. . . . Nurse's aides are already in skilled jobs. . . . hospital service workers also have a skill: we don't take applications without a health and social welfare BEP now,[9] and even maybe a bit more, we often ask for a bit more. But that said . . . I can foresee contracting out maintenance, the hospital service worker's job.

As is happening at the national level, the number of hospital service workers employed by our case study hospitals was stagnating or even dropping, and application requirements were rising. One private clinic, for example, had adopted a "degree" policy when hiring not only nurse's aides (replacing retiring nurse's aides who had not had a degree with those with a degree) but also hospital service workers (requiring a basic vocational training degree). The public hospital just cited also said it would not hire a hospital service worker without a degree.

Of course, the search for cost reduction through outsourcing and the use of nonpermanent staff also exists as a countertrend. But it seemed to be held in check among our case hospitals by staff resistance and quality constraints. The productivity-quality strategy seemed to be prevailing, except in one private clinic—which in fact was in some difficulty—and the one public hospital with a monopoly in its area.

An Industrial Rationalization of Housekeeping? Breaking with the classic profile of the hospital service worker described earlier, several hospitals have sought to refocus their hospital service workers on cleaning tasks and to apply standard industrial criteria regarding surfaces to clean, a specialization in housekeeping, and limited contact with patients. In one of the private clinics, the hospital service workers, while remaining attached to a unit, no longer distributed meals. Two public hospitals and one private hospital had chosen a system in which hospital service workers specialized in housekeeping tasks and were regrouped in a central department. For the public hospital, this choice came about when the new building shared with a private clinic opened. For the private establishment, the choice was part of the recent decision to subcontract a specialized business for all housekeeping, food preparation, laundry, and check-in tasks.

It is clear that the contrast between public and private does not allow for a simple differentiation of organizational choices. It is not possible to distinguish clearly how one or another strategic choice mentioned before accounts for an organizational option. There is in fact great hesitation regarding organization. The private hospital that decided to subcontract was not sure that its choice was technically or economically sound. One of the public hospitals had followed the classic model but then reorganized its hospital service workers into a specialized central pool. At the time of the survey this hospital, after trying out that system for five years, had just abandoned it, and the hospital service workers had been returned to the units. The hospital had returned to its old system under pressure from unit managers, hospital service workers, and union organizations. A satisfaction survey conducted among the staff had shown a clear preference for returning to a classic form of organization.

Although these innovations, which resemble the solutions adopted by English and German hospitals, may be called "low-road" in terms of job description, unlike in Germany they are not accompanied by a significant reduction in wage levels. At a deeper level, hesitations about organization point to a fundamental question, which remains open to this day: is it possible in a hospital to separate care operations from "pure" hotel services? Only the case study private hospital with a system of generalized subcontracting answered in the affirmative. Everywhere else, the question was a matter of debate.

A Heavier Workload The final trend—present everywhere and showing no real gap between the public and private sectors—is toward increased productivity through heavier workloads.

The question of working conditions and workload is particularly sensitive in hospitals. Since 1998, indicators in national surveys have pointed to significant deterioration in employees' perceptions of their working conditions (Le Lan and Baubeau 2004). Comparative European surveys note increased health risks and burnout in France (see also Baret 2002; Mosse and Arrowsmith 1999; Estryn-Behar, Le Nézet, and Jasseron 2004). In our case studies, we find more or less the same phenomena: frequent complaints (especially from nurse's aides) about work injuries (backaches, accidents associated with lifting patients), growing problems in relationships with patients and their families, and lack of time to perform the job correctly (Sainsaulieu 2003). One private hospital nurse's aide said:

> We're tired. Emotionally, because the patients have become a burden, the patients are always watching, well, there are charming people, but there are people who've become suspicious. So whether it's due to TV programs or magazines, people know better than you do now, and I feel like it's hard to take care of those people.

In addition, if we consider the absenteeism attributable to work accidents or illness as an indicator of poor working conditions, we find that it was relatively high in most of our case study hospitals, both public and private. In full-time equivalents (FTEs), it represents between 5 and 9 percent, with a minimum of 2.4 percent.[10]

We do not have precise indicators for measuring workload. In the case study hospitals, nurse's aides were responsible for between eight and twelve patients, with the exception of one public hospital (eighteen beds). Hospital service workers were assigned seven to ten rooms and sometimes, depending on the case, common areas to be cleaned. Another exception was one public hospital that assigned fifteen rooms. (It was also one of the clearest cases of specialized housekeeping for hospital service workers.) That workload is lower than what is found, for example, in retirement homes or some hotels, as was quickly pointed out by the staff we met who had experience elsewhere. It is the intensity of the work more than the volume that accounts for the perception that working conditions are deteriorating, as recorded in the national surveys and in our interviews.

How should we interpret these complaints? We can identify five factors contributing to the deterioration of working conditions, and they are sometimes linked to the restructuring strategies mentioned earlier.

1. *The impact of the compulsory thirty-five-hour working week.* There has been only partial compensation in terms of job creation. For a 10 percent reduction in work hours, the number of staff has increased 6 percent at maximum. In addition, the new jobs are usually for nurses.

2. *An increase in the patient turnover rate.* Shorter hospital stays result in more dependent patients requiring closer monitoring and more help with mobility and feeding, which increases the workload of nurses and nurse's aides. With higher turnover, hospital service workers and nurse's aides must make up rooms more frequently, disinfecting them when patients are released and reconfiguring semiprivate rooms.

3. *A quest for greater profitability of high-tech equipment.* Two solutions are possible: better coordination of this equipment in relation to hospitalization services and adoption of a just-in-time strategy (but in the opposite direction when compared to practices in the industrial sector), which imposes industrial constraints on the units regarding their use of the equipment. In hospitals, the need to adjust to the scheduling of exams or surgeries increases uncertainties about admissions and releases and about the transportation of patients (in terms of the availability of stretchers, for example, or delays in mealtimes).

4. *The role of various monitoring tools and the paperwork associated with the fixed-rate system and accountability.* These increase the amount of data collection and the level of dependence on computerized tools (monitors, beeps), which intensifies the need for immediate attention and response.

5. *The "consumerist" trend in patient and family behavior.* This phenomenon, though more noticeable in private clinics, is also affecting public hospitals. Conflicts or squabbles about the quality of care and about hotel services are becoming more common: our interviewees mentioned demands for private rooms, for immediate access to a television and telephone, and for better quality and choice of meals.

An increase in pathologies involving a vital prognosis (AIDS, cancer, terminal care for the elderly) is also mentioned as a stress factor.

The Resilience of the Employment System

On the whole, the foundations of the employment system seem to be largely unaffected. We have seen that rules regarding remuneration and principles of seniority endure. The few efforts to individualize wages have been ineffective, and in two of the private clinics employee profit-sharing was abandoned in favor of a year-end bonus equivalent to a month's salary and automatically granted to everyone. At the time of writing, national discussions had begun at the Ministry of Finances to reorganize the wage scale and increase wages in the lowest job categories (especially hospital service workers and nurse's aides) in public hospitals. We may assume that these discussions will also have an impact on private hospitals. Recently as well, it has become possible to earn credit toward a nurse's aide degree through on-the-job experience, which ought to reduce the time and cost of training, increase the prospects for promotion among hospital service workers, and thus reinforce the workings of the internal work market.

CONCLUSION

The chief characteristics of the French model are concentrated in the hospital sector, despite many distinctive features in its operations and structure. There is a negligible incidence of low-wage work, internal labor markets are resilient, central institutions are bypassed to build the reserve labor pool, and various trade-offs are made between wages, jobs, and working conditions.

Compared to the highly feminized sectors of retail or the hotel industry, hospitals offer attractive employment conditions. Objectively, this attractiveness stems from slightly higher wage levels (on this point, see the chapter on the hotel industry) and work schedules that are more favorable to a balance of work and family life. The prospect of job stability also plays a role. The attractiveness is also a "symbolic" one, in two ways. The first reason lies in the value given to care or to relationships with patients. Standard among nurse's aides, strong feelings about their caregiving role also prevail among hospital service workers as a form of "distinction" (and struggle) in the face of the social devaluation of housekeeping jobs. The second lies in the prospect for promotion. The little door open to the hospital service worker who wants to become an nurse's aide, or to the nurse's aide who wants to be a nurse, was kept in sight on the horizon by the youngest of our interviewees, valued by those who had made the transition, and regretted as a lost opportunity among older workers. This twofold attractiveness of hospital jobs serves as a "compensatory advantage" in the face of generally deteriorating working conditions. It explains the relative ease with which hospitals find job applicants, the broad margins they give themselves in managing their labor pools (especially hospital service workers), and probably as well the lack of innovation in the area of human resource management.

Of course, the transformations under way and still to come are increasing the pressure on the traditional employment model, but the main pillars of that model remain. The resilience of labor market institutions, and especially the influence of public employment in hospitals (closely linked to French public employment generally), account in part for that resilience. There is, in addition, the role of health institutions (both financing and quality control) in combination with consumer pressure, which may have an impact on quality standards and norms and may limit low-road strategies.

Is it possible to clearly identify establishment "good practices" strategies and correlate them with the characteristics of our sample? At this stage the response is, most likely no. The first variable chosen (public versus private) functions in terms of level (wage, proportion of temporary jobs), but not in terms of the basic principles of organization and operation of the labor market or in terms of the reorganization under way. The second variable (situation of the labor market) appeared even less operative, except concerning the use of government work programs by public hospitals. On the one hand, even with a relatively low unemployment rate in certain areas, unemployment in France remains high for unskilled or low-skill categories. On the other hand, hospitals are generally attractive enough as workplaces to maintain wide margins for maneuvering. Moreover, because of the recent character of some of the changes (especially the method for financing hospitals), we still lack the proper distance. Hospitals are in a trial-and- error phase. Strategies are mixed, sometimes contradictory, and shift back and forth. Yet the standard model seems to persist.

Is this model sustainable from the standpoint of the job categories that concern us, the nurse's aide and hospital service worker?

In an international comparison, given the efficiency of the French hospital sector, the response is, most likely, yes. The sustainability of the model will depend in part on the social consensus about medical costs and the role of hospitals in the chain of care. It will also depend on how the labor market develops in relation to that chain of care.

In considering the likely developments in employment or skill structures, we may formulate the following hypothesis. Especially for nurse's aides, the rise in skill level will continue in hospitals, which more and more constitute the "technical" core of the chain of care. Nurses will increasingly take charge of new medical procedures. Logically, and consistent with the principles of "dirty work" (Hughes 1996), a portion of their workload will fall to nurse's aides, who will take over certain procedures on the borderline between treatment and care, as they are sometimes doing already. There will thus be a rise in skill level for nurse's aides, who may abandon certain tasks to other staff. In that case, and again consistent with the principle of "dirty work," these tasks will be transferred to hospital service workers. For example, hospital service workers will be increasingly involved in hygiene and cleaning areas near the patient. Some of our hospitals have already increased their application requirements for that job category. Outsourcing, a further step in the "industrial rationalization" of housekeeping tasks strictly defined, is thus not assured.

More fundamentally, we must keep in mind that hospitals are only one link in the chain of care. As the most technical and most professional link, they may also transfer the most routine and least skilled care activities to other institutions. That is where the future of low-skill, low-wage work will be played out for nurse's aides and hospital service workers.

APPENDIX

Table 4A.1 Characteristics of the Case Study Hospitals

	A	B	C	D	E	F	G	H[a]
Sector	Public	Public	Public	Public	Private	Private	Private	Private
Labor market	Soft	Tight	Soft	Tight	Soft	Tight	Soft	Tight
Structural information								
Beds (number)	440	654	128	749	159	251	268	133
Medical, surgical, and obstetric specialization	63%	43%	61%	54%	100%	100%	100%	100%
Subcontractors[b]	No	No	L	No	K	K/L/part C	K/L	K/L/C
Public-private partnerships	Yes	Yes	Yes	Yes	No	?	Yes	Yes
Activities								
Rate of beds occupied	78%	89%	104%	83%	88%	98%	91%	81%
Proportion of outpatient care	1.7	0.5	1	0.8	0.6	0.6	0.5	0.3
Days per bed (medical units)	4.7	6.4	5.5	6.5	8.9	4.9	5.5	6.5
Days per bed (total)	6.2	12.6	8.6	10.6	5.3	4.8	4.4	10.6

Table 4A.1 (Continued)

	A	B	C	D	E	F	G	H[a]
Staff full-time equivalent (FTE), excluding doctors								
Nurses	232	459	66	530	63	123	140	86
Nurse's aides	231	313	113	497	49	125	146	48
Hospital service workers	84	169	31	224	64	95	56	49
Total full-time equivalent	1,074	1,529	312	1,918	245	458	503	223
Staff per 1,000 days								
Nurse	2	2	1.3	2.3	1.3	1.5	1.7	2.1
	(1.6)[c]	(2.4)	(0.6)	(2.4)	(1.4)	(1.9)	(1.9)	(1.4)
Nurse's aides	1.9	1.4	2.2	2.1	1	1.6	1.7	1.2
	(1.5)	(1.8)	(0.9)	(1.8)	(1.3)	(1.3)	(1.3)	(1.3)
Hospital service workers	0.7	0.8	0.6	0.8	1.3	1.2	0.6	1.2
	(0.6)	(0.7)	(0.5)	(0.7)	(0.8)	(0.8)	(0.8)	(0.8)
Human resource management indicators								
Part-time nurse's aides	39%	23%	31%	20%	27%	28%	6%	4%
Part-time hospital service workers	60	12	5	14	5	22	1	8
Absenteeism, full-time equivalent[d]	7	7	5	6	n.a.	9	7	6

Source: Authors' compilation from hospital case studies.
[a] Before outsourcing of housekeeping tasks.
[b] K/L/C = kitchen, laundry, cleaning.
[c] National average for institution of the same size is in parentheses.
[d] Illness and accidents, no maternity leave.

NOTES

1. The authors would like to thank Direction de la Recherche des Études de l'Évaluation et des Statistiques (DREES), particularly Marc Collet and Romuald Le Lan, for making these surveys available.
2. This contrast is relative, given the high unemployment rate in France, particularly for the least-skilled categories.
3. We use the term "licensed" here to designate civil servants in the public sector. By extension, it is also used to designate workers with an open-ended contract in the private sector. That was the word used by everyone we met to differentiate permanent workers from those with fixed-term contracts.
4. It should be noted that the duties of hospital service workers do not strictly correspond to those of "housekeepers."
5. Some public hospitals do their own laundry but provide the same service to other hospitals or retirement homes.
6. In one of the private clinics, by contrast, a grievance from the staff led the labor bureau to intervene and to turn some fixed-term contracts into open-ended contracts.
7. In the extreme case of hospital B, the waiting time for hospital service workers could be as long as eight years.
8. The contrat emploi solidarité (CES, or solidarity employment contract), one of the government work programs set aside for the unemployed, is a half-time contract at minimum wage.
9. A vocational training degree that involves two years of full-time postsecondary education.
10. At the national level, for public hospitals alone, absenteeism in the lowest job categories reached more than 20 days in 2003 (on the decline), including 15 for illness, 4.5 for maternity leave, and 1.7 for accidents.

REFERENCES

Appelbaum, Eileen, Peter Berg, Ann Frost, and Gil Press. 2003. "The Effects of Restructuring on Low-Wage, Low-Skill Workers in U.S. Hospitals." In *Low-Wage America: How Employers Are Reshaping Opportunity in the Workplace*, edited by Eileen Appelbaum, Annette Bernhardt, and Richard J. Murnane. New York: Russell Sage Foundation.

Arborio, Anne Marie. 2001. *Un Personnel invisible: Les aides soignantes à l'hôpital* [Invisible Personnel: Nurse's Aides in Hospitals]. Paris: Anthropos.

———. 2004. "Climbing Invisible Ladders: How Nurse's Aides Craft Lateral Careers." *Ethnography* 5(March): 75–105.

Baret, Christophe. 2002. "Hôpital: Le temps de travail sous tension: Une comparaison Belgique, Italie, France, Grande-Bretagne, Pays-Bas et Suéde" ["Hospitals: Working Hours Under Tensions: A Comparison of Belgium, Italy, France, Great Britain, the Netherlands, and Sweden"]. *Sciences Sociales et Santé* 20(3): 75–105.

Brahami, Abdenor, Agnès Brizard, and Sophie Audric. 2002. *Les Rémunérations dans les établissements de santé privés: Évolutions récentes et comparaisons avec l'ensemble du secteur hospitalier* [Salaries in Private Health Establishments: Recent Changes and Comparisons with the Whole Hospital Sector]. Working paper 25. Paris: Direction de la Recherche des Études de l'Évaluation et des Statistiques (DREES).

Brown, Claire, Bengt Arnetz, and Ove Petersson. 2003. "Downsizing Within a Hospital: Cutting Care or Just Costs?" *Social Science and Medicine* 57(9): 1539–46.

Carroll, Marylin, Damian Grimshaw, Karen Jaehrling, and Philippe Méhaut. 2006. "Shaping and Reshaping the Work Organization: Including or Excluding Low-Skilled Labor? The Case of the Nurse Assistant in Germany, France, and the United Kingdom." Paper presented to the eighteenth meeting of the Society for the Advancement of Socio-Economics (SASE). June 30–July 2, 2006, University of Trier.

Chevandier, Christian. 1997. *Les Métiers de l'hôpital* [Hospital Jobs]. Paris: Éditions La Découverte.

Collet, Marc. 2005. *Les rémunérations dans les établissements de santé* [Salaries in Health Establishments]. Working paper 45. Paris: Direction de la Recherche des Études de l'Évaluation et des Statistiques (DREES).

Direction de l'Hospitalisation et de l'Organisation des Soins (DHOS). 2004. *Données sociales hospitalières 2003* [Social Hospital Data 2003]. Paris: DHOS.

Direction de la Recherche des Études de l'Évaluation et des Statistiques (DREES). 2005. "Les Établissements de santé, un panorama pour 2003" ["Health Establishments, a Panorama for 2003"]. In *Données sur la situation sanitaire et sociale en France* [Data on the Sanitary and Social Situation in France]. Paris: La Documentation Française.

Doeringer, Peter B., and Michael J. Piore. 1971. *Internal Labor Market and Manpower Analysis.* Lexington, Mass.: D. C. Heath.

Estryn-Behar, Madeleine, Olivier Le Nézet, and Carine Jasseron. 2004. *Santé, satisfaction au travail et abandon du métier de soignant* [Health, Work Satisfaction, and Abandonment of the Health Care Profession]. Étude PRESST-NEXT, January 2004. Accessed at http://www.sante.gouv.fr/oudps/estrynbehar.pdf.

Hughes, Everett C. 1996. *Le Regard sociologique: Essais choisis* [Sociological Glance: Selected Essays]. Paris: Éditions de l'École des Hautes Études en Sciences Sociales.

Imbert, Jean, editor. 1982. *Histoire des hôpitaux en France* [*History of Hospitals in France*]. Toulouse: Privat.

LeGrand, Julian, and Will Bartlett. 1993. *Quasi-Markets and Social Policy*. Houndmills, U.K.: Macmillan.

Le Lan, Romuald, and Dominique Baubeau. 2004. "Les Conditions de travail perçus par les professionnels des établissements de santé" ["Working Conditions as Perceived by Health Care Professionals]. *Études et Résultats* 355.

Maillard, Christian. 1986. *Histoire de l'hôpital de 1940 à nos jours: Comment la santé est devenue une affaire d'État* [*History of Hospitals from 1940 to the Present: How Health Has Become an Affair of the State*]. Paris: Dunod.

Mosse, Philippe, and James Arrowsmith. 1999. "Les Temps de travail dans les hôpitaux en France et au Royaume Uni" ["Working Hours in Hospitals in France and the United Kingdom"]. *Travail et Emploi* 77: 67–77.

Sainsaulieu, Ivan. 2003. *Le Malaise des soignants: Le travail sous pression à l'hôpital* [*The Malaise of Health Care Workers: Working Under Pressure at Hospitals*]. Paris: L'Harmattan.

———. 2005. La Communauté de soins en question, le travail hospitalier face aux enjeux de la société [The Health Care Community in Question, Hospital Work in the Context of the Stakes for Society]. Paris: Lammarre.

Vassy, Catherine. 1997. "Le Travail en équipe à l'hôpital: Comparaison de l'organisation de six services de neurologie en Allemagne, France, et Grande-Bretagne" ["Teamwork at Hospitals: A Comparison of Organization at Six Neurological Services in Germany, France, and Great Britain"]. Ph.D. thesis, Institut d'Études Politiques, Paris.

———. 1999. "Travailler à l'hôpital en Europe: Apport des comparaisons internationales à la sociologie des organisations" ["Working at Hospitals in Europe: The Contribution of International Comparisons to the Sociology of Organizations"]. Revue Française de Sociologie 40(2): 325–56.

CHAPTER 5

Housekeepers in French Hotels: Cinderella in the Shadows

Christine Guégnard and Sylvie-Anne Mériot

France, with its leading role in tourism, has been one of the world pioneers in the hotel industry ever since its first luxury hotels sprang up in the 1920s. This sector has never been much of a pioneer, however, with respect to the social progress of its workers. Indeed, quite the opposite is true: collective bargaining has always been a complex and lengthy up-and-down process, and it took thirty years for its main collective agreement to get onto the statute books in 1997. Annette Bernhardt, Laura Dresser and Erin Hatton (2003, 35) have defined the hospitality industry in the United States as a "classic low-wage, labor-intensive service industry, employing large numbers of low-income people, especially workers of colors and immigrants," with subcontracting and flexible staff. These features also prevail in the hospitality industry in France, which has its own set of paradoxes in a specific institutional and policy environment.

Indeed, the hotel industry differs from other French industries on more than one count. Remaining mostly family-run and bound by tradition, it is often marked by long working hours, a watered-down application of collective agreements or labor rules, and even undeclared work. The predominance of very small independent establishments (80 percent of hotels employ fewer than ten employees), fragmented employer and worker organizations, and a very low rate of trade union membership (2 percent) are just some of the obstacles for more positive labor regulations. As a result, the hotel and catering trade is famous for the weakness of its negotiations in favor of employees and for its large number of employer dispensations from the French Labor Code—this last point underlining the strength of the employers' lobby and employers' electoral weight with French politicians. For years cafés, hotels, and restaurants, considered vital meeting points between voters and their elected representatives, have held a key position in French political life.

The hotel and catering industry, which accounts for 3.5 percent of the working population, employs 27 percent of its workforce on low wages and offers many part-time or short-term contracts, primarily to cope with yearly fluctuations.[1] Jobs with prospects are not always available, since the industry's workforce has little scope for professional development. Employment in this sector has been developing in France at an average rate of 2 percent in the last two decades. Its cripplingly high staff turnover rate—half of all employees stay with their employer for less than six months—has made the permanent search for manpower endemic. These recruitment tensions are in part due to the particularly hard working conditions. In addition, the low wage rates are among the lowest in the market, partly because the work activities require very little qualification, as in the retail industry and community services (Beauvois 2003). The hotel industry continues to be France's emblematic low-wage sector.

In the hospitality world, the housekeepers differ from other hotel employees: they are almost invariably women, relatively old (thirty-five to forty-five years old), overwhelmingly of foreign extraction, and often with no qualifications. They tend to be stable in their jobs and are paid wages that hardly enable them to support a family as breadwinners. The bedroom is at the heart of the hotel business, and the quality of room cleaning is strategically important to the success of hotels, yet invisibility is crucial to housekeepers' activity. Finally, these are jobs that technological developments, training courses, and the unions pass by. Any real career prospects are remote, even though in a few hotels management has been making some positive initiatives. Housekeeping in France is a female activity, and indeed, it is the lowest-paid of all the hotel jobs that are kept behind the scenes. Thus, the housekeepers symbolize the hotel industry's low-wage workers. The unequal access to full-time and permanent work underlines an increasing dualism in the labor market of which housekeepers are victims. It is difficult for them to escape from the vicious circle that links precarious employment to low earnings, like a modern-day Cinderella.

These paradoxes for housekeepers are addressed here as a story from three different interlinked angles that correspond to the three sections of this chapter. First, how have competitive economical conditions, critical events, and institutional regulations changed the hotel industry? Second, what is housekeeper job quality really like? Is housekeeping a temporary or sideline position with no

Figure 5.1 Dynamics of Hotel Jobs for Room Attendants

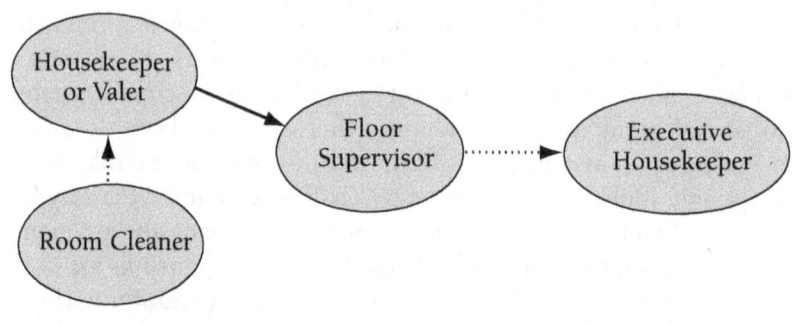

Source: Authors' compilation.

prospects for a captive labor force? And finally, how have firms' strategies affected the quality of working conditions and career ladders? For example, what is the effect on room cleaners themselves of hotels' choice either to manage them directly or to subcontract this service?

This research was conducted in two phases to answer these main questions. One study of the main trends and characteristics of the hotel industry in France (see also Guégnard et al. 2005) is followed by a case study of eight hotels. The criteria used (see table 5.1) when selecting the hotels were category (four high-service-quality, three- to four-star hotels and four medium-service-quality, one- to two-star hotels), location (four in Paris, four in provincial towns), status (three independents, five chains), and size (ten or more employees only). Interviews were held with the managers, middle management, and floor staff of each hotel. They were supplemented by interviews with sector representatives, unions, the main hotel chains, and training organizations, for a total of sixty-five individuals interviewed, including thirty-three room attendants. There are two kinds of room attendants: the "housekeepers," or "valets," who are responsible for the daily cleaning of guestrooms and bathrooms, and the "room cleaners," who tend to be in charge of cleaning the common areas of the hotel and who help the housekeepers (with carpet cleaning, laundry transport, and so on). In addition, the large hotels have a layer of middle management, including one or more "floor supervisors" and an "executive housekeeper" who organize the cleaning of the bedrooms and common areas and manage the floor staff reporting to them.

Table 5.1 The Case Study Hotels

Location	Midmarket: One- to Two-Star	Upper Market: Three- to Four- Star and Deluxe
Paris		
Chain	H5: Two-star; 195 rooms; 63 employees; *one room cleaner, three housekeepers, two floor supervisors, one manager*	H3: Four-star; 294 rooms; 141 employees; *four housekeepers, one floor supervisor, one executive housekeeper, one HRD manager, one manager* H6: Four-star; 384 rooms; 163 employees; *four housekeepers, one room cleaner, one floor supervisor, one manager*
Independent		H4: Three-star; 72 rooms; 15 employees; *one housekeeper, one manager*
Provincial towns		
Chain	H7: Two-star; 46 rooms; 13 employees; *three housekeepers, one floor supervisor, one assistant manager*	H2: Four-star; 134 rooms; 130 employees; *three housekeepers, one executive housekeeper, two floor supervisors, one manager, one HRD manager*
Independent	H1: Two-star; 31 rooms; 10 employees; *one housekeeper, two managers, one outsourced manager* H8: Two-star; 34 rooms; 10 employees; *one room cleaner, two housekeepers, one manager*	

Source: Authors' compilation, case study hotels.
Note: Italics represent staff interviewed in each hotel.

THE FRENCH HOTEL INDUSTRY IN THE TWENTY-FIRST CENTURY

Historically, small independent units, low rates of staff representation, and governance by employers have largely characterized management in the French hotel industry. The mid-2000s have been economically crucial

Table 5.2 The French Hotel Industry

	Chains		Independents		Total	
	Rooms	Hotels	Rooms	Hotels	Rooms	Hotels
No-star	49,934	690	17,353	1,329	67,287	2,019
One-star	9,032	154	24,046	1,450	33,078	1,604
Two-star	78,096	1,181	196,165	8,550	274,261	9,731
Three-star	55,147	588	113,559	3,165	168,706	3,753
Four-star and deluxe	33,064	188	25,512	589	57,288	777
Total	225,273	2,801	376,635	15,083	601,908	17,884

Source: Institut Nationale de la Statistiques et des Études Économiques (INSEE), Direction du Tourisme (2006).

for the hotel and catering industry, not only with higher room occupation numbers but also in social terms: major negotiations resulted in three simultaneous changes: new working conditions, new wage-calculating rules, and a new right to continuing training (not specific to the branch).

A Two-Stream Market with Ever-Deepening Segmentation

France has Europe's fourth-highest hotel room capacity, with over 602,000 rooms on January 1, 2006 (table 5.2). For several years the French hotel fleet has stabilized at around 18,000 establishments, with an average of thirty-three rooms per hotel. These numbers have benefited large chain hotels at the expense of the smaller independent hotels,[2] which suffered from four main trends: the sluggishness of the rural and mountain tourist industry, their own lax management, their failure to make enough investments, and increased market pressure from the chains, which caused a permanent price war. Independent hotels still account, however, for the lion's share of the market, both in establishment numbers and revenues, despite the continual inroads made by both the associative and integrated chains.

The independents have the highest number of establishments and the greatest accommodation capacity (half the hotels and 48 percent of rooms). They are often family-managed businesses whose assets are mainly held by the hotelkeeper (or the hotelkeeper's relatives). The integrated chains are relentlessly gaining ground and already account for 37 percent of rooms (or 16 percent of hotels). The best-known names are Formule 1, Ibis, Novotel, Mercure, Sofitel (under the Accor umbrella, the leading group with 1,300 hotels in

France), Campanile, Première Classe, and Concorde (in the Louvre Hotels group, which has 800 hotels).[3] Given the inroads being made by these chains, many isolated independents have formed groups called "volunteer chains" in order to benefit from promotional and sales initiatives under the same banner and to acquire commercial visibility and the endorsement of a label for their clientele. Logis de France, Agil, and Châteaux et Hôtels de France are examples of such "fake" chains of hotels that are in fact managed independently (and account for one-third of hotels and 15 percent of rooms).

Establishments employing fewer than ten employees still account for 80 percent of French hotels and hire almost 40 percent of industry workers. The pattern of distribution of no-star to four-star hotels varies from one part of the country to another and from one tourist region to another.[4] The capital, Paris, where one-quarter of all hotels in France are located, has a strong showing in the highest categories. But two-thirds of hotels are so-called affordable hotels, among which the two-star category alone accounts for half the accommodation capacity. The two-star hotels are popular with all guests who are concerned about the best value for their money, whether business or tourist guests, whereas foreign travelers predominantly stay at hotels at the top of the range (four-star and over), which amount to only 4 percent of all establishments and 10 percent of the total accommodation capacity. Foreign customers are more sensitive than national customers to changes to the socioeconomic context and world events (exchange rate changes, political events, and so on).

The chain hotels, concentrated in the upper and lower market segments, account for over half the four-star rooms and three-quarters of the no-star rooms. They registered a considerably higher room occupancy rate than the traditional independents in 2005 (67 percent compared to 54 percent).[5] Since the chains are less subject to seasonal fluctuations, they can combine the benefits of higher occupancy and relatively longer stays by primarily accommodating business customers at often-higher categories than those of the independents: 54 percent of business nights compared to 33 percent for the independents (Direction du Tourisme 2006).

Developments That Change Hotel Job Profiles

Generally speaking, the hospitality industry is extremely dependent on national economic activities; international, political, and monetary events have also led to particularly strong fluctuations in hotel business activity during the last few years. According to the Union des Métiers et des Industries de l'Hôtellerie (UMIH, Union of Hotel Professions and Industries), the French hotel industry went through a recession between 1991 and 1996, primarily because of overinvestment (due to the fast development of many large hotel chains); currency undervaluation in many countries that compete with France for tourists; changes in the habits of customers, who became more unpredictable and selective, choosing their hotels on the basis of cost-effectiveness; and economic crisis that made hotels unable to make necessary investments in renovating the hotel network (UMIH 2003). Furthermore, the regulatory provisions for the development and promotion of commerce and the trades have had a hand in curbing hotel construction: since July 1996, the Raffarin law, whose aim is to curb the risks of hotel overcapacity, has forced all investors to submit their construction permit applications to a special regional commission if the building is to offer more than thirty rooms in the provinces or more than fifty rooms in the Paris region.

Hotel occupancy gradually picked up again after 1997, fueled by the return of foreign guests. This improvement was dealt a harsh blow, however, by the attacks of September 11, 2001; it was further blunted by the American conflict in Iraq, and then by the SARS epidemic. Business recovered after October 2004 and reached 192 million bed-nights in 2006. Business primarily went to the hotels at both ends of the comfort range, the four-stars and the no-stars (Le Garrec 2007). This increase in activity is explained by the return of foreign guests; meanwhile, the average length of stays by French clients is shortening, particularly since the thirty-five-hour working week act came into force. At the start of 2006, earnings per available room, described by the famous international RevPar indicator (revenue per available room), increased both in the provinces and in Paris, where top-class establishments produced their best performances (with €135 RevPar (US$191.20), that is 18 percent more than the last year) (Cosson 2007).

In the long term, the hotel industry will have to adapt to changes in the structure of the population and its demands: people are living longer, more of them are engaging in travel and leisure activities, health and physical fitness have become priorities, as well as good value for money, and there is increasing awareness of environmental problems and the need for cleanliness and traceable products (Guégnard, Giffard, and Strietska-Ilina 2001). These new customer expectations and relevant technological investments may lead to added demands for hotel information and/or facilities and, naturally, impeccable room hygiene, which could call for reorganization efforts inspired by the need for quality assurance. As a result, some hotels are gaining control of the quality of their service by phasing out the outsourcing of room cleaning or reinforcing their housekeeping teams. Some budget and small hotels are even trying to develop occupational multiskilling.

Given the growth in hotel room supply both nationally and internationally, marketing developments tend to gravitate around a differentiated room rate approach for groups, seminars, trade fairs, or local customers. This approach—which also involves considerable diversification of room rates during off-peak periods to defray major overhead costs—has its roots in "yield management," which was initiated in the air transport sector. The hotel groups are keen on refining their marketing strategies by, for example, creating loyalty cards for their customers or developing online reservation sites, such as Travel Accor Reservation System (TARS), which offers common room availability and rate visibility, simultaneously and in real time to Accor group hotels and different central reservation channels (web and travel agencies). The burgeoning of Internet bookings has led to competitive advantage, and even some independent hotels are joining forces with local authorities or marketing sites to give their offerings greater visibility.

Technological changes in hotel administration have already had an impact on all jobs. Computerized reservation and back-office activity, sometimes including electronic cashiers (a technology now being tested at the 700-room flagship Ibis hotel in Paris), make for clear, direct transmission of room availability information to the floor staff. The hotels that target business customers, primarily the chains, instigated this movement, but many small hotels, including family hotels, have invested in Internet website and administration software (Guégnard and Mériot 2005). Computerization also enables the deluxe hotels to update their information on the preferences of regular customers, for use both to enhance customer visits and in marketing initiatives. Automation can lead to job cuts as well: in the lower market segment, for example, the reception desk can now more easily be closed during off-peak hours because electronic key cards are issued by a bank card–controlled dispenser.

Very few technological changes have affected housekeepers, beyond ergonomic changes. Some chain hotels have made efforts that affect these jobs, such as having staff wear safety shoes or placing equipment at a convenient height to avoid medical problems. Modifications made to the services offered to guests have more to do with strategic policy on the quality of amenities: putting bathrobes in all rooms, distributing more hospitality packs, providing more services in the room, and so on. Automated communal washroom cleaning systems, which are primarily found in no-star hotels, could also transform the jobs of room cleaners.[6]

Belated Social Progress

Because there are so many small independent hotels, organizations representing the employers (four employers' associations)[7] and workers (five trade unions)[8] are fragmented, and unionization rates are low, the hotel and catering industry took its time in negotiating social progress for its personnel (Mériot 2006). This sector is organized around one major employers' association, the UMIH, which represents roughly 90 percent of hotel, restaurant, café, and discothèque employers affiliated with a union. In the French industrial relations system (see chapter 2), the legal minimum wage (SMIC) is set by the government and the law, and the specific working schedules can be negotiated between employers' associations and trade unions in national branch collective agreements.

Social bargaining has always been a complex and lengthy process, and the employers' lobby has been historically reluctant to negotiate wage and social advancements. Their strength is underlined by the large number of dispensations from the Labor Code on issues such as the legal minimum wage, working hours, and employment contracts. For instance, even though the adoption of the thirty-five-hour working week came into force on January 1, 2002, the hotel industry would only accept a drop to thirty-nine hours per week (as against fifty-three hours before 1997, then forty-three hours). Until July 2004, the hotel industry minimum wage was lower than the real value of the interprofessional SMIC (the national legal minimum wage) because employers were allowed to deduct a number of in-kind benefits, such as meals and accommodation. The agreement in force makes no provision, however, for an automatic seniority allowance and gives no occupational seniority rights to redundancy payment and no compensation for working on Sundays or on many of the public holidays.[9]

The latest branch agreement, signed in July 2004, not only introduced the thirty-nine-hour week and a sixth week of annual holiday but also created an insurance scheme for all employees, defined executives' wage rates, and regulated night work. In the words of one industry journal, it was "a historical agreement of the kind signed only once every thirty years in the field of hotels and restaurants." Despite opposition from two trade unions and one employer organization, the French government decided to authorize this agreement, which came into force on January 1, 2005. Recently, at the request of one trade union (Confédération française des travailleurs (CFDT)), the Supreme Administrative Court (Conseil d'Etat) canceled the adoption of the thirty-nine-hour working week, but the government immediately adopted measures allowing the industry to keep its hourly basis until a new agreement is reached.

In fact, at the national level, discord persists between trade unions and employers and even among employers' representatives who lobby the government. The origins of this pressure and these contradictions in industrial relations go back to the development of the cafés during the French Revolution. French cafés, hotels, and restaurants, by tradition, have played a large role in political debates: for instance, the Resistance during the two world wars, major demonstrations, strikes, and important peacetime decisions have all emerged from these venues. They are important sites where the people and their representatives share a social and political life. This lobby may explain why the present government, while tending to promote wage and schedule negotiations, voted a €697 million (US$988 million) subsidy for hotel and catering employers in November 2006 to promote the "extra" contracts—the most precarious working status.

At the workplace level, the trade unions are weak or absent, primarily because 80 percent of hotels employ fewer than ten employees and employees' representation is compulsory only in firms with more than ten employees. (Works councils are compulsory in firms with more than fifty employees.) Another reason is that the hotel industry is one of the sectors with the lowest union membership in France—only 2 percent—while 5 percent of private sector workers are unionized. In all the hotels visited, employee membership rates are low and trade unionists make very few demands at the firm level.[10] We will see that the low level of union membership partly stems from staff structure: hotels offer many short-term contracts and have high turnover rates, and staff tend to be low-skilled, young, female, and often of foreign extraction.

A Heterogeneous Workforce

In the last decade, the French hotel and catering industry has seen its numbers grow by 14 percent. It employs more than 800,000 people—over 3.5 percent of the working population. One-third of industry employees work as waiters or waitresses and one-quarter work as cooks. The third-largest occupational group is that of room attendants (European Foundation for the Improvement of Living and Working Conditions 2004).

A Young and Poorly Qualified Workforce   Half the workforce is under thirty (excluding students and apprentices), and three-quarters do not hold the baccalaureate (high school leavers' certificate), compared to an average of only two-thirds in other branches. The hospitality industry offers these young people an entry point into the labor market (Guégnard and Perret 1997). There are three possible reasons for this: the demand in this sector for unskilled, low-paid employees gives many young people with few qualifications a gateway to the labor market; there is a large demand for temporary seasonal workers; and the relatively poor conditions (low wages, long operational hours) make older people reluctant to stay in this sector, where jobs often involve physically demanding work. Nevertheless, few people with low qualifications ever manage to reach the top by dint of hard work and enthusiasm.

A Low Number of Managers   Nearly two-thirds of employees are clerks (waiters, room cleaners) or blue-collar workers.[11] In addition, one-quarter of the hotel industry's employees work part-time, compared with 17 percent in other sectors. Part-time jobs go mostly to the lowest category of employees—women and young people—and 60 percent of part-timers would like to work more. Hotel employees rarely achieve much seniority: nearly 50 percent have less than six months' seniority, compared with less than one-quarter in the private and semi-public sectors.

Staff Characteristics   Women traditionally play an important role in this sector and account for half the workforce. Despite their numbers, they occupy the lower ranks in the sector's professions, have few possibilities for advancing their careers, and are paid less than men. The hotel industry also attracts noncitizen workers and illegal immigrants—again, because many of the jobs in this sector do not require many qualifications.[12] However, the whole profession suffers from the fact that many workers are not properly declared or are only partly declared; some are also subject to an unfair and excessive use of precarious contracts or to intentional miscalculations of working times. Illegal immigrants are especially liable to accept any kind of contracts or schedules and at times work under conditions that are not far from exploitation. According to the latest published data on undeclared work in hotels and restaurants (ministère de l'Emploi, du travail et de la cohésion sociale 2005), issued by the Délégation interministérielle à la lutte contre le travail illégal (the Inter-Ministerial Delegation on Combating Undeclared Work), 35 percent of all the labor regulations passed in 2004 have led to fines, and a growing number of violations were sent to court (2,211 in 2004 compared to 336 in 2003). In some southern French regions, one-third of hotel and restaurant employers break the law.

The traditional constraints on hotel industry workers—long operational hours, low wage rates, and variable, seasonal jobs with relatively low social status—make hotel jobs unattractive to potential employees. Almost half of the hotel industry's employees work every Sunday, and another one-third occasionally work on Sundays (Labor Force surveys, 2000 to 2002, INSEE). Sometimes workdays can be very long, depending on the season. In addition, employees are occasionally obliged to stop work for several hours in the middle of the day, which increases the length of their workday. Moreover, employees often have to start work very early in the morning or end very late at night.

Against this industry backdrop, housekeepers, who account for almost 20 percent of the labor force, are different on more than one count. They have more occupational seniority in their jobs and are older—on average, they are thirty-five to forty-five years old.[13] Another peculiarity is that, according to hotel managers, their recruitment is easy and turnover is low, in contrast to many other hotel job categories. In the next section, a range of interview statements describe the characteristics of this undervalued, low-wage, often marginalized occupation dominated by women.

BECOMING A HOUSEKEEPER: THE "WORKER IN THE SHADOW"

Housekeepers occupy a special place in the hotel industry: working in a subordinate position within the ranks, they are invisible to the guests as they carry out a tedious and servile activity. Feminization and ethnic concentration are the very foundations of this profession. Most housekeeping employees have no qualifications and are easy to retain, which makes for a captive and docile workforce.

A "Cosmopolitan" Workplace

Most housekeepers are foreign nationals or of foreign extraction. The H2 executive manager sums it up this way:

> We have to deal with many different ethnic groups: I have Muslims, Algerians, Moroccans, Poles, Chinese, Madagascans, Mauritians, many Comorians... Their private lives are often a shambles, lots of children, their husbands are not always there or kind to them... They are often illiterate and their only experience is in cleaning, maybe domestic cleaning.

Some hotels employ more people from certain regions or ethnicities—from the Far East, for instance, or North and Sub-Saharan Africa—a practice that encourages recruitment by cooption, but the locally available workforce often varies. The myriad profiles and career paths of housekeepers highlight their cosmopolitan quality. Some are escaping from poverty, while others have fled a conflict in their home country. Few had been to secondary school before migrating.

One feature common to all housekeepers is the need to work to earn money, however tedious the occupation: "At Marseilles, there is a supply of housekeepers because there are people who need the job if they are to eat," says a deputy supervisor at H2. What they have in common is that they are captive in the job; in addition, many of them have great difficulty speaking French.[14] Some young French women, often with foreign parentage, accept this work for a short time. Given their difficulties in entering the job market, this first job gives them a little financial independence, but they often aspire only to other unskilled jobs in sales or service, since they feel invisible and are frustrated by the "dirty work." Will they succeed in leaving their stopgap jobs?

Taking a housekeeping job, associated with being a "domestic," is often a Hobson's choice, because no other occupation is open to these women. To be sure, men are also assigned to clean in some hotels, but these room cleaners are given different tasks: cleaning public areas and backing up the housekeepers by performing the harder tasks, such as carpet cleaning, or handling linen or guests' luggage.[15] Therefore, there is a division of labor by gender within the cleaning segment. Housekeeping remains the province of women in a sector that purports to be mixed.

Over and above the gender issue, the profile is not defined in terms of qualifications; as an H3 manager states: "The person must be serious, inconspicuous, and cleanliness is an essential criterion. A housekeeper does not need to have any special skills—she just needs to know how to use the color codes, namely, read figures."[16] Thus, even in deluxe hotels there is no real need for any qualifications. There are very few housekeepers around who hold a hotel or catering diploma, such as a CAP/BEP—a two-year French vocational training course for fourteen- to sixteen-year-olds. But previous experience in a hotel, catering company, hospital, or cleaning company is a strength for those seeking to be hired.

Training is generally done on the job, by observation; for no more than one to two days, depending on the hotel category, the new employee imitates and shadows an experienced colleague.[17] From the third day onwards, the new employee is expected to work independently and to work as fast as experienced staff. Applicants are not in short supply. In both Paris and the provinces, managers receive unsolicited applications every month. These and the social networks of existing staff are the most common recruitment paths. While housekeepers appear to abound in the employment market, employers set more store by the supervisors who in the luxury segment go by the epithet of "rare gems." Occasionally they are promoted internally, but more often than not they have received hotel training.

"It's the Bed, the Dusting, the Bedroom . . ."

Housekeepers and valets, their male peers (who are rare birds within the profession), are responsible for hotel room cleanliness, tidiness, and comfort and sometimes for the public areas or reception areas as well. Every morning the housekeeper is issued a work schedule that indicates which rooms need to be cleaned up, sometimes in order of priority or in response to guests' expectations. Her daily workload is thirteen to eighteen rooms (but up to twenty-four rooms in one hotel), to be cleaned at the rate of two to four rooms per hour, depending on the hotel category. The number of housekeepers varies not only with fluctuations in hotel capacity but also with the hotel classification, the type of rooms (duplex, suite, VIP), the distance between rooms or the number of floors, the presence of a utility room on each floor, and the possibility of delegating public area cleaning tasks to a room cleaner or inspection tasks to a supervisor. Thus, the practice of self-checking is increasingly in demand, although certain deluxe hotels prefer to bolster their supervisor teams to avoid any risk of lowered quality, given their unskilled workforce and the keen competition in the hotel industry.

The fine details of these well-defined tasks are differentiated, according to a supervisor in H3, a luxury hotel, by the "technical side of the job to be learned, the manner, and the behavior." Housekeepers' jobs are given greater consideration in deluxe hotels, where they often have a well-defined work pace. The floor staff competencies analyzed and presented in figure 5.2 give a first glimpse of the unsuspected diversity of floor staff activities. The housekeeper job comprises tasks that require communication skills, organizational or managerial responsibilities (concerning room supply and work instructions), and many technical duties (from arranging rooms to cleaning rooms and sometimes linens, room checking, and other cleaning or maintenance). Of course, not all room attendants carry out all of these activities, and many of the tasks that require communication skills are limited to managerial positions. Nevertheless, the diversity of the housekeeper position, on the one hand, and the difficult working conditions and low pay, on the other, make this marginalized job a paradoxical one as well.

In large hotels, where "each housekeeper has her own floor," management of the room attendants is delegated to several supervisors. Thus, the only real managerial contact for the housekeepers is the executive supervisor; it is their own supervisor who administers the organization of work, makes schedules, handles absences, hires temporary workers, and quite often is involved in recruitment, in which case the management plays only an administrative role (including checking ID cards or residence permits).

Occasionally housekeepers work to targets, and some managers take advantage of this to set unachievable goals. An H3 housekeeper states: "Personally I find that the thirty minutes we are allowed per room, for a four-star hotel, isn't fair, as it takes at least forty minutes to get a room spic-and-span. Because I often decide to clean one or two rooms thoroughly, so that everything is done, sometimes it takes

Figure 5.2 Floor Staff Competencies (from Housekeeper to Executive Housekeeper)

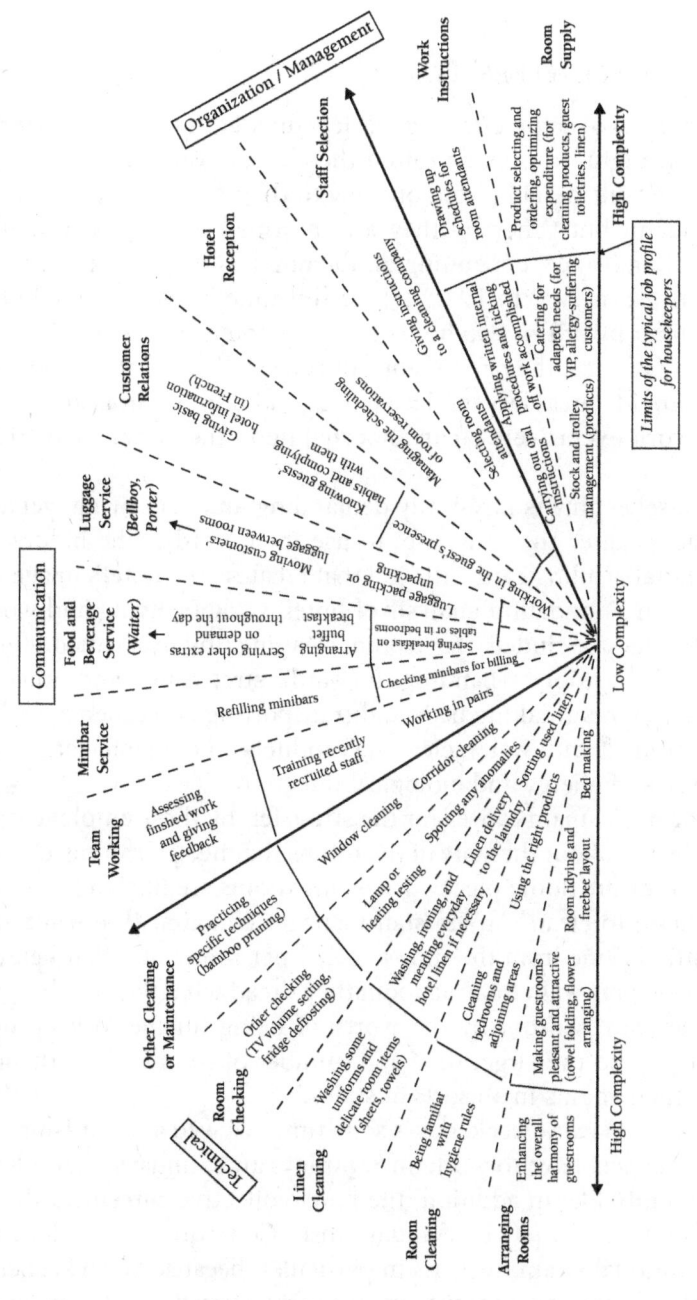

Source: Authors' compilation, case study hotels.

twenty minutes just to do the dusting and vacuum properly under the beds."

The Housekeepers' Labor

In the deluxe sector, cleaning work is divided into at least two shifts, day and night, to provide round-the-clock coverage. Working times can vary considerably from one day to the next, with the employees' agreement, but generally they are informed between two and four weeks in advance, depending on the hotel. Hours tend to be 8:00 AM to 4:00 PM or 2:00 to 10:00 PM for full-time housekeepers, but they may differ by one or two hours between hotels. In the hotels without evening service, the permanent full-time staff starts at 6:30 AM, when they provide breakfast service coverage, and finish around 4:00 PM; if they work exclusively on an allocated floor, the hours are 8:30 AM to 5:30 PM.

Housekeeping is physically demanding and very tiring, yet all the managers agree that it is also, to use their words, "the hidden job," "the hotel's calling card," the job that creates "the hotel's image." The European Foundation analysis of hotel workers' living and working conditions concluded that room cleaning involves uncomfortable physical positions (bending forward, stretching, and kneeling), heavy weights (making beds and transporting equipment), and constant contact with water, cleaning products, and disinfectants, entailing a risk of allergy and biological infection.

One of the main causes for the stress felt by these employees is apprehension about the state of the rooms that need cleaning, especially when they are doing piecework; some rooms are likely to be particularly hard to clean. An H6 staff manager concurs: "We realized that the stress came from the time allowed per room, and that before the housekeepers walk into the room they dread what they might find. So they are stressed out by the worry of being unable to keep up the work pace to the target time and number of rooms, since the guests leave their rooms in all sorts of states."

Having to work weekends is sometimes viewed as a hardship: when housekeepers have to work on Saturdays and Sundays, that interferes with family life; in addition, the hotel collective agreement does not provide for extra pay for Sunday work. Consequently, job location is an additional strain. In Paris in particular, because housekeepers seldom live in the center of the city or near the prestige hotels where they work, their travel time can be long—typically between one hour and one and a half hours each way. In the provinces the chain hotels are often located outside the built-up area, which poses problems for people who use public transport: their workplaces are not always well served, especially on Saturdays, Sundays, and strike days. This stress has to be added to the physical toll of the work.

As Inconspicuous as Dust

Both housekeepers and the technical staff are excluded from face-to-face contact with the guests in a service activity centered on customer relations (Monchatre and Testenoire 2004). How well housekeepers do their jobs is of strategic importance to the success of the hotel, yet they are invisible as domestics. Rooms must be cleaned when the guests are out, to avoid disturbing them with their presence, so housekeepers are instructed to remain inconspicuous, or even to apologize, when they come across a guest. In most hotels, housekeepers are isolated and kept on the fringe of the collective life of the establishment; reduced to spending many hours alone, they may only occasionally meet their colleagues or supervisors. In the deluxe hotel segment in particular, only the supervisor is authorized to address the guests, primarily to answer their requests. Housekeepers like being able to organize their own work, as is generally the case, but they are also dependent on the guests.

The division of labor assigns housekeepers to an occupation that is often referred to as degrading "dirty work" (Hugues 1996). Other jobs, such as serving at tables or kitchen work, entail coming into contact with dirt, but that is only one element of the job. Dealing with dirt is central to housekeeping, however, and sometimes even the only task assigned to them. There is a social divide between receptionists and waiters, on the one hand, and the room attendants in charge of the "dirty work" on the other hand. Housekeepers and their colleagues are also separated organizationally. The upper floors where housekeepers work are geographically remote from the ground floor, the area where the establishment buzzes with life. Each housekeeper is isolated in her own corridor, carrying out the work alone and seldom with a coworker.

Furthermore, their relations with customers reveal complex attitudes toward tipping. Generous sums left behind are experienced as a mark of recognition, although such tips are tinged with ambiguity because they also point to the subordinate position of the housekeeper. Housekeepers in the deluxe sector have grown accustomed to getting tips, which can amount to a considerable supplement to their earnings. They are inclined to associate lavish tips with tourists and foreign guests. The practice is tending to fade out, primarily in the chains, but some claim that they still receive pleasant surprises of between €2 and €10 (US$2.83 and US$14.18). However, housekeepers view paltry tips—just a few cents left in the ashtray—as showing contempt.

Despite all these difficulties, some housekeepers said that they enjoy their job, especially in hotels that provide a friendly family atmosphere. They enjoy being part of a team and particularly working on their own. These housekeepers appear to be proud of their work and to appreciate the contact with regular customers. Work recognition and autonomy appear all the more important since these employees feel stigmatized in their domestic and subaltern positions.

Employment Contracts: "There's Nothing Extraordinary About Being an Extra!"

With a large pool of housekeepers available, hotels can use a whole range of contracts, from "extra" workers or "seasonal" contracts at the bottom, to fixed-term and open-ended (or permanent) contracts (see chapter 2). Employees can also be divided between full-timers (thirty-nine or thirty-seven hours per week) and part-timers. Whereas "extras" often work for only a few hours a day, stable part-time workers are generally guaranteed around thirty hours per week in the hotels under study. This reinforces a tension between permanent and nonpermanent staff and between part-timers and full-timers. Getting a stable full-time job—which goes hand in hand with access to better working hours and work that is more regular—is a real competition. Advancement through merit is thus a matter of earning a right to work, since the number of rooms allocated per day per person starts off very low and only permanent hotel staff can be sure of getting a decent wage through their daily work.

The deluxe hotels visited offer hardly any part-time work. On the contrary, almost all the staff are on permanent full-time contracts, and during a few temporary peaks in activity fixed-term contracts are used (for people who, for instance, come in for three months to help out). This contrasts with the midmarket hotels, both chain and independent, which mainly employ their floor staff on a part-time basis, with the exception of the supervisors. This time arrangement meets the need for flexibility, but housekeepers' opinions are divided about it. Some of them would like to have a permanent job or to work longer hours for a decent wage, while others appreciate being able to achieve a life-work balance through part-time work.

Apart from standard fixed-term and open-ended contracts drawn up in keeping with the most recent legislation, the hotel industry uses two other arrangements. The first, the "seasonal" contract (between one and nine months), is used for jobs in seaside or mountain tourism (not found in the eight hotels visited). "Extra" status, the second arrangement, is specific to the hotel and catering industry: the "extra" worker is routinely paid on the basis of the hourly SMIC rate for housekeepers, regardless of work experience. The extra contract covers a period of at least one hour but not more than sixty days during the same quarter. (Otherwise, the employee would be allowed to claim a permanent contract.) Employers are allowed to give the staff their extra contracts within forty-eight hours, which prevents the Labor Inspectorate Services from monitoring them and may encourage undeclared work, especially in small units.

Most hotels hire extras in the interest of management flexibility when room occupancy rates fluctuate. But some of them also use this contract to take their time in selecting the best staff they can find. An extra has to wait for a vacancy to come up if she is to get a stable job and thus prove that she is highly committed to her work. This may take several years. Sometimes after an assignment a housekeeper is offered a part-time permanent contract, which she may find hard to refuse, even though she may lose out financially.[18] They also have to make themselves available, at the risk of being passed over for other assignments. One deluxe hotel supervisor in the provinces openly asks her extras not to sign up elsewhere so that she can count on them. She knows full well that all the hotels in town filled up at the same time. Housekeepers are thus forced to stay in the unstable situations this supervisor offers, at the risk of losing the few advantages they may have.

An H2 hotel director, along with many of his peers, admits that he is tempted to restrict the number of stable contracts, because "sometimes the people we hire lose their appetite for work." In an area blighted by unemployment, he finds it easy to recruit extras and thus prefers to keep a large pool of workers available on unstable contracts. These workers are so dependent that they accept any type of requests and working hours or objectives in terms of numbers of rooms to clean within a preset time, even if this time is unrealistic. While some housekeepers are content with the status of extra because it enables them to refuse work when they want, many more are desperate about their insecurity and would agree with the woman who describes herself as a "permanent extra." ("There's nothing extraordinary about being an extra!" she adds.) She tells the following story: having arrived in France twenty years before, she took a two-month short course in the French language, then became a cleaner for several employers simultaneously (in a cleaning company). She worked up to thirteen hours a day, then took a vocational course and reverted to being an extra hired by a hotel this time, despite her qualification and professional experience.

A Minimal Wage for an Essential Mission

The room is at the heart of the hotel business, and room-cleaning quality is decisive for customer loyalty. However, housekeepers are the lowest-paid of all hotel staff, and the eight case study hotels are no exception. Wages are usually pegged to the national legal minimum wage, and only individual negotiations or bonuses such as the payment of a thirteenth month make a slight difference. The net gross monthly wages declared by the interviewed housekeepers are in the range of €800 to €1,200 (US$1,134.12 to US$1,701.18) for the permanent workers (working part- or full-time between thirty and thirty-nine hours per week). One housekeeper who works thirty-nine hours per week at H6, a chain hotel, declares: "I think it's true when they say it's a hard job. They could pay us more. But we get the SMIC. . . We get just under €1,200 net per month." In fact, in budget hotels, where work intensity is at its greatest, the hourly wage for cleaning four rooms is the equivalent of €1.50 to €2.00 (US$2.13 to US$2.83) per basic room—in other words, the price of a cup of coffee. Some employees are particularly vulnerable and dependent on their employers. For instance, in hotel H3 one extra works at most eighteen days and earns €100 to €120 (US$141.74 to US$170.09) per month less than the stable full-time staff in the same hotel.

In the hotel industry, wage rates, unrevised since 1997, have become inapplicable because they have been overtaken by the SMIC rate. Accordingly, most employees up to the executive level are paid the SMIC

Table 5.3 The Gross Monthly Wage in the Hotel Industry (for a Thirty-Nine-Hour Working Week), 2005

	Monthly Wage
SMIC employees	€1,286
Housekeeper	1,350
Waiter	1,463
Receptionist	1,515
Average hotel employees	1,608
Cook	1,617
Executive housekeeper	1,683
Manager	3,109

Source: Authors' compilation from ConsoCHD, 2005 survey of a sample of hoteliers and restaurant owners, 342 establishments; *L'Hôtellerie* supplement no. 2930, May 23, 2005, pg. 16.

wage exactly, with no benefits, and even those who work full-time or have seniority are no better off. A number of historical and recent surveys present the same findings. The most recent survey, conducted in 2005, emphasizes that the gross monthly mean wage for housekeepers (€1,350 (US$1,913.56)) is considerably lower than for all the other hotel occupations (€1,608 (US$2,278.03)) (see table 5.3). Other data show that about 27 percent of hotel employees can be considered low-paid workers, compared to 10 percent of the total working population (see table 5.4). Moreover, this share is increasing (23 percent in 1995), whereas the general trend in France is a drop in low-wage workers (see chapter 2). Women represent about two-thirds of the workforce considered low-paid. These results are underestimated because these data do not include undeclared or illegal work and family help. Wages in

Table 5.4 Share of Low-Wage Workers in the Hotel Industry

	1995	2003
Hotels with a restaurant	21.1%	17.9%
Hotels without a restaurant	17.6	21.2
Low-skilled employees	23.4	26.7
Total hotel industry	19.9	20.4
Total all sectors	12.7	10.4

Source: Déclarations Annuelles des Données Socials (DADS) 1995 and 2003, Institut Nationale de la Statistique et des Etudes Économiques (INSEE), calculated by Cepremap.

the hotel and catering industry are lower than in most other French sectors, partly owing to the low job skills and the weakness of labor market regulation.

Finally, many attributes of women's occupations in France are combined in the housekeeper job: continuity between their domestic and workplace activity, short-term or part-time contracts, and low wages. However, if chain and deluxe hotels want to achieve high service quality, it may be in their interest to garner the loyalty of their floor staff. At H6, for example, there are incentives for housekeepers, as explained by a supervisor: "We operate a points system. Every task is worth a one- or two-point credit, and these one or two points are worth euros." The measure is very popular with this low-paid staff. What other business initiatives or managerial policies can be identified that are favorable toward housekeepers and offer them opportunities for career development? That is the main issue developed in the next section.

MANAGERIAL STRATEGIES TOWARD HIGH-ROAD PRACTICES?

While large hotels tend to rationalize the work, the small establishments reveal the cottage-industry style of the French hotel industry: the family-run micro-enterprise model prevails, and it encourages paternalistic managerial relationships as well as greater autonomy for the floor staff. Located beside other professionals, housekeepers have little chance for career promotion, despite the initiatives some hotels have taken on their behalf. In fact, being a housekeeper can be considered a dead-end job that is difficult to find a positive way out of.

THE PREVAILING COTTAGE INDUSTRY MODEL

Hotel management in France is dominated by the family micro-enterprise model, which makes for entrenched, highly paternalistic relationships. Management turns out to be a key element in this sector, and the hotel director's personality plays a fundamental role (Guégnard 2004). Working for a chain is often experienced as opting for more institutional relations in which compliance with current regulations (adherence to the Labor Code or collective agreement, abiding by the predetermined working hours or schedules) is better. Dependency relationships, with regard to the director or any other single member of the management, are bred by the domestic nature of the work, even in major hotels (Triby 2004). However, even when directly managed by a chain, hotel establishments enjoy considerable freedom, and the establishment's labor relations may stem from the director's personality. "The hotel and catering industry sets particular store by its small-scale features and personal involvement of its individuals" (Mériot 2000, 4).

Each of the criteria selected in this research project that differentiated between hotels in category, location, status, and size turned out to be relevant on more than one count, even if the impact of the criteria on housekeeper job quality is often combined and interlinked. In the hotel industry, however, variations in managerial practices especially depend on the manager's profile and his goodwill.

THE SIREN CALL OF CHAIN HOTELS

The tendency for hotels to concentrate, linked to the development of chains, is leading to some wage improvements and to some high-road managerial practices. Accor, for example, was the first to adopt the thirty-nine-hour week several years ago. Primary differences in management strategy are related to whether a hotel is an independent or a chain, and these variations create a kind of dualism (see table 5.5). In addition to the benefits of working for a chain (payment of a thirteenth month, sickness and pension schemes, surety bond, profit-sharing, help with travel expenses, subsidized meals at the workplace, gift vouchers), Accor group collaborators indicate that they have better working conditions and that management is compliant with legislation, including the thirty-nine-hour working week, public holidays, bonuses, continuing training, and occasionally improved career prospects, which are sometimes lacking in the independent hotels.[19] Furthermore, employees' work schedules are given to them in advance, making the work-family balance easier, as witnessed by the Equilibre project instigated by Ibis.[20]

Through the example of one of the Paris-based Sofitel hotels, the group is seeking to innovate on behalf of the housekeepers by developing social monitoring (including a social worker), limiting tediousness, isolation, and stress by making it possible to work in pairs, encouraging good postural habits, and using innovative equipment (such as the "ergolit" system, which raises beds at the press of a pedal). These practices were proposed and initiated when the

Table 5.5 Job Quality Management for Housekeepers

	Chain Hotels	Independent Hotels
Housekeepers' characteristics	Women, mainly of foreign extraction, low-skilled or unskilled	Women, mainly of foreign extraction, low-skilled or unskilled
Type of management	Directly managed; paternalistic and hierarchical management in large hotels; controls or self-controls for room cleaning (for senior workers); in large hotels; some male room cleaners do physical tasks (carpet cleaning, stairs or window cleaning, laundry transportation)	Directly managed, family-owned businesses; paternalistic management; direct control of room cleaning by the manager-owner
Number of rooms to clean per day	Thirteen to eighteen rooms	Fourteen to eighteen rooms
Subcontracting practices	Used for common areas (lobby, meeting rooms, window cleaning) and for outside areas or gardens; sometimes used for room cleaning, except in deluxe hotels	Internalization or externalization of room cleaning and other common areas

Labor contracts		
Up-market segment	Full-time permanent contracts (based on thirty-nine or sometimes thirty-seven hours per week) and some "extra" contracts	
Midmarket segment	Combination of part-time contracts (permanent and fixed-term for thirty hours) and an increasing number of "extra" contracts	Regardless of the market, many full-time permanent contracts based on thirty-nine hours per week) and some "extra" contracts
Wages and other benefits	Basic pay; a thirteenth month after one year, sickness and pension schemes, profit-sharing, travel card offering discounts in the chain brands; a continuing training program	Basic pay; specific bonus may exist for loyalty or for very specific opportunities (such as Christmas); unlike on-the-job training, continuing training is not a priority
Career ladders	Few opportunities	Few promotional opportunities and none toward managerial positions when occupied by the owners
New practices	Developing social monitoring and communication practices; organizing work-family balance; innovating multiskilling; introducing working in pairs	Developing a social watch and guidance

Source: Authors' compilation, case study hotels.

MyBed concept was introduced and resulted in some difficulties for the housekeepers, who described the system as creating "pains in the arms."[21] In some up-market hotel chains, there have been recent moves to improve housekeepers' working conditions, while in low- to mid-range hotel chains some managers are testing new forms of multiskilling (for instance, combining cleaning and reception activities). However, housekeepers' wages tend to be pegged to the legal minimum wage, and hotel chains are only a little more generous by awarding a yearly thirteenth month and social benefits. The same managers may combine elements of the high and low roads in a profitable and flexible way, offering simultaneously career prospects for some of their employees and unstable part-time contracts for others, such as housekeepers.

Location-related differences stress the existence of local labor market tensions and highlight the nature of the available labor, which sometimes included a higher proportion of foreign-born workers. We visited four hotels in Paris where the supply of hotel rooms is greater and the cost of living makes it hard to hire quality employees at low wages. In contrast, two of the four provincial hotels selected are in typical rural regions while the other two are on the French Riviera, an interesting area in that it has a high influx of tourists coupled with a high rate of unemployment. The local market is fairly decisive: if it is dynamic, hotels have no difficulty hiring available workers, even when they have no hotel industry qualifications. Hotel locations also differentiate leisure guests from business clients who stay for shorter periods; this difference has a bearing on the work of housekeepers. The Parisian and hotel chains tend to adopt leaner organizations and adapt to high staff turnover, which is rare in the provinces or the family-run firms.

THE THREAT OF SUBCONTRACTING

Hotels may choose to outsource part of their staffing requirements through temporary work agencies or subcontracting in order to remove the burden of managing the industry activity fluctuations. Employment contracts are thus essentially part-time requirements.[22] In practice, the use of temporary work agencies for room cleaning is an exception and limited to situations where there is a real dearth of manpower. For instance, hotel H1 used temp workers when it faced a staff shortage. Hotel H7 took on an agency worker to fill in for a housekeeper on sick leave because other staff were off at the same time. Employers tend to consider temp agency use costly and risky, since the agency is responsible only for selecting the staff and completing the administrative formalities relating to the employment contract but provides no supervision, which is essential.

In contrast, hotels resort to subcontracting to tackle the cleaning of common areas such as halls and meeting rooms, the external environment, and particularly special surfaces (such as big bay windows that call for special skills and equipment). Subcontracting is almost always used for guest linen care or delicate outfits, such as uniforms, in contrast to housekeepers' pinafores or dustcoats, which they wash themselves. Subcontracting is used in one in the two budget hotels in the Group Louvre Hotel for room cleaning. However, the market leader Accor has recently reversed its practice after its commercial image was dented by major industrial unrest at one of its subcontractors, Arcade. In 2002 the employees of this cleaning company went on strike to improve their working conditions and work rates: while the Accor group staff housekeepers had to clean sixteen rooms in eight hours, the cleaning company employees had to clean twenty to twenty-three rooms in six hours (and were paid €7.16 (US$10.14) per hour, only 49 centimes more than the SMIC rate).

It needs to be emphasized that in a sector where silence reigns and union membership is rare, these tensions and the claims made by housekeepers with unstable, captive jobs emerged where they were least expected. Cleaning company employees earn very low wages (Puech 2004). Like housekeepers, they are often migrants, with no certificates or qualifications, and many live in unstable family situations. This unusual strike hit Accor out of the blue. Since then, it has internalized part of the cleaning of its hotels and taken on former cleaning company employees. At the start of 2003 the Accor group management and the unions signed a protocol on the use of subcontracting that aimed to guarantee better industrial conditions for the group's cleaning service provider employees.

Hotel managers do not choose between directly managing and subcontracting cleaning services for financial, administrative, or pay considerations alone.[23] Only one independent out of the hotels surveyed still uses a cleaning company that was in place when it took over the establishment. Another director has just stopped using the services of a cleaning company known to him that was also in place when the hotel was purchased. Two of the chain hotels had internalized room cleaning and hired former subcontractor employees in the same way as Accor did. They believe that this decision had a positive impact on their organization, work rhythms, wages, and social relations.

Subcontracting for some employers is part of their policy to seek flexibility and rein in costs as tightly as possible. For others, the decision to internalize cleaning also aims at cost reduction (a drop of 30 to 40 percent), since a contract with a service company may be based on mean occupancy rates and thus invariable in the short term, while others appreciate paying per room, at the lowest price. Direct management may also promote greater flexibility and better staff retention. The human factor is important; indeed, some guests insist that their room be on a particular floor because they want the services of a specific housekeeper. As one manager notes: "In a hotel sector where we are competing on value-for-money, charm may come up trumps."

Little Hope of Promotion

Most housekeepers either have no certificate (or only a certificate obtained abroad that is not recognized in France) or their qualifications are too low to hope to benefit from a career, especially since geographical mobility may be the factor that clinches access to a supervisor's job but for many housekeepers such work flexibility would conflict with their family situation. When they are unable to free themselves temporarily from their family obligations to pursue a course of study, or they have learning difficulties in some subjects, such as French or English, they soon throw in the towel. However, housekeepers do hope to become supervisors one day—or even "a real supervisor"—since they cannot see any other opportunities for turning their professional experience to good use. Even when they know that their chances of pulling off this ambition are slim, they try to remain hopeful for the long term, since hope alone may be what makes their daily lives easier to handle.

Some hotels are exceptions to the rule and award promotions, if not by deliberate strategy, at least during periods when manpower is scarce. The deluxe hotel H3 had promoted one individual to "first housekeeper" after giving her half a day's training; that promotion had enabled another person to become a floor supervisor (although she remained classified as a clerk) on the basis of a two-day, in-house vocational training course. Another small hotel had promoted an employee to the "first housekeeper" level and given her a new administrative role, but it insisted that she retain her hourly cleaning rate of three rooms as before. In a recent study for Accor (Bosse and Guégnard 2005), a former housekeeper told a story reminiscent of the Cinderella fairy tale. Of African origin, she arrived in France at the age of twenty and started working in a three-star hotel: moving up from room cleaner to executive housekeeper to trainer, she traveled widely from Russia to Cuba, Egypt to Latin America, before settling down in France as the head of a hotel.

The in-house career possibilities are few and far between and largely symbolic. They are limited to the positions of assistant supervisor and executive housekeeper, which only large establishments can offer. Since many hotels are small and headed by their owners, as in the case of family-run hotels, there are few possibilities of being promoted to supervisor (this function usually being held by the hotelier's wife). Few hotels offer any training that really enables their housekeepers to move on in their jobs. Ibis hotels, to mention some of the good practices in this area, offer the "Acteurs 2003" vocational development approach and encourage their housekeepers to learn a second trade in the hotel industry and to move to frontline jobs (for example, housekeeper and waitress or housekeeper and receptionist). Nevertheless, to move upward in their careers these employees must demonstrate ample availability and be prepared to meet the hotel's multiskilling requirements—which often involves moving sideways first.

THE ROLES OF EMPLOYEES IN TRAINING

Continuing training is less widely practiced in the hotel industry than in other sectors, mainly because most of the firms are so small. In 2004 only one-quarter of employees had participated in at least one course financed by their employer, compared to 38 percent of all employees in other industries (Céreq continuing training survey). The mean duration of the training courses was twenty hours, versus thirty-one hours in all the other sectors combined. However, these statistics mask some disparities, since only large firms, such as chain hotels, actually showed percentages well above the legal minimum. At the Accor group, for example, continuing vocational training is central to human resource management policy, and the firm devotes sums amounting to 2 percent of its wage bill to this item. (Firms with ten or more employees are obliged to spend a sum equal to at least 1.6 percent.) The Accor Academy, the first corporate university to be created in Europe, aims to give all "collaborators" access to the career ladder and to give each employee "one vocational training course per year."

Training for housekeepers is almost nonexistent in small hotels. Only a handful of the hotels in our case study offer any initiatives for the room attendants such as training on ergonomic postures, room-cleaning techniques, reception in deluxe hotels, or building customer satisfaction awareness.[24] Most training sessions have operational objectives and do not lead to skills certificates that are recognized throughout the industry. They are aimed at retaining manpower and making sure that staff are integrated by learning the house style and increasing in-house dialogue rather than at letting the housekeepers make any real managerial progress or rise in rank. The main training requirements, defined for the whole hotel and catering industry nationwide by the employers and unions, are totally irrelevant to housekeepers because they cover food safety, IT, environmental awareness building, and foreign language skills (ministère de l'Emploi et de la Solidarité 1997). The independent sector as a whole appears to have little commitment to investing in employee training, especially when any such investment extends beyond a hotel's immediate operational needs.[25]

Turning to initial training, the French Ministry of Education runs a range of training courses tailored to the hotel and catering industry.[26] One rather striking aspect of the hotel training system is the stability of the enrollment patterns. The CAP (certificat d'aptitude professionnelle) and apprenticeship schemes, the two-year vocational training programs, continue to attract much larger numbers than other vocational training courses. As far as room cleaning is concerned, the BEP (brevet d'études professionnelles hôtellerie-restauration [hotels and restaurants]) targets a specific field of activity, whereas the CAP employé technique de collectivité (employees in collective settings) is less specifically oriented toward the hotel industry.[27] Both courses nevertheless teach cleaning rooms, making beds, and serving breakfast and other meals. The BEP offers an option that goes by the name of production de services (services production); this euphemism is intended to avoid discouraging students from applying for what is in fact a housekeepers' vocational training course. These two certificates, the CAP and BEP, are held by housekeepers in the hotels surveyed that had orientation training. Most employers, however, either do not ask for these certificates or are uninterested in them. They feel that there was no need to train for two years to do this job and they give preference to more practical considerations when recruiting housekeepers (whether they live nearby, can work even during public transport strikes, accept staggered working hours, have family constraints, and so on).

Likewise, floor supervisor or executive housekeeper jobs are prepared from the baccalaureate level through the BP (brevet professionnel gouvernante) or the baccalauréat technologique (also including reception and waiter service). But applicants who have two years of higher education, such as the BTS (brevet de technicien supérieur) in hotel and catering management, improve their chances, especially because they will have better foreign language skills. Because there are far fewer career opportunities in the hotel industry than in catering, BTS holders sometimes accept a job as a housekeeper in the hope of fast-track promotion to the rank of supervisor.[28] Continuing training just cannot fill the yawning gap between the jobs of housekeeper and executive manager. The branch has created a professional qualification, the CQP (certificat de qualification professionnelle d'employé d'étages [certificate for housekeepers]), which it issues to only about fifty people per year, and it makes no difference to their pay.

INNOVATIONS FOR ROOM ATTENDANTS?

Other initiatives for housekeepers aim to make the working atmosphere friendlier or to include them more in company life. Thus, some chain hotels have launched group breakfasts and encourage staff to take part in induction days, get involved in hotel festivities (even the extra-status workers), and self-manage their holiday dates. In other independent establishments, guidance is given on interpersonal relations through regular one-to-one interviews and organized meetings or breakfasts. When Sofitel France introduced MyBed, some housekeepers were invited to take part in a product testing that involved a free night and meal at the hotel.

Some deluxe hotel managers, under pressure from the keen competitive environment, have also opted for a special wage policy in which they draw up their own grid, sometimes offering exceptional bonuses to deserving staff for high-quality work or for coping with extra difficulties (for instance, when there was an excessive influx of guests during the heat wave). Nonetheless, these benefits and practices are usually directed at all hotel staff and largely depend on the director and his individual managerial policy. Whereas functional multiskilling (doing both reception and waiting, or both service and cooking) is on the increase within the hotel industry, few hotels supplement the floor staff's basic service by allocating them to other tasks within the establishment, although such assignments would enable them to be less captive in their jobs.

CONCLUSION

The hotel industry continues to be France's emblematic low-wage sector. It stands out from other sectors because of its particular industrial and institutional regulations and its powerful employers' lobby facing the government and the trade unions. The predominance and fragmentation of very small independent establishments, which tend to be represented by the employers' union UMIH, and the very low rate of trade union membership are just some of the obstacles to more positive labor regulations.

Hotel industry employers, including chains, have managed to convince the political and institutional authorities that any social progress is a risk, because it might favor undeclared or illegal work or lead to an increase in the unemployment rate. The government incentives frequently given to the hotel industry are in contrast with other sectors, especially since the industry is growing and creating jobs. The hotel sector has so much clout that it can be absolved from many otherwise binding state regulations. In fact, cafés, restaurants, and hotels are vital meeting places that give their owners some degree of social and political influence. This is one more reason why politicians are very sensitive to hotel employers' complaints, particularly in the run-up to important elections.

Moreover, the hotel industry remains marked by tradition and its connection to domestic work. In addition to harboring illegal work, hotels do not always strictly apply collective agreements at the company level. Collective agreements do not provide for any increase in wages linked to seniority, but they do offer flexibility to employers, including a range of insecure contracts, such as those for "extras," that the French government has recently subsidized in order to favor development in the industry. Small independent hotels continue to make inroads in the sector despite increasing standardization of work procedures and the services provided to guests. This rationalization has been undertaken by chains, which emphasize high service performance quality as central to the work of housekeepers. The organization of schedules appears to be the result of pressure from competitors and increasing financial constraints. In an attempt to be more flexible and to reduce salary costs, hoteliers across the industry employ both part-time workers and extras. As a result, the gap has widened between housekeepers with permanent contracts and casual workers and is reinforced by a second level of division between those employed on a full-time basis and part-time workers.

There is no shortage of available housekeepers in France, and in this context managers also adopt other practices that border on illegality: paying wages according to objectives (number of rooms cleaned instead of actual working hours) and refusing to pay overtime (at best overtime can be made up if an agreement is negotiated with the manager). In this institutionalized context with few rules, housekeepers, many of whom are untrained and uninformed about their rights, have few means available to fight the intensification of work or the imaginative application of labor law, especially when employers have made individual arrangements that divide them. Most employees are vulnerable and undemanding about working conditions, and they easily become dependent on the employer owing to their lack of employability on the market. Thus, they remain a docile labor force, confined to the status of low-wage workers for whom their jobs seem to be a trap leading to exclusion and a dead end. Housekeepers find themselves in a spiral that links insecurity and low wages and is reinforced by managerial demands for flexibility, as favored by some employment policies in France.

The research conducted in the United States (Bernhardt, Dresser, and Hatton 2003) and in the other European countries under study—Denmark, Germany, the Netherlands, and the United Kingdom—reveals many similarities. Across the Atlantic, the profession of housekeeper is also female-dominated, undervalued, and low-skilled. It attracts a population of poorly educated people of foreign extraction who are consequently vulnerable and captive. In all these countries, although the room is at the heart of the hotel business, a booming industry, low pay is a good reflection of the subordinate status of housekeepers, who have few opportunities for career advancement. Many case studies show the connections between low wages, job insecurity, and heavy workloads. Hotel directors are ready to admit that the housekeeping job is tedious and badly paid, but few adopt strategies that would benefit their staff. Against this backdrop, hotel chains sometimes appear like a mirage, especially in France. However, the status of extras in France is comparable to that of the "on-call" workers who are described by the American researchers as "employees who are not regularly scheduled but are available on an as-needed basis."

Housekeepers are responsible for cleaning rooms—"scrubbing bathtubs and toilets, mopping and vacuuming floors, changing sheets, towels, making beds"—but what is the true picture? Housekeepers' stress also comes out as a crucial common element. This stress deserves deeper analysis, especially since the daily number of rooms to be cleaned differs. In the United States it ranges from fifteen to seventeen rooms and has risen in the deluxe hotels included in the research. In contrast, in France this number is thirteen to eighteen rooms across all categories of hotel and is dropping in the upper market segment. There is little evidence that the notion of higher productivity that prevails in the United States ("doing more work with fewer people") is found in the French hotels studied (with the exception of the subcontracting situations); in the French hotel industry, "doing better with fewer people" would be a more apt expression.

Nevertheless the studies point up differences. Elsewhere, the trade unions seem to be influential, especially in Denmark and to a lesser extent in the United States; this is not the case in France. Among all the European industries under study, the lowest rate of unionization (2 percent) occurs in French hotels, which are more characterized by small establishments. Mainly migrants and part-time workers, housekeepers are not represented by the unions, and the only social unrest that the Accor group recently experienced in mainland France was a campaign led by insecure cleaning company employees who were vulnerable, poorly trained, and badly informed about their rights. It would thus be expedient to go deeper into the analysis by comparing working conditions, work paces, and career opportunities not only for housekeepers in hotels but also for employees of cleaning subcontractor companies, in relation both to union representation in these various countries and to their industry models. French housekeepers employed at low hotel industry wages, working for independent employers and in cottage businesses, could find themselves in an even more precarious situation than their American or European counterparts. Indeed, the American hotel industry is based on wage earners, franchised hotels, and chains more than in France (Gadrey et al. 2002).

Moreover, the hotel industry in these countries does not appear to be such a particular case as it is in France, with its powerful employers that benefit from labor law dispensations concerning working hours, employment contracts, and, until recently, the legal minimum wage. Furthermore, on-the-job training for housekeepers may at times be more formal and structured in the United States. According to the dual market theory (Doeringer and Piore 1971), however, in all these countries housekeepers have secondary-market jobs in that they are low-paid, labor under backbreaking working conditions, and have few chances of promotion. The following question must be asked: why is there so little professional mobility for housekeepers in this industry? The research work could be supplemented by a comparative in-depth look at career paths in order to identify when, where, how, and why these jobs might be valued to a greater or lesser degree and socially recognized. In other words, which country offers its housekeepers career prospects worthy of the Cinderella fairy tale?

> The research was funded by a grant from the Russell Sage Foundation, and this chapter has benefited greatly from comments made by Annette Bernhardt and Tom Cook. Research assistance from the following is gratefully acknowledged: Nathalie Bosse (Céreq-IREDU/CNRS, Dijon), Samira Malhaoui (Céreq, Marseille), and Armelle Testenoire (GRIS, Rouen). The authors would like to thank the Accor and Louvre Hotel groups for their support, as well as all the interviewed persons

NOTES

1. Low wages are defined as less than or equal to two-thirds of the median wage (see chapter 2 and table 5.4). The net hourly cutoff corresponded to an average of €5.09 (US$7.21) in 1995 and €6.23 (US$8.82) in 2003, with all sectors being taken into account (DADS surveys, INSEE).
2. The independent hotels decreased in number by 50,000 rooms within

seven years, thus losing 12 percent of their capacity (INSEE, direction du Tourisme).

3. The Louvre Hotels group was formed by the merger of Envergure (budget hotels) and Concorde Hotels (deluxe) in 2002, which was in turn bought in the summer of 2005 by Starwood Capital.

4. In the French system of hotel classification, hotels are awarded between zero and four stars ("deluxe") on the basis of their equipment, comfort, and services. The criteria for this state classification, carried out by the French Tourism Ministry, are more demanding than in other countries, where a hotel from the same chain is generally awarded an additional star. Cleaning quality has never been included in the classification criteria or even in quality assurance standards such as "Hotelcert"—a recent certification now held by two hundred hotels that guarantees their quality of service, reception, infrastructure, and environment.

5. The occupancy rate across the eight hotels varies from 63 to 90 percent. It was higher in the chain hotels, partly owing to the high number of business customers (who account for 40 to 70 percent of occupancy across the eight hotels).

6. The installation of automated washroom cleaning in some no-star hotels may have reduced the need for housekeepers, since the device performs the disinfection function, but human intervention will always be required to clean off or scrub stubborn stains.

7. The Union des Métiers et des Industries de l'Hôtellerie (UMIH), created in 1946, includes 80,000 hotel or restaurant employers, among them 12,000 independent hotel and 1,600 chain hotel employers. Other organizations, less preponderant, are: the Confédération des professionnels indépendants de l'hôtellerie (CPIH), created in 1970; the Syndicat national des hôteliers restaurateurs, cafetiers et traiteurs (SYNHORCAT), with 10,000 members; and the Fédération autonome générale de l'industrie hôtelière touristique (FAGIHT), which was founded in 1968 and has 6,500 members.

8. The five trade unions concerned are Confédération générale du travail (CGT), created in 1895; Confédération française des travailleurs chrétiens (CFTC), founded in 1919; Confédération française des travailleurs (CFDT), created in 1964; Confédération française des cadres (CGC), created in 1944; and Force Ouvrière (FO), founded in 1947. Few of the confederations have specific sections for the hotel industry and even none for room attendants.

9. Although May 1 is a public holiday in France, article L. 222-5 of the Labor Code states that hotel, restaurant, and café managers are exempted from applying this rule and allowed to schedule their employees to work on May 1 without having to pay them double wages.

10. In three hotels, three trade unions were represented on the consultative bodies. Only one manager claimed that up to 5 percent of his staff were unionized, and one at a deluxe hotel mentioned that the hotel had been affected by a very temporary strike: "It was only a two hour strike to protest the cut in working hours, but as soon as the housekeepers realized that they were not being paid, they came back and have never been on strike since."
11. In fact, 71 percent of full-time staff are either clerks or blue-collar workers, compared with an average of 61 percent in other private and semi-public sectors (DADS survey, 2002, INSEE).
12. Nearly 38 percent of room attendants are of foreign extraction, compared to 12 percent of the French workforce (Labor Force INSEE, 2004, calculated by Cepremap).
13. According to the managers interviewed, the only people who left housekeeping jobs were either those who were retiring or employees who had health problems (caused in some cases by the difficult work activities) and hadn't "got the strength to carry on."
14. Since she has been in her job, reports an H5 supervisor, she has not received a single application from a French-born national. Managers at some of the hotels express a need to recruit more people who could speak fluent French or understand it.
15. For example, four room cleaners and twenty-six housekeepers work at H6, and four room cleaners and fifteen housekeepers work at H5. In our survey sample, two male room cleaners were interviewed.
16. In the many hotels visited, the housekeepers have color-coded boards for identification purposes. The rooms "marked in blue," explains an H6 supervisor, "are the rooms due to check out, and in yellow, the rooms that will be slept in again . . . and the crew is highlighted in orange."
17. Of the thirty-three floor staff we interviewed, only two had been hired through an apprenticeship for a twelve-month housekeeper training course.
18. For example, having been employed as an extra, an H6 housekeeper was hired on a part-time permanent contract to clean ten rooms a day (her full-time colleagues cleaned fifteen rooms) and said she thus earned less: "I was paid more as an extra: fifty-four euros net for the day, and now I'm paid thirty euros per day. All in all I earn five hundred fifty euros per month."
19. In October 2004, thirty-five French firms, including Accor, signed a "charter of diversity." In 1997 Accor had signed a nondiscrimination agreement, which was ratified by the five largest trade unions. These initiatives to promote equal opportunities were not mentioned during our interviews with the housekeepers; the directors were the only ones to mention them in passing.

20. Equilibre is a project of Equal, a community initiative program backed by the European Social Fund (see http://www.equal-equilibre.com). It is based on a set of experimental actions carried out from 2002 to 2004 to reconcile arrangements between work and personal life on a local level, foster career development through qualifying training, build awareness, and train managers in more flexible schedule management (Guégnard 2004).
21. The MyBed concept came from the United States. "A new way of sleeping and dreaming" the advertising promises, but making this bed with a featherbed, thick comforter, and four down pillows takes twelve to twenty minutes according to the housekeepers.
22. One-third of cleaning company employees work part-time, compared to one-quarter of those in the hotel industry (Labor Force surveys, 2000 to 2002, INSEE).
23. About outsourcing, an H1 manager declares: "This arrangement saves us from having to draw up the pay-sheets ourselves, and the managerial tasks (such as recruitment and dismissal procedures) are handled elsewhere. . . It is increasingly unusual to recruit hotel cleaning staff directly these days in France" (quoted in Guégnard and Mériot 2005).
24. In one chain hotel, H7, all the housekeepers had been on two to eight short vocational continuing training courses.
25. The prestige independent hotel H3 hired adults who had come out of the Association nationale pour la formation professionelle des adultes (AFPA) as housekeepers or supervisors from the private school at Poligny (which brings students to BEP level in two years).
26. In 2004 almost 13,300 secondary school pupils and 11,300 apprentices were in their final year of initial training in the hotel and catering field (Guégnard and Mériot 2005).
27. There were 5,800 students and 1,800 apprentices in their final year of the BEP production de services in 2004, while the CAP employé technique de collectivité had only 600 students and 3,200 apprentices (Reflet base, Céreq).
28. A young woman from Reunion Island, whose travel was funded by the French Agence Nationale pour l'Insertion et la Promotion des Travailleurs d'Outre-Mer, was employed by the Accor group in the United Kingdom. She discovered, as did several classmates who finished studying the same year, that she had absolutely no prospects because she was assigned to a two-star hotel cleaned by subcontractors where it was impossible to speak English because she had no contact with the guests and all her housekeeper colleagues were of foreign extraction. Consequently, she gave up her one-year commitment to her contract to take up her studies again, in the hope of getting into hotel management.

REFERENCES

Beauvois, Martine. 2003. "L'hôtellerie, la restauration, et les cafés: Un secteur très spécifique en termes d'emploi et de remuneration" ["Hotels, Restaurants, and Cafés: A Specific Sector Regarding Employment and Wage"]. *INSEE Première* 889(March): 1-4.

Bernhardt, Annette, Laura Dresser, and Erin Hatton. 2003. "The Coffee Pot Wars: Unions and Firms Restructuring in the Hotel Industry." In *Low-Wage America: How Employers Are Reshaping Opportunity in the Workplace*, edited by Eileen Appelbaum, Annette Bernhardt, and Richard J. Murnane. New York: Russell Sage Foundation.

Bosse, Nathalie, and Christine Guégnard. 2005. *Mixité, carrières, et performances* [*Mixed Employees, Carriers, and Performances*]. Céreq-IREDU (Institut de Recherche sur l'Education: Sociologie et Economie de l'Education)/CNRS report.

Cosson, Claire. 2007. "Février 2006 : progression des RevPar pour l'hôtellerie française" ["February 2006: Progressions of RevPar in the French Hotel Industry"]. *L'Hôtellerie* 2972(April): 10.

Direction du Tourisme. 2006. "L'hôtellerie de chaîne de 1999 à 2006" ["Hotel Chains from 1999 to 2006"]. *Tourisme Infos Stat* 2006-2.

Doeringer, Peter B., and Michael J. Piore. 1971. *Internal Labor Markets and Manpower Analysis*. Lexington, Mass.: Heath Lexington Books.

European Foundation for the Improvement of Living and Working Conditions (Eurofound). 2004. *EU Hotel and Restaurant Sector: Work and Employment Conditions*. Dublin: Eurofound.

Gadrey, Jean, Faridah Djellal, Camal Gallouj, Florence Jany-Catrice, Sylvie-Anne Mériot, and Thierry Ribault. 2002. *Hôtellerie-restauration: Héberger et restaurer l'emploi (les cas français, américain, et japonais)* [*The Hotel and Catering Industry: To Accommodate and Restore Employment (Based on French, American, and Japanese Cases)*]. Paris: La Documentation Française.

Guégnard, Christine. 2004. "À la récherche d'une conciliation des temps professionnels et personnels dans l'hôtellerie-restauration" ["In Search of a Balance Between Professional and Personal Schedules in the Hotel and Catering Industry"]. *Relief* (Céreq) 7(September): 5-25.

Guégnard, Christine, and Sylvie-Anne Mériot. 2005. *French Hotel Industry: First Case Study*. Report for Russell Sage Foundation. New York: Russell Sage Foundation (March).

Guégnard, Christine, and Cathy Perret. 1997. *Les trajectoires professionnelles des jeunes de Bourgogne: Enquête auprès des sortants des filières automobile, hôtellerie-restauration, commerce* [*Professional Paths for the Young People in Burgundy. Survey of School Leavers from the Automobile, Hotel-Catering, and Trade Fields*]. Céreq-IREDU (Institut de Recherche sur l'Education: Sociologie et Economie de l'Education)/CNRS report.

Guégnard, Christine, André Giffard, and Olga Strietska-Ilina. 2001. "Forecasting Training Needs in the Hotel, Catering, and Tourism Sector: A Comparative Analysis of Results from Regional Studies in Three European Countries." *Training and Employment* (Céreq) 42(January–March): 1-4.

Guégnard, Christine, Sylvie-Anne Mériot, Nathalie Bosse and Danièle Roualdès. 2005. *French Hotel Industry: Traditions and Social Developments*. Report for Russell Sage Foundation. Céreq, Iredu/CNRS Report.

Hugues, Everett C. 1996. *Le Regard sociologique* [*The Sociological Glance*]. Paris: Éditions de l'École des Hautes Études en Sciences Sociales (EHESS).

Le Garrec, Marie-Anne. 2007. "L'hôtellerie et les campings en 2006: une bonne année pour le haut de gamme" ["Hotels and Camping Sites in 2006: A Good Year for the Top of the Range"]. *INSEE Première* 1125(March): 1-4.

Mériot, Sylvie-Anne. 2000. "Employment Prospects in the Hotel and Catering Trade: A Franco-American Comparison." *Training and Employment* 40(July–September): 1-4.

———. 2006. *Nostalgic Cooks: Another French Paradox*. Netherlands: Brill Academic Publishers.

Ministère de l'Emploi, du travail et de la cohésion sociale. 2005. *Examen de l'état d'avancement du plan national de lutte contre le travail illégal* [*Addressing the Challenge of Fighting Illegal Work*]. Paris: Commission Nationale de Lutte contre le Travail Illégal.

Ministère de l'Emploi et de la Solidarité. 1997. *Hôtellerie, restauration, cafés: analyse et enjeux en matière d'emploi et de formation professionnelle* [*Hotels, Restaurants, and Cafés: Analysis and Stakes for Employment and Vocational Training*]. Prospective formation emploi, La Documentation française.

Monchatre, Sylvie, and Armelle Testenoire. 2004. "Les carrières entre mirage et réalité" ["Careers Between Mirage and Reality"]. *Relief* (Céreq) 7(September): 39-67.

Puech, Isabelle. 2004. "Le temps du remue-ménage: conditions d'emploi et de travail des femmes de chambre" ["Cleaning Time, Protest Time: Employment and Working Conditions for Hotel Maids"]. *Sociologie du Travail* 46(2): 150–67.

Triby, Emmanuel. 2004. "Le travail entre le professionnel et le domestique" ["The Work Between the Professional and the Servant"]. *Relief* (Céreq) 7(September): 27-38.

Union des Métiers et des Industries de l'Hôtellerie (UMIH). 2003. "L'industrie hôtelière en France 2002." Accessed at http://www.umih.fr/.

CHAPTER 6

Working Hard for Large French Retailers

Philippe Askenazy, Jean-Baptiste Berry, and Sophie Prunier-Poulmaire

The leading global retailer Wal-Mart and the German hard discounter Lidl are both subjects of wonder because of their overall business performance. They are also criticized as threats to society, especially by trade unions. These firms, their business, and their human resource models have been discussed in a large number of studies and papers. Paradoxically, the major French food retail chains, or indeed the nonfood chains, are not given much coverage. Nonetheless, France has some giant distributors, in particular the Carrefour Group, the world's second-biggest retailer. Also, a distinctive feature of French high-volume retailing lies in the importance of nonspecialized hypermarkets. They are similar to American "supercenters," and their size may reach 20,000 square meters—about 200,000 square feet. As in the United States, unionization is low in this sector, and the proportion of low-wage labor is high—twice the national level. It is thus worthwhile studying French retail working practices, especially in human resources.

This chapter focuses on large food retailers and their workers, as well as on shops with a high turnover in electrical and electronics goods (including hypermarkets). These firms account for half of French retail trade. Special attention is given to low-skilled and a priori low-wage jobs: cashiers, delicatessen sales staff, and electrical and electronics sales staff.

A striking fact is that, contrary to American practices, most large French retailers still offer hourly remuneration significantly above the legal minimum wage, while hard discount food stores pay rock-bottom wages. The main objective of this chapter is to analyze and explain these "high roads" for low-skilled occupations. Actually, two different stories emerge: one for food retailing and one for electrical and electronics retailing.

In food, high entry barriers generate "rents" for firms. High-end employers redistribute part of this rent to attract workers with specific social skills to support high-quality customer relations. These employees need to have the social and ethnic characteristics expected by customers, especially when they sell food. A relatively high hourly wage rewards demanding work requirements: variable and dispersed hours, a greater intensity of work, a lack of autonomy, and marked physical constraints.

In the growing electrical and electronics sector, high demand for efficient sales staff and pay incentive schemes have pushed wages to twice the minimum wage. This can be observed in both high-end and discount stores, even for workers with poor options outside the sector. Workers also have quite some room for maneuver compared to the food sector: rather than merely being subject to work constraints, they participate in shaping conditions by, for example, choosing their working hours during periods when customer flows are heavy.

In both sectors, it may be asked whether existing models are sustainable, given the rise of discount chains, the arrival of new competitors, and the current changes in the regulation.

We begin by describing store formats and contrasting the oligopolistic food retailers with the competitive electrical and electronics goods retailers. The next section provides a general picture of the low-skilled occupations and depicts the role of France's (lifeless) unions. Workplace organization and human resource management are detailed in the following section. We then go on to highlight occupational health issues and provide key indicators of the high-road strategies. We conclude by discussing the future of low-wage work in food and electrical and electronics outlets.

This chapter is based on an overview of the sector and on case studies conducted from 2004 to 2006. In each case (see the appendix), we followed a common methodology, and the result was 150 interviews with top human resource managers, store directors, store managers, sales staff, cashiers, and workers' representatives. In addition, we carried out an ergonomic work analysis of workplace activity for most stores and interviews with the occupational health doctors who covered the stores and workers. These in-depth studies give us detailed, qualitative, and quantitative information on working conditions, especially physical and psychological workloads.

For food retailing, we tried to compose a generally representative sample of this oligopolistic sector; the chains studied represent super discount stores and high-end stores and about 50 percent of total employment (or sales) by large food retailers in France. The only typical case not studied is the high-end franchisee. For electrical and electronics stores, the hypermarkets and specialized chains studied represent about 20 percent of the market. However, because of the strong heterogeneity of the firms operating in this sector, we cannot consider the case studies for this sector more generally representative; even when we find similar descriptions of sales staff occupations in our different cases, that actually suggests a rather homogenous profession.

NONCOMPETITIVE FOOD RETAILING VERSUS COMPETITIVE ELECTRICAL AND ELECTRONICS RETAILING

The French retail market is broadly divided into two types of outlets: large stores retailing food products or nonfood goods, often located on the outskirts of towns and cities, and smaller, traditional, inner-city outlets. The former are dominated by major supermarket and hypermarket chains as well as by specialist chains retailing a variety of goods, from clothing to home improvement, leisure, and cultural goods. Food retailing and electrical and electronics markets are two polar cases. Food retailing is oligopolistic, with important entry barriers; as such, it is dominated by French supermarket and hypermarket groups. Electrical and electronics retailing is a continuously changing sector with many competitors. Both sectors, however, face a similar growing pressure from discount retailers, especially from German firms.

LARGE-STORE FORMATS IN FRANCE

French statistics distinguish between two types of large food stores: hypermarkets, with a surface area of over 2,500 square meters, and supermarkets, which measure between 400 and 2,500 square meters. Supermarkets are generally split into two subcategories: "classic" supermarkets and "super discount" stores, which also consist of smaller stores (around 300 square meters) owned by super discount chains.

Offering a range of services to their customers, hypermarkets and classic supermarkets account for 53 percent and 40 percent of employment, respectively, in large food stores in 2005. Hypermarkets, which dominate food retailing with about one-third of the market, typically have a size range of 5,000 to 20,000 square meters. Classic supermarkets hold about one-fifth of the market; their average surface is 1,200 square meters. Choice in hypermarkets and classic supermarkets is extensive: 10,000 to 50,000 products are offered, and the wide variety of nonfood goods on their shelves make hypermarkets accountable for about 15 percent of nonfood retailing in France. All categories of products are present, from low-quality and low-price goods to quality products on pleasant shelving. Stores offer convenience with easy car access and vast parking lots or proximity to public transport in city centers. High-end stores generally provide some rayons traditionnels (food sales staff who offer artisanal services in selling fish, delicatessen products, bread, pastry, fresh cut cheese, and meat). In city centers, stores provide free home delivery for larger purchases. Most chains propose their own credit cards or customer loyalty programs that offer regular customers significant rebates, air travel miles, and so on. Contrary to many other European countries, France has no restrictions on shop opening hours, except on Sundays: typically a hypermarket is open between 9:00 AM and 10:00 PM, Monday to Saturday.

Super discount stores accounted for only 6 percent of employment in large food retailers in 2005, but for about 13 percent of food sales turnover; this share rose to 50 percent in the poorest urban zones. Super discount stores offer no services to their customers and generally have no rayons traditionnels, and they usually close at 7:00 PM. The mean store size is 600 square meters, though stores range from 200 to 2,000 square meters. The choice is restricted, on average, to 1,300 products. Hard discount stores offer only nonbranded and low-quality products; in soft-discount stores a limited choice of quality products is available at deeply discounted prices. While hypermarkets and classic supermarkets have a mix of customers, super discount stores in France clearly focus on less affluent French consumers: low-paid workers, the unemployed, and poor or retired people. Consequently, ethnic minorities are the basic clientele.

Paradoxically, the prices of "best price" products in high-end hypermarket chains could be lower than prices in discount stores. But the "one need–one product" model is appreciated by customers because it helps them avoid the temptation—ever-present in classic stores—of buying high-priced products. The motto of the super discounter Leader Price, "In our store, you also save time," summarizes a second advantage for customers of this no-choice model and of the "human size" of its stores. The absence of customer services leads to lower staff levels: according to the Institut Nationale de la Statistique et des Études Économiques (INSEE)'s *Sales Outlet Survey 2006*, employment per square meter is half the rate of classic supermarkets, for similar sales values. In addition, inventory costs are reduced; large sales volumes put strong pressure on producers, generally medium-sized suppliers.[1] In non-affluent areas, the business model of discount stores ("soft" and "hard") provides far higher profitability than that of high-end stores.

The nature of low-/high-end segmentation is specific to each market. Especially for electrical and electronics goods, there is no real price difference between different outlets for a given product. Customers are well informed about prices, for example, through the Internet. Numerous stores reimburse differences in purchase prices if a customer finds lower prices elsewhere. Discount stores, often located on city outskirts, offer a choice of low-priced products and have low-end customer assistance policies. Shop assistants have to encourage purchases of targeted products, which are chosen each week by the marketing department of the chain. The objective is making not the best choice for the customer but the best choice for the firm's margins. The value-added for customers lies in immediate product availability, given large inventories. In high-end chains, there are no such top-down prescriptions for sales staffs, who are there to help and inform customers. These chains target the most affluent clientele, mainly in inner cities, and the number of shop assistants they employ per square meter is twice that found in other outlets.

In addition to the high-end versus discount dimension, stores specialize or not in electrical and electronics products. An important share of the market is captured by stores offering complementary products, such as cultural goods associated with electronics or furniture linked to electrical goods. Hypermarkets are also major players in this market, generating 20 percent of sales with either a high-end or discount strategy—for instance, hypermarkets may be high-end for food products (employing numerous *rayons traditionnels*) but low-end for electrical and electronics goods, for which they offer no customer service.

COMPETITIVE ELECTRICAL AND ELECTRONICS GOODS RETAILERS VERSUS OLIGOPOLISTIC FOOD RETAILERS

The multiplicity of actors ensures a competitive market for electrical and electronics goods. Historically, because small businesses in this sector rapidly disappeared in the 1980s, local politicians and lobbies have not significantly slowed the development of nonfood stores and subsequent competition. Some French chains have been bought out by foreign distributors; for example, Darty, the leading electrical and electronics retailer in France, is owned by KESA.

The keener competition of recent years, however, has induced a decline of sales margins.[2] The market has witnessed the arrival of new foreign discount companies, such as the German firm Saturn. In addition, e-commerce has been growing rapidly. In 2006 about 7 percent of electronics goods (especially computers, at 10 percent) were sold via the Internet at discount prices. Now most firms sell via the Internet, including both subsidiaries of brick-and-mortar retailers and pure Internet players. Competition is uncertain, owing to permanent product renewal. Firms are mainly concerned about handling the exceptional growth in sales volumes linked to rapid price declines. Despite growing markets, these constraints, along with proliferating discount offers, are challenging the business model of the actors in this market.

Hypermarkets face growing competition in the electrical and electronics sector. The rise of super discount stores is also changing the environment for food retailing. However, competition is still limited in this sector. The five main food groups in France are all French, and they account for about 85 percent of the total super- and hypermarket turnover and about 30 percent of total retail turnover. To improve their market power, firms merged massively during the 1990s, the most notable being the merger in 1999 between Carrefour and Promodès. This linkup has created the second largest retail group in the world. The French market is now structured around three major groups (Carrefour, Auchan, and Casino) and chains of independent stores (Leclerc, Intermarché, Système U). The two main challengers are the German hard discounters Lidl and Aldi, which still account for less than 7 percent of the French food market.

REGULATIONS: PUTTING LIMITS ON FOOD STORES' SALES SURFACE AREAS

Legal barriers to entry in food retailing are important in France. According to the OECD's regulation database, in 2003 France had the most restrictive regulation for new, large outlets and the most protec-

Figure 6.1 Barriers for New, Large Retailers, in 2003: OECD Index of Specific Regulation of Large Outlets and OECD Index of Protection of Existing Firms

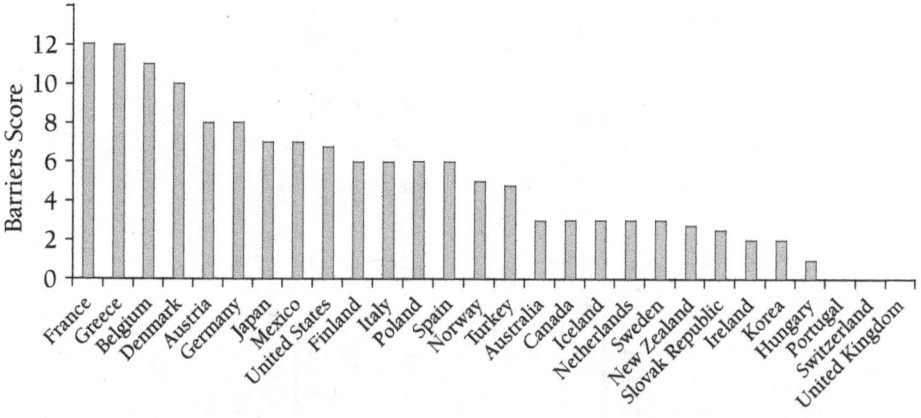

Source: OECD indicators of product market regulation.

tive regulation for existing retailers (see figure 6.1) (for methodology, see Boylaud and Nicoletti 2001).

Retail zoning regulation was introduced in 1973 (the Royer law).[3] The creation of any new, large retail establishment now required approval by a regional zoning board composed of store owners, consumer representatives, and regionally elected politicians.[4] From April 1993 to 1996, new authorizations of large stores were partly frozen by conservative governments. Finally, the limits were restricted to a threshold of 300 square meters in 1996 (the Raffarin law), which is low by international standards, while large outlets (6,000 square meters) became subject to special investigations. These laws also changed the composition of zoning boards, giving more power to the elected representatives of small retailers. The freeze and the Raffarin law led to a dramatic drop in store creations (see table 6.1).[5]

The law has increased the market power of existing groups, protecting this sector against the entry of innovative competitors.[6] During the second half of the 1990s, only thirteen new hypermarkets were opened, and the number of approved supermarkets declined substantially, despite annual growth in consumption of 3 percent and

Table 6.1 Regulations Dramatically Reduced Creation, 1993 to 2004

	1993	1994	1995	1996	1997	1998	1999	2000	2001	2002	2003	2004
New hypermarkets or extensions (thousands of square meters)	327	246	289	165	65	103	132	173	157	321	180	236
New supermarkets (excluding super discounters) (thousands of square meters)	81	75	92	49	33	31	32	42	42	50	31	50
New super discounters (thousands of square meters)	170	225	160	133	94	50	50	32	73	74	73	94
Total growth per inhabitant	4.1%	3.8%	3.6%	2.1%	1.0%	0.9%	0.9%	1.0%	1.1%	2.2%	1.1%	1.7%

Source: Authors' compilation from Institut National de la Statistique et des Études Économiques (INSEE) trade database.

relatively cheap land. The Raffarin law has especially slowed the development of hard discounters: their growth was reduced by 60 to 80 percent. Overall, the development flow of new surfaces per inhabitant in France was about half the flow of creations by Wal-Mart in the United States. To avoid the authorization threshold, super discount chains have recently developed small stores in city centers, targeted at a mixed clientele. Therefore, progressively, the super discounters have gained new market shares, from virtually zero in 1990 to 13 percent in 2006. French groups have developed their own discount outlets to meet the rise of German chains. This subsector is also oligopolistic: Lidl (German), Leader Price (Casino), Ed (Carrefour), and Aldi (German) generate 85 percent of sales by discount outlets.

Price regulation also has important consequences for profit margins. A specific law aimed at restoring the balance in producer-retailer relationships was passed in 1996: this law prevents retailers from setting the price of a good below a certain threshold, defined as the unit price invoiced by the supplier of the good, plus transport costs (Allain and Chambolle 2004). The law has had a direct effect: it forces retailers to increase the prices of the goods they previously sold at below-cost price. Empirical studies conducted by INSEE and the Ministry of Finance suggest that prices rose by 5 percent following the introduction of the law. The law was partially abrogated in 2006 and 2007, and prices have declined slightly since, but there has still been no price war.

Discount Stores: A Challenge to Profit Growth in France

Despite the progressive emergence of German hard discounters and increases in the legal minimum wage (the SMIC; see chapter 2), concentration, low competition, and growing rebates have been correlated with a dramatic rise in the profits of super- and hypermarkets (see table 6.2). Conversely, labor's share in value-added dropped by twelve percentage points between 1995 and 2002. These changes contrast with a small increase in labor's share in the rest of the retail sector. These huge margins have helped French groups finance growth in numerous foreign markets.

However, the main French companies expect tougher competition in the future, with the expansion of hard discount stores, especially German competitors, and the current reforms of retail trade regula-

Table 6.2 Labor's Share in Value-Added: Falls in Hyper- and Supermarkets, 1994 to 2002

	1994	1995	1996	1997	1998	1999	2000	2001	2002
Share in retail trade	67.0%	67.1%	6.4%	67.8%	66.9%	66.5%	65.5%	65.1%	65.0%
Share in hyper- and supermarket trade	79.3	79.0	78.6	76.4	74.2	73.5	70.3	68.4	67.1

Source: Authors' compilation from Institut Nationale de la Statistique et des Études Economiques (INSEE) trade database (2005).

tions. Therefore, even if they have still kept their traditional business model, especially relating to human resources, insider food and electrical and electronics retailers are being challenged by the emergence of such new competition.

WORKERS AND UNIONS IN LARGE FOOD RETAILERS

Our work focuses on three low-skill occupations: cashiers (the main occupation in food outlets), delicatessen sales staff, and electrical and electronics sales staff. This section presents their main characteristics, wages, and union activities, as well as the collective agreements that cover them.

NOT SUCH LOW WAGES

According to the Labor Force Survey, workers in these retail jobs generally have similar educational achievements: about 10 percent—mainly students—have some college education, 45 percent have the French baccalaureate (France's general or vocational high school diploma), and 45 percent are less educated.[7] In large cities or in tourist zones during summers, students can represent up to 20 percent of the workforce. However, students are not the sole workers on short-term contracts, which cover on average one-fifth of the workforce.[8]

French Women in the Food and Mixed Electrical and Electronics Sectors
Not surprisingly, cashiers are mostly female. According to the Labor

Force Survey, 80 percent of food sales staff in supermarkets are female, and 70 percent in hypermarkets are also female. Furniture and household equipment staffs are more balanced, with 60 percent men and 40 percent women. Our case study provides similar figures: about 60 percent male for electronics staff and 60 percent female for electrical staff.

According to the Labor Force Survey, the share of foreigners among cashiers is significantly higher in supermarkets and discount stores than in hypermarkets; our case study suggests that this gap is explained by the fact that in discount stores the proportion of foreign workers, as well as visible minorities, is greater than in high-end stores.

Relatively High Hourly Wages in Hypermarkets and High-End Supermarkets Overall, 18 percent of workers in general retail stores were low-wage earners in 2003—about twice the national level (see table 6.3). However, there is a clear distinction between supermarkets and discount stores compared to hypermarkets. The share of low-wage workers is declining in hypermarkets but rising in supermarkets, possibly because of the development of hard discounters. Consequently, the share of low-wage workers in the workforces of hypermarkets (greater than 2,500 square meters) is generally similar to the share in all private firms, while it is twice as big in supermarkets, including super discount stores (table 6.3). Our cases suggest that the gap is greater between large hypermarkets (greater than 5,000 square meters) and pure hard discounters.

Hard discounters offer rock-bottom wages. In the discount stores we studied, 60 to 90 percent of the workforce were on low wages in 2005 and were actually paid at the national minimum wage. Moreover, profit-sharing and performance bonuses were almost nonexistent in the franchise outlets. Consequently, contrary to the example of Wal-Mart in the United States (Carré, Holgate, and Tilly 2005), hypermarkets and very large retail outlets in France are mostly high-end stores, offering comparatively high wages and high average hourly pay rates. There is also a wide gap between occupations: low-wage work in large food stores affects 30 percent of female cashiers and 25 percent of food sales staff.

Table 6.3 Incidence of Low-Wage Work, by Sex, 1995 and 2003

	1995	2003	Male	Female
Private sector and state-owned firms in the competitive sector	12.7%	10.4%	8.9%	12.6%
Retail trade in general stores	20.1	18.0	15.8	19.1
Cashiers	36.8	29.1	27.8	30.3
Food sales staff	25.1	20.4	6.1	24.7
Furniture and household equipment sales staff	5.1	3.3	3.2	4.6
Supermarkets (including hard discounters)	24.2	26.4	13.1	33.2
Hypermarkets	17.3	11.2	10.2	11.7

Source: Authors' compilation from Institut Nationale de la Statistique et des Études Economiques (INSEE), Déclarations Annuelles des Données Sociales (DADS).
Note: Low-wage workers are defined as those earning less than two-thirds of the median net hourly wage of full-time staff. These figures are based on hourly wages and include collective bonuses but exclude profit-sharing schemes.

High Wages for Electrical and Electronics Sales Staff Conversely, only 3 percent of electrical and electronics sales staff are on low wages. In the four chains we studied, the average gross wage for a full-time worker was €2,000 to €2,500 (US$2,858 to US$3,573) per month (including performance bonuses and profit-sharing earnings), which was twice the monthly minimum wage. Because of differences in individual performances, gross wages of full-time staff ranged from €1,500 to €3,500 (US$2,144 to US$5,003), which are very high wages for low-skilled workers. Average wages are similar in high-end and low-end stores. Because the electronics sector is more active than the electrical market, the wages of electrical sales staff are 10 to 20 percent lower than for sellers of electronics. This has induced a slight gender gap among electrical and electronics vendors. These workers are also relatively young (see table 6.4).

Cashiers Are Mostly Part-Time Workers Cashiers and food sales staff are also young, but often work part-time, thus earning low monthly wages. So the monthly wage gap between cashiers or delicatessen sales staff and electrical and electronics staff is huge—by a factor of one to three or four—while these workers have similar educational levels.

Laws passed in the early 1990s led to a rapid extension of this part-

Table 6.4 Part-Time Work and Age Structure, 2003

	Part-Time	Younger Than Thirty Years Old	Older Than Fifty Years Old
Private sector and state-owned firms in the competitive sector	16.5%	18.3%	27.0%
Retail trade in general stores	48.0	43.0	19.9
Supermarkets (including hard discounters)	50.2	42.9	20.0
Hypermarkets	45.5	43.0	19.9
Cashiers	66.9	52.5	14.6
Food sales staff	34.6	33.8	23.1
Furniture and household equipment sales staff	18.4	32.5	13.5

Source: Authors' compilation from Institut Nationale de la Statistique et des Études Économiques (INSEE), Déclarations Annuelles des Données Sociales (DADS).

time work to cut social security contributions. Despite the subsequent removal of these laws, firms have kept up such practices.

UNIONS AND COLLECTIVE AGREEMENTS

Relatively high wages in some sectors of retail trade can a priori be directly linked to favorable collective agreements. But paradoxically, unions are weak in retail trade.

Lifeless Unions Union membership is particularly low in retail trade, about 2 percent compared to 5 percent in the private sector generally. Some structural factors have caused this phenomenon, such as high job turnover and a young workforce. The anti-union policies of some firms have also effectively kept union membership low, particularly in discount stores. For example, despite having forty-five workers (employers are legally obliged to organize elections of representative for firms with ten or more workers), a franchise store studied here had neither workers' representatives nor unionized workers. According to the store director:

> An employee who joins a union has to be fired immediately. We find a virtual fault as justification. In any case, the legal proceedings in labor tribunals [prud'hommes] are long.... Actually, I have no room for

maneuver in this area. I too am a salaried worker. If I do not fire a union member, I will be fired. But currently, the ambiance is good; nobody has tried to join a union.

However, in chains of integrated discount stores, unions are progressively gaining a hold. Food discount retailers have become an area of development for unions. But workers' representation is still particularly weak here: as a twenty-five-year-old cashier in a classic supermarket remarked, "There's also the defeatism. I told F., who had a problem, that we would all offer help and that we were right behind her. She said it wouldn't do any good and that she was worried about losing her job."

Numerous outlets have fewer than ten workers, and so the absence of a workers' representative is legal. The presence of a health and safety committee (mandatory in establishments with fifty or more workers) is exceptional. Franchise stores are union deserts. Interviews with workers revealed quite similar situations in high-end stores: one thirty-two-year-old cashier in a hypermarket said, "Few people join unions because of fear. I am a union member. Fear of losing your job takes people's spirit and consciousness away. . . . Even people with work-related illnesses don't talk about it, because they're afraid of losing their jobs and being stuck with loans to pay back."

Where they do exist in larger food stores and in nonfood retailing, unions and workers' representatives do not seem to be very active. Strikes are rare. At the store level, representatives assist workers in cases of individual sanctions; they may make some basic recommendations if a health and safety committee exists (in large outlets). Surprisingly, in some high-end food and electronics chains, unions are partly financed by employers (around €7 (US$10) per voter), who may also provide personal benefits (such as career advancement) for national representatives.

Unions have different objectives. Low union membership tends to favor first movers and unions that have less effect on employers. Consequently, the Confédération Générale du Travail (CGT), which historically is linked to the Communist Party and is France's largest union at the national level, has a strong public voice but is relatively weak in retailing. It should also be noted that in elections for staff representatives the main "unions" in retailing are "independent" lists of non-unionized workers, some of whom are directly linked to the company's management.

Finally, one reason for union lifelessness in high-end food and electrical and electronics stores could be the relatively high wages. Actually, most of the agreements at the national legal branch level propose minimum wages below the national minimum wage (the SMIC). They are therefore largely pointless, since agreements at the company level may provide earnings that are clearly above the SMIC. For pay, company or group agreements are indeed worth something. Different agreements exist within a group: for example, the Carrefour group includes Carrefour hypermarkets, Champion supermarkets, and Ed super discount stores. Table 6.5 shows key elements of the collective agreements in each chain, with Carrefour hypermarkets offering far better hourly wages and benefits than Ed.

In Carrefour hypermarkets, a cashier with one year of tenure earned at least 25 percent more than the hourly SMIC in 2005, as did cashiers in most hypermarket chains in France. Actually, hypermarket chains provide various bonuses to workers with minimal tenure, such as holiday bonuses and a thirteen-month wage, or profit-sharing. Workers also receive bonuses linked to the performance of their store and chain. They also receive a 100 percent premium if they work during exceptional opening hours on Sundays. For workers who work regularly on Sundays, most company agreements include small bonuses (about 5 percent). This leads to important variations in compensation between stores and from one year to another. For example, in one outlet we studied, the collective "store" bonus was zero in 2006, compared to 15 percent in 2005.

According to the REPONSE survey of 2005, 75 percent of integrated hypermarkets (90 percent of the workforce) provide such collective bonuses. Therefore, the share of low-wage workers in very large retailers is concentrated among new hires and students. Large chains of integrated stores have also developed worker shareholding schemes. For example, workers own about 15 percent of the capital of Auchan.

Given their small size, profit-sharing or performance bonuses are not mandatory in franchise discount outlets, and few exist. Workers at integrated stores benefit from mandatory schemes, but these are less favorable and more restrictive (compare Ed and Carrefour in table 6.5). It is likely that in the absence of national minimum standards, wages in these stores would be lower. But the legal minimum wage does not seem to be an obstacle to employment in these outlets. Indeed, the logic of such stores is to provide minimal services and as-

Table 6.5 Working Time and Wages in Three French Nonfranchise Subsidiaries of the Carrefour Group, 2005

	Carrefour Hypermarkets	Champion Supermarkets	Ed Super Discount Stores
Working time			
Full-time (except managers)	35 hours per week (effective work) + 1.75 hours for breaks		
Minimum part-time (except for students and for medical reasons)	29 hours + 1.45 hours for breaks	28 hours + 1.40 hours for breaks	26 hours + 1.30 hours for breaks
Maximum weekly positive or negative variation in worked hours (except overtime hours)	+/−6 hours (full-time) +/−4 hours (part-time)	+5/−7 hours full-time +/−4 hours (part-time)	+13/−35 hours full-time +/−4hours (part-time)
Paid vacations		At least 2.5 days per month	
Benefits			
Vacation bonus	0.5 × basic monthly wage (if working at least three months between January and June in a Carrefour hypermarket)	0.1 to 0.5 × basic monthly wage (if tenure greater than one year in the Carrefour group)	Less than 0.15 × reference monthly wage (if tenure greater than one year in the Carrefour group)
Annual bonus	One basic monthly wage (if working at least three months between June and December in a Carrefour hypermarket)	One basic monthly wage (if tenure greater than one year in a Champion supermarket)	One basic monthly wage (if tenure greater than one year in the Carrefour group)

Collective bonuses for nonmanagerial workers	0% in 2005 (linked to turnover performance; tenure greater than three months in a Carrefour hypermarket)	Proportional to hours worked, about €400 for a full-timer in 2005 (linked to turnover, theft levels)	Two types (linked to turnover, theft levels): 0 to 8% (all workers) and 0 to 8% (tenure greater than one year in the Carrefour group)
Profit-sharing scheme, Carrefour group		6.5% in 2005 (tenure greater than three months)	
Wages			
Minimum gross hourly wage for a cashier		€8.03 (= minimum wage)	
Minimum gross hourly remuneration for a cashier if tenure less than one year	€10.17 (= 127% minimum wage)	About €9.85 (= 123% minimum wage)	€9.79 (= 122% minimum wage)
Minimum gross hourly wage for food staff if tenure less than three months	Linked to the counter's performance, but at least €9.55 (= 119% minimum wage)	€8.03 (= minimum wage)	(no delicatessen)
Health insurance paid	About 2%	About 2%	1% to 2.6%
Employer participation in social activities	0.5% of total wages	0.5% of total wages	0.45% of total wages
Other significant benefits	Six to nine paid days per year for taking care of sick children	—	—

Sources: Company collective agreements and authors' calculations.

sistance with a minimal workforce; despite increases in the minimum wage, profit rates in this sector are high, and super discounters are constantly planning expansion; given the characteristics of customers, Keynesian effects of the minimum wage are probably strongest in this submarket.

The generosity of company agreements seems proportional to the rate of union membership. However, the causality is not so clear. Even in hypermarkets, unions have never been able to conduct strikes with a significant proportion of workers. It is hard to believe that such limited power could massively influence wage policies, even if the large rents associated with French retail regulations should lead to less pressure on firms, and hence on wages. High-end retailing could be a high-road subsector, but unions are not the main reason. Our interviews with top human resource managers suggested that high-end chains have their own interests in providing relatively high wages. The next section examines these interests, which explain the coexistence of clearly "low-road" discount outlets and high-end chains.

The national food retail branch agreement is more useful for working time arrangements. The share of part-time jobs had been continuously rising but is now decreasing because the collective branch agreement increased the minimum number of hours worked from twenty-two to twenty-six (except for students), and the thirty-five-hour working week has lowered the full-time limit. Actually, all workers in food retailing now officially work thirty-five hours per week. The 2001 agreement sets out a statutory reference of 1,600 hours of work per year, computed on an annual basis and excluding overtime (see chapter 2). Employers thus do not have to pay overtime hours until the average number of hours worked in a year exceeds the contractual limit. The implementation of the thirty-five-hour week provided an opportunity to formalize such practices in the sector.

It is harder to generalize in the electrical and electronics sector. Firms operating in this market are covered by a variety of collective branch agreements. However, for wages at least, most national agreements can be considered not binding, since the pay of sales staff is far higher than the minimum wage. In hypermarkets, electrical and electronics sales staff may be considered the "aristocracy" of shop assistants and are numerically limited; they are not the priority for workers' representatives. In more specialized stores, unions are present at the national level, but only occasionally at the store level. In our case studies, health and safety committees were inactive. The main concerns of unions are wages and, more precisely, incentive schemes. Actually, most firm agreements have introduced profit-sharing schemes and partial percentage fees for sales staff. As competition between firms to keep or capture the best salespersons remains strong, firms may be seen to be converging on best practices in the area of working conditions, including the thirty-five-hour week.

HIGH-PERFORMANCE WORK

In the retail trade, working conditions are first of all determined by sales flows: in electronic goods, customers are unfailingly attracted by new technology products sold at the most attractive prices; in food retailing, zoning rules have caused continuous rush hours in super- and hypermarkets. For example, the hypermarkets studied here had an average of between 10,000 customers on Tuesdays and 25,000 on Saturdays.

As a matter of fact, stores selling electrical and electronics goods, hypermarkets, and a majority of classic supermarkets have extended opening hours, not only to absorb massive customer flows but for the convenience of customers. Stores are also open five Sundays per year (more in tourist zones) and on nonworking days. Ongoing reforms will liberalize opening on Sunday. Despite these schedules, stores are not able to handle both significant customer assistance and shorter waiting times.

Strikingly, French retailing has exceptional labor productivity.[9] According to Eurostat, in 2003 the value-added per worker in French retailing was about 30 percent higher than the EU-15 average (see table 6.6).

A corollary of this high productivity is fewer jobs. The retailing share of total employment is 20 percent lower in France than the EU-15 average. It should be noted that there is a correlation between low employment in retailing and the level of entry barriers (table 6.6). Even if we do not have robust statistics, productivity seems high in outlets selling electrical/electronics goods, while the food distribution subsector leads in retailing efficiency (MGI 2002).

DECOMPOSING THE EXCEPTIONAL PRODUCTIVITY OF FRENCH FOOD RETAILING

Given that standard supermarkets and giant stores are retail fixtures in both France and the United States, as well as long opening hours,

Table 6.6 Employment in Retailing Nomenclature of Economic Activities in the European Communities (NACE 52) in the European Union, 2003

	Employment (in Thousands)	Value-Added per Worker (in Thousands of Euros)	Percent of Total National Workforce	Barriers to Entry
Denmark	2.289	27.9	8.0%	8%
Germany	184	28.8	7.0	10
France	1.538	35.9	6.4	12
Netherlands	626	23.8	8.0	3
United Kingdom	2.920	24.4	10.7	0

Source: EUROSTAT, OECD (graph 1).

it is possible to compare large French and American retailers. Assuming that one euro equals one dollar (as it did in 2004), the value of sales per hour worked in large stores is about twice as high in France as in the United States.

A first, obvious point concerns price differences. The anticompetitive laws should have caused higher prices in France. However, their cumulative impact is estimated to be less than 5 to 10 percent (Canivet 2004). A second source of productivity could be the high level of the minimum wage (and thus of labor costs), which would lead to choices of fewer services per store and then less labor-intensive organizations (Gadrey and Jany-Catrice 2000; Piketty 1998). Nevertheless, the only significant service that is not available in France is bagging: baggers and greeters, who are the lowest-paid workers in American retailing, simply do not exist in France. Thus, employment does differ owing to the minimum wage, by up to 10 percent (for United States figures, see Carré, Holgate, and Tilly 2005). However, for a similar surface area, retailers in France use more labor (in terms of hours worked) than in the United States (see table 6.7), even though most French stores are closed at night and on Sundays, unlike American stores. The managers we interviewed thought that, because of high productivity, the minimum legal wage was not too high for their sector, and again, the Keynesian effect of the minimum wage seems dominant in this market, especially for discount stores. The minimum wage should have more consequences in other retail sectors.

Table 6.7 Labor Performances of Large French and U.S. Food Retailers, 2004 (€1 = $1)

	Annual Sales per Sales Square Meter	Sales per Hour Worked	Workers per Ten Sales Square Meter	Hours Worked per Sales Square Meter	Gross Margin	Total Labor Costs per Hour
French super-hypermarkets	€9,800	€200	0.33	50	21 to 23%	€13.70
United States supermarkets/centers	$4,200 to $6,500	$120 to $140	0.25 to 0.35	35 to 46	25 to 29	$12.10 (2005)[a]
Wal-Mart US	$4,700	$110	0.25	42	24	$10.40 (2005)

Sources: French retailers: *Données sociales de la FCD* and Institut Nationale de la Statistique et des Études Economiques (INSEE); U.S. retailers: Food Marketing Institute, *Progressive Grocer*, Food Industry Center, Dube, Eidlin, and Lester (2005); Wal-Mart: estimates using various Wal-Mart reports (accessed at http://www.walmartstores.com).

Notes: French supermarket = food store greater than 400 square meters; U.S. supermarket = food store turnover more than $2 million (about 500 square meters or greater). Data for France come from exhaustive or representative surveys. Data for the United States are corporate figures from Wal-Mart or results from private panels, except for total labor costs estimated by Dube, Eidlin, and Lester (2005).

[a] Retailers with 1,000 or more workers.

Third, high labor productivity is the mirror of the exceptional sales per square meter in France, up to €30,000 (US$42,886). Super- and hypermarkets are often overcrowded between 5:00 PM and 8:00 PM and on Saturdays or Sundays (if stores are open). When all checkout positions are open, waiting in line thirty minutes is common in France, and waiting for the rayons traditionnels is systematic. According to high-end store directors, they cannot physically install more checkout positions and the associated cashier jobs or increase staff in rayons traditionnels. Customer flows are the main organizational concern of managers.[10] Consequently, services per square meter are similar to the United States, but assistance per customer by French retailers is lower.

The zoning rules that have limited the opening of new outlets and the expansion of existing stores are the main causes of the relative deficit in retail food stores. Marianne Bertrand and Francis Kramarz's (2002) results support this argument. Using a unique database of regional variations in decisions on store creations, they find that the first zoning laws have slowed down employment growth in retailing (food and nonfood).[11] For example, the sales per full-time-equivalent worker in a city of 22,000 inhabitants with a sole supermarket are 50 to 60 percent higher than in another store owned by the same chain but operating in a three-city area with a competitor in each city.

To conclude, most of the apparently striking productivity of workers in large French food retailers is linked to real performance. Conversely, despite recent improvements in American retail productivity, which have contributed to growth in the United States (McGuckin, Spiegelman, and van Ark 2005), we believe that American retailers still have room to enhance productivity. Indeed, stores in France have built particular business, organizational, and human resource models that make workers hyperproductive. Our case studies reveal a continuum of models from giant hypermarkets with a large variety of goods, some assistance, and relatively high wages to discount stores with limited choice and poor services.

How can the high productivity of French workers be explained?

Assessing the French High Performance Puzzle

Hiring: From Discrimination in High-End Food Retailing to the Search for "Geeks" in Electronics Sales   A first explanation for the high productivity of French retail workers is the selected hiring process in the different outlets. In large food outlets, store managers receive hundreds of unsolicited applications (via mail or the Internet) or unemployed persons selected by the ANPE (National Public Employment Service). Store managers often choose females who are in fragile personal situations. For example, in a store located in a city with few job opportunities, single-parent women are preferred because keeping their job is a necessity. But in a store on the city outskirts, such women are considered a source of absenteeism (due to children's illnesses) and so are banned. Given the general shortage of qualified labor, specific skills requirements are relaxed in recruiting staff. Generally, recruiters search for workers with few other employment possibilities who will therefore put up with the working conditions and apply themselves to the work at hand, thus guaranteeing maximum productivity.

For food vendors, "commercial" discrimination along racial line seems "normal" in high-end stores and is "justified by customers' preferences"; black people are rare in meat, delicatessen, or cheese departments but accepted at fish counters. For cashiers in high-end stores, ethnic discrimination is also clear, but it disappears if the worker is well educated; black or North African students with master's degrees are welcome because they are appreciated for the quality of their commercial skills, especially with affluent customers. Some of the chains we studied have signed "diversity charters," but we found that these had had poor impact at the store level, contrary to real efforts to employ some heavily disabled persons.

In fact, the job market is segmented for store workers who have direct contact with the public, and this is associated with a segmented sales market (affluent customers versus poor customers). This segmentation is even more visible in super discount stores, where minorities are massively present both as workers and as customers. Here store directors face some hiring difficulties because of the negative image of super discount stores. Recruitment is based on the labor market segment in which employees have fewer outside options, and thus store managers focus on hiring low-educated and ethnic minority workers.

For electrical and electronics sales staff, each manager supervises the hiring process, which is validated by the store director. The sales staff are recruited according to their interest in entering the sales field and on the basis of their sales skills rather than their specific technical skills. Actually, sales abilities have become crucial. While being specialized in audio or photographic products was a prerequisite ten years ago, the rapid pace of innovation and product "convergence" (for example, all-in-one goods) has dramatically accelerated the obsolescence of such skills. Education is not the basic criterion for employers. For technological goods, personal interest (in electronic games, for instance) is a key criterion, while sales staff recommendations are also a source of recruitment. The very high-end chain we studied could be more selective about educational background because it received about four thousand unsolicited external applications per store each year.

Discount stores also offer the very rare opportunity of high-wage jobs to relatively low-educated persons. Most workers were hired on permanent, full-time contracts in the four chains we studied. There was no discrimination according to race, but again, we observed partial gender specialization: women were more present in white-goods departments (washing machines, and so on).

In-Service Training to Ensure Immediate Availability A second source of high performance is the brief training that workers receive. In food retailing, initial training is very limited and mostly informal. In the four case studies, after a rapid presentation on the "in-house culture," cashiers were trained directly on a cash register by senior cashiers for a couple of days. If a cashier already had experience, such training might take just a few minutes. However, one of the case study stores offered workers optional training in posture and movement, provided by outsider trainers.[12] Some other stores also had in-house posture and movement training. All the chain stores we studied provided continuous training in customer reception and conflict management.

Globally, training expenditure in electronics retailing is high in the different outlets, accounting for 2.5 to 4 percent of labor costs, including training in standard, specialized sales techniques. For example, training can be provided for six days for two or three employees who will become internal trainers. Internal trainers have to be regularly informed of progress in electrical and electronics goods via intranet, which provides more than one hundred training programs. Internal trainers pass on information to colleagues at "training and work meetings." Every three months there is an evaluation of technical and sales training programs. Because this sector provides up-to-date products, there is not enough time to compile internal training material. In addition, affluent customers generally learn about product characteristics through the internet before making purchases: so basic training in a high-end chain is provided by suppliers that specify forthcoming products to the internal trainers or directly to the sales staff.

Illegal Practices   Another source of high performance by large retailers lies in the use of illegal practices. These seem "natural," as managers described them during interviews, even if we still find significant differences between chains. Lack of respect for the compulsory medical visits is just one example, among others, of illegal practices in high-end establishments. We also witnessed some flagrant, prohibited behavior: for example, canceled breaks, employer pressure not to declare work-related injuries (in two stores), and workers who were coerced into coming to work even while on sick leave. In another store, there were clear mobbing practices—pushing targeted workers to resign or excluding children whose parents participated in strikes from company vacation camps. Another generalized illegal practice was expecting middle managers to work very long hours, about sixty hours per week (the European limit is forty-eight). Work-life balance problems were acute for such staff. It should also be noted that neither store directors nor workers recalled any labor inspections having taken place.

Illegal practices are also used positively to favor electrical and electronics staff. To optimize pay, staff may resort to such practices with the implicit complicity of their employers: for instance, in one chain we studied, if sales were flat, some employees volunteered to be ill and obtained medical certificates under false pretenses. They then received 80 percent of their average wage from the national social security program. Under this arrangement, the remaining shop assistants increased their own personal turnover and hence their wages. This illegal practice was not costly for the employer and ensured higher revenue for the sales staff.

That said, the main causes of the outstanding productivity among French retailers are to be found in workplace organization and technology as well as incentive payment schemes.

Computerized and Permanent Control of Checkout Productivity
Again, because of the strict zoning rules, numerous stores face mas-

sive customer flows, especially on Saturdays. The efficient checkout of customers is then crucial. About 25 percent of workers in food stores are cashiers. In large stores (typically greater than 1,500 square meters), most cashiers are specialized. Productivity norms are strict, ranging from twenty to forty scanned goods per minute. In case of exceptional customer flows, managers can help with bagging and thus increase the pace of cashiers' work, or they can replace a cashier.

Following the collective branch agreements, cashiers have a three-minute paid break per hour. Using individual records in three stores, we estimated that in food retail outlets a cashier handles about 1,100 pounds per hour. In the chains we studied, cashiers received their own daily productivity figures compared to the ones of their colleagues. Some stores ran competitions for the highest sales per cashier. However, wages were never connected to individual performance, partly so as to avoid workers stressing this indicator too much and forgetting other tasks that would ensure quality of service. To achieve the high-end objective, many formal and informal tasks were added, from the classic SBAM (Smile, "Bonjour," "Au revoir," "Merci") to bagging goods for senior citizens. Also, one essential task is to stop theft. Coping with these contradictory formal and informal tasks can be a source of psychological strain.

"Mystery shoppers" and "mystery shoplifters" check that cashiers are following the required, minimal job specifications; failure to do so may be cause for dismissal. Hierarchical control (including video) is also permanent; other cashiers have to control their colleagues. In fact, food retailing managers aim to hire employees who are ready to suffer such severe work constraints.

Autonomy in Electronic Goods Retailing   While cashiers are oversupervised, electronic sales staff are autonomous. The forms of compensation determine the working atmosphere in the sector, as well as the choice of working hours. Because pay on a commission basis leads to real rivalry, sales staff are managed through informal strategies and subjective rules of the game. Intense competition may result as colleagues become rivals. The working atmosphere can apparently become quite tense, although there are informal processes that set workers' schedules in order to limit competition between them. Each worker's objective is to work Saturdays, when about 30 percent of sales occur. High-performing salespersons organize these bargaining processes, whereas managers just ensure that at least one worker is present at any time.

One high-end chain stood out as an exception: in its unionized stores, sales staff tried to avoid working during stressful periods, since wages were not correlated to sales. In this case, priority depended on seniority, so that less-experienced workers generally worked when there were the most customers. But in a non-unionized store of the same chain closed on Sunday, which we studied in depth, working on Saturdays and Mondays (days with higher customer flows) and on the three other days was mandatory. This is an illegal practice, because the collective agreement imposed two consecutive days off per week.

In the different chains, the sales process was the same, whether salespersons earned commissions or not. It appeared to be a subtle mixture combining sales strategies, know-how, and technical skills: salespersons were constantly analyzing how customers' behavior revealed their desire to buy. Except for white goods, product innovation had a substantial impact on job content. For example, at a constant sales value of LCD or plasma TV, the 30 percent drop in prices between 2004 and 2005 led to about 20 percent more transactions (the TVs bought being 10 percent larger), leading to more intensive work in this department. At the same time, self-service buying increased dramatically in the mature market for MP3 products, lowering pressure on workers.

Flexible Working Time and Hard Working Conditions to Ensure Maximum Productivity in Food Outlets While sales staff in electronics retailing have room for maneuver in their work schedules, compulsory flexible working time is the rule in food retailing. All workers in the large food retailers (including discount stores) have thirty-five-hour-week contracts, but this limit is not binding for the 40 percent of cashiers who are part-time workers. According to our interviews, some (nonstudent) cashiers wished to work more: the problem was less acute in local labor markets where students provided extra workers during evenings and on Saturdays. But according to managers, part-time work was a requirement to adjust staff levels and labor costs. Indeed, higher customer flows were concentrated in only fifteen hours of the week. The national branch agreement has fixed that workers should be informed of their schedules seven days in advance. But in reality, we observed workers often being informed just a few hours ahead. Moreover, employers may offer extra hours to part-timers (generally up to 10 percent above usual hours) paid at a normal rate; in the four high-end stores we studied, these hours could be decided at any time. This flexibility of working time, however, had adverse effects on workers, who were mainly women with long commuting times. Scheduling problems were even more acute in food sales occupations, and work schedules were harsh. One shop assistant described her schedule:

> I do mornings. I arrive at work and deal with orders at 4:00 or 5:00 AM, depending on the day. Monday is stock-taking day. On Saturday evenings and Monday mornings, I do the department. We put the stock-taking tags on everything and do all the stock lists. We have to put in the orders and then put the products away in order to maintain the cold chain, so that everything is chilled. After that, I go to the department, at 8:30 or 8:45 AM, because I have a fifteen-minute break, just for coffee. Afterwards I go back down again and add up the stock lists with the department manager and then, around midday, we normally leave.

The high productivity in super- and hypermarkets is achieved by innovative workplace organizations. Stores use supply-chain management and merchandise management. Inventory levels have been lowered. Information and Communication Technology helps to achieve this goal and to improve the control and supervision of workers. Just-in-time processes also function in the sales areas. Space in shelving for each product has been reduced to increase variety or to cut sales areas. Thus, workers have to fill shelving more regularly. Work intensity for cashiers is high in discount stores: the norm is forty scanned articles per minute, compared to twenty to thirty in high-end stores. This rate is sustainable since memorizing the bar code position is easy (indeed, bar codes on own-brand products are located in the same place on all products to facilitate the scanning process) and the products do not change (there are only 100 to 200 new ones per year, out of an average of 1,500).[13] In addition, multitasking is imposed: cashiers have to stock shelves, clean the store, and load garbage bins. Monitoring by management is permanent: cameras may control both potential shoplifters and workers: for example, the official title of one chain's directors was "inspector." But working conditions are not necessarily worse than in high-end stores: in particular, super discount stores are typically open from 9:00 AM to 7:00 PM, compared to 10:00 PM for hypermarkets. Work schedules are more predictable, so female workers have fewer problems combining their work and private lives. Despite lower wages, these nuanced working conditions and the poor outside options associated with labor market segmentation explain why worker turnover is globally similar in low- and high-end retailers.

Scheduling systems also enhance productivity by increasing the checkout speed and aligning staff and local production to demand. Staff schedules are defined in fifteen-minute slices. Computerized scheduling systems use historical data on customer flows and can be fine-tuned to account for everything from weather conditions to TV programs. The management of checkout operations aims ideally to eliminate slack by ensuring that customer waiting remains strictly positive. This technology has been used in hypermarkets since the mid-1990s (see Prunier-Poulmaire 2000). Nonetheless, schedules are still defined manually in supermarkets because computer systems are not efficient for small organizations.

HARMFUL WORKING CONDITIONS BUT SOME HIGH ROADS

Large retailers have thus developed organizations close to the ones used in manufacturing. These work organizations drive the working conditions and have an impact on workers' health. They are also one of the keys to understanding why some chains offer wages that are not rock-bottom.

WORKING CONDITIONS: CASHIERS AND FOOD STAFF VERSUS ELECTRONICS SALESPERSONS

Our case studies of two hypermarkets and two high-end supermarkets include in-depth ergonomic observations that highlighted the consequences of various customer relations on working conditions.

Cashiers have to cope with high-pressure work rates brought on by the drive for productivity and monotonous work carried out under strict hierarchical control: one item must be handled every two or three seconds, and one client every three minutes. As a twenty-seven-year-old cashier in a classic hypermarket noted, "It's really tiring. The job is repetitive and insignificant. I no longer look at what I do. I can escape or daydream at times. I'm used to the gestures and think of nothing. It's a way of coping."

Poor checkout desk design associated with the physical work environment (which may include cold, drafts, noise, and so on) makes the work disagreeable. Psychological and mental demands are strong, as shown by customer relations. Cashiers often have to put up with troublesome remarks by customers who are in a hurry and rarely understanding, while management orders are often contradictory; in the resulting double bind, "clients are always right, even if you know you are because you're following regulations to the letter." The job is also characterized by very limited freedom and a negative social image: "As soon as five or six people are standing in line, people suffer," commented a twenty-five-year-old cashier in a classic hypermarket. "They don't understand, they see us as robots and not as individuals. You always have to work faster." In super- and hypermarkets, multiskilling is informal. It is imposed, not chosen, on the spur of the moment to meet the store's immediate needs. As a result, rather than raising employees' interest in their work by breaking the routine, the imposition of multiskilling creates anxiety, since workers do not always know what they must do.

Delicatessen sales staff face particularly hard working conditions. Apart from the early hours, the factors contributing to harsh conditions at cold-cuts counters include intense physical demands (carrying loads, repetitive product handling, frequent movement in the store) and poorly adapted equipment and intensified work (product diversification and increasing hygiene requirements due to recent European regulations, severe time pressure, understaffing). Workers have to develop their own strategies for regulating their work to avoid the risks linked to equipment and products and preserve their own health and safety, while respecting customers' demands. But such strategies remain uncertain, especially because of the high work rates and the strict deadlines. We have measured a delicatessen sales vendor walking two kilometers per hour and handling twenty plates that weigh four kilograms on average.

An example of severe working conditions for delicatessen sales staff was an operator who worked from 7:00 AM to 11:30 AM in a 37 to 41°F refrigerator. Her tasks consisted of making an average of five hundred sandwiches of all kinds before selling them at lunchtime (11:30 AM to 1:00 PM) in the shopping center as an informal cashier and vendor. The workstation of this female operator had previously been located in a food laboratory next to the rayon traditionnel, and the sandwiches were sold in the delicatessen department. Subsequently, the store management decided to create a "workstation" in a refrigerator in order to redevelop the "sandwich area," achieve sales objectives, and better respect food regulations (such as the cold chain) rather than labor regulations. Since then, this "female sandwich" no longer had any contacts with her coworkers, was not able to take any breaks because of her isolated situation, and had no social recognition. She worked for one and a half hours as a cashier without any legal protection or any bonus, and her physical and mental health was declining (constant colds, musculoskeletal disorders in her legs, symptoms of depression). Moreover, when her son suffered from meningitis, the manager refused to allow her to take a break to meet him at the hospital.

Among electronics sales staff, significant differences exist in work strategies, depending on the types of remuneration, which shape how the job's demands are accepted. Salaried workers on commission described themselves as clients' "hunters." All contact was reduced to a sales transaction, which had to be "quickly done": "I've got used to jumping at clients."

The majority of salespersons believed that clients had changed considerably in recent years, becoming more demanding and better informed: "They've mainly become more aggressive and impatient." These changes had modified working conditions. Customer contact was viewed with ambivalence, as a source of satisfaction but also of stress and fatigue. A twenty-seven-year-old salesperson in a high-end electronics had this to say:

> On Saturdays, clients surround me like a whirlwind. It gives me vertigo.... They stare at you, get impatient, push into you, follow you around everywhere for fear of losing you and argue amongst each other. It's unbearable ... a sort of tidal wave. I can't describe it, but there are days ... when it's really frightening.... I'm a search engine: people click on me to hear my sales pitch. There used to be dialogue—now you're just a reference catalog.

The dazzling speed of product change and Internet access had also affected workers' views of the job: "Digitization killed the job, and the taste and passion I used to have for the work." Employees felt a high level of stress and regularly suffered from anxiety. They admitted that conflicting relations with clients, tension among colleagues, pressure to raise sales, and long working hours each day all had a negative impact on them, affecting their private lives.

"Fifteen years ago, this was small-time retailing," said one salesperson. Shop staff were autonomous, they met traveling salespersons, and they were responsible for placing orders. Today new forms of work organization have emerged: buying is centralized, and staff are directed purely at selling. Some chain stores, however, have recently started to make sales staff check out their customers' purchases in order to lighten the load at checkout desks.

Occupational Health Issues in Low-End Versus High-End Stores

The optimization of the production process has intensified work for retail and intermediary staff, including cashiers, sales staff, and workers in self-service areas. Besides the standard pressures, such as being on one's feet for long periods (table 6.8), new psychological and physical strains increased during the 1990s.

These trends are confirmed by the recent evolution of occupational injuries and illnesses in retailing. According to France's social security authorities, the rate of occupational injury increased by 20 percent between 2000 and 2003 (CNAM 2005). At the same time, the severity of these injuries (measured in average working days lost) also rose by 20 percent. Illnesses, especially musculoskeletal disorders, are growing by 20 percent per year. Occupational doctors working in the stores have confirmed these trends. These problems recently attracted attention in food retailing at the branch level. The Federation of Commerce and Distribution signed an agreement with trade unions in 2003 on workplace health and safety. It recognized the particular risks of some occupations in the sector, as highlighted by the medical literature (Leclerc et al. 2004; Van der Windt et al. 2000). As a result, the period between two compulsory medical visits was cut to one year for these occupations, compared to the standard two years. However, our case studies show that these statutory measures are not applied: workers on short-term contracts were not protected, and medical visits for permanent cashiers generally occurred every three years. In addition, we observed that a majority of delicatessen vendors and many cashiers suffered from musculoskeletal disorders, but only a small minority of workers actually claimed to

Table 6.8 Increasing Physical and Psychological Strains for French Retail Staff, 1984 to 2005

Percent of Workers Claiming to Face:	1984	1992	1998	2005	Supermarket Including Discount	Hypermarket
Being on one's feet for long periods	75%	77%	76%	75%	76%	64%
Long or recurrent walks	16	34	45	38	47	49
Handling heavy loads	29	47	57	60	73	66
Painful postures	12	27	46	33	51	43
Psychological strain						
Irregular job rotation linked to company activity	n.a.	n.a.	29	30	40	30
Not being able to perform job correctly because of insufficient staff	n.a.	23	29	32	38	32
Tensions with customers	n.a.	39	49	44	40	44
Irregular schedules	18	20	29	37	48	30
Working on Sundays	14	19	17	17	19	18

Source: Authors' compilation from French working conditions surveys.

suffer from them. Workers may have suffered from muscle and joint pains but did not associate these with their work. Others were aware of the cause, but afraid of losing their jobs if they admitted such pains to company doctors. According to our interviews, company doctors were also reluctant to declare illnesses officially, because French labor law states that an employer may dismiss a worker who is recognized as disabled.

A recent epidemiological survey found that 12 percent of female workers in stores suffer severe mental depression (Dousson et al. 2002). Depression is also an increasing source of absenteeism, affecting 10 percent of cashiers. We found no significant disparities on this point between high-end and low-end outlets. However, workers in one high-end hypermarket seemed to be significantly less stressed and to suffer fewer illnesses than those in a second high-end hypermarket, though we did not observe any differences in workload. Actually, the former store had developed a type of stress management, with systematic controls of workers and pressure not only coming from the store director but being put on him as well. Thus, the quality of the management as defined by top managers seemed to be an important determinant of workers' health and satisfaction. Surprisingly, however, insensitive management did not seem to be associated with higher labor turnover or absenteeism, nor with better productive or financial performances.

The case studies confirmed that the health of checkout staff is indeed worrying: the cumulative impact of biomechanical, managerial, and commercial constraints threatened their physical and psychological health. Repetitive work carried out under strong time pressure, carrying heavy loads, and the poor adaptation of workstations all contributed to spreading musculoskeletal disorders:

> I think I will get my carpian canal operated on. . . . It's worst for your arms, neck, and shoulders. They are always being used in the same way. It wakes me up at night. I haven't seen the company doctor, but I've done an X-ray, and an ultrasound scan. . . . The trouble is that it means taking fifteen days off. I'm on a short-term contract [CDD], and this isn't the time to be ill.

Special time arrangements (unexpectedly longer hours during work surges, the uncertain organization of breaks) and the lack of organized multiskilling all led to more illness: "Saturdays, we finish at 9:00 PM. I'm exhausted," said a thirty-year-old hypermarket cashier. "As it's back to work on Monday mornings, we've only got Sunday to rest."

Apart from purely biomechanical problems, company doctors worried about the problems arising from other practices: banning the consumption of liquids while working (leading to cystitis and other urinary problems), favoritism, privileges, sexual or moral favors, and harassment. Sleep and digestive problems and recourse to psychotropic drugs can all be linked to these practices, which come on top of the violence of arguments with clients, tense relations with management, and limited social support. Yet job insecurity or precariousness seemed to prevent work accidents and work-related illness from being declared and were an obstacle to the recognition of health problems: "I'll tell you, but you absolutely mustn't pass it on," cautioned a thirty-nine-year-old cashier in a hypermarket. "If they knew that I'm not well, I would lose my job. This is all I have to feed two children whose father regularly forgets to pay child support." The harshness of such work-related constraints affects employees' personal lives.

In-depth studies have revealed that repeated work accidents and illnesses are very often linked for food sales staff to the use of their normal working instruments (such as meat slicers), the lack of protective equipment (not having gloves to operate pizza ovens leads to numerous burns), and poor knowledge of cleaning products (causing allergies and burns). Awareness of the risks of accidents and other health issues is generally low and minimized by all company staff (employees as well as management). In short, staff working at cold-cut counters have even more difficult working conditions than cashiers. But irregular hours and frequent and unexpected extensions of shifts discourage workers at cold-cuts counters from requesting transfers to cash registers. An examination of staff characteristics in the stores we studied partly explains this phenomenon: delicatessen staff largely consisted of single women who were often isolated and had children to care for. Their personal situation could not easily be reconciled with the demands of fluctuating part-time work, which was often imposed, even if accompanied by higher monthly wages.

The ergonomic study revealed some permanent physical characteristics for electronics vendors. Among the inherent constraints, workers in this sector cited handling heavy loads, much standing (pedometric measures indicated that the average salesperson walked only one kilometer per hour), and a noisy environment (around eighty-five decibels, except in one store that sought to provide customers with a pleasant environment and so salespersons were also protected from noise). Up to two-thirds of electronics sales workers claimed to suffer from backache and to regularly consume anti-inflammatory drugs. Women workers were more concerned about blood circulation disorders and leg pains. That said, the company's official social indicators of the working atmosphere described a generally satisfactory situation: according to these figures, staff turnover was minimal, workers were generally in good health, absenteeism was very low, and there were very few accidents.

Turnover

According to human resource managers, these working conditions, compelled flexibility in scheduling, and the need to manage the work-life balance are the main sources of the high—and growing—labor turnover in large hypermarkets (table 6.9).

In addition, workforces in super- and hypermarkets are seg-

Table 6.9 Labor Turnover in Super- and Hypermarkets

	Hyper- and Supermarket, Including Super-Discount		Total Private Sector	
	2000 to 2002	2003 to 2005	2000 to 2002	2003 to 2005
Labor turnover	67.4%	69.3%	40.1%	40.5%
Fewer than fifty workers	66.7	67.9	42.5	42.8
More than 250 workers	53.1	53.4	32.0	31.9
Entries on normal contracts	15.2	15.9	26.8	27.2
Entries on short-term contracts	79.4	79.7	64.1	64.9
Exits from short-term contracts	68.4	69.0	55.2	55.3

Source: Déclarations Mensuelles de Main-d'Oeuvre-Enquête Mensuelles de Main-d'Oeuvre (DMMO-EMMO) French Ministry of Labor, authors' calculations.

mented. The high turnover rate contrasts with the 80 percent proportion of workers with tenure of more than a year and the 80 percent with permanent contracts. It may be noted that because of significant "natural" labor turnover in all types of stores (about 15 percent for permanent workers), all of the human resource managers we interviewed thought that France's strict employment protection legislation had no significant impact on their business.

But the main management concern is the absenteeism in high-end stores. Hard working conditions and related health problems induce important, unexpected rates of absenteeism, up to 25 percent among the checkout cashiers in one of the hypermarkets. In "lean" organizations that deal with large customer flows, the absence of a food vendor or a cashier can rapidly induce congestion at the rayons traditionnels or even the outlet. Absenteeism is of less critical concern in discount stores because all workers in these stores carry out multiple tasks and service is poor.

UNDERSTANDING THE HIGH ROAD

Overall, working conditions for cashiers and food sales staff in high-end food retailers are as hard as in discount stores. Yet classic supermarkets and hypermarkets offer better hourly wages to basic workers than do discount stores. What are the sources of this difference? Why do high-end stores take this high road? Our case studies reveal numerous complementary factors that explain why it is important that wages in these stores be higher than in discount chains.

First, in discount outlets the relative predictability of work schedules allows part-time workers to perform a second part-time job to ensure a decent monthly wage. This is impracticable for workers in super- and hypermarkets because of the unpredictability of work schedules, which also causes them difficulties in managing the work-life balance. To provide cashiers and sales staff with a minimal income—or the possibility, for example, of paying an occasional babysitter while they work some evenings—these stores must pay hourly wages that are above the legal minimum wage.

Second, maintaining their public image is important to high-end outlets. The risk in paying their workers poor wages is that the workers would then have to do their own shopping in hard discount stores. (High-end chains generally provide a 2 to 5 percent rebate to their workers.) Moreover, super- and hypermarkets also have to attract workers who are not in the segment of the workforce with the least opportunities. According to a high-end human resource manager, wage bonuses compensate for the hard working conditions. Discrimination (employing a white sales staff, and so on) also has a cost.

Third, unlike in discount stores, workers who have contact with the public (cashiers, sales staff, and employees in self-service areas) must create real commercial relationships with customers. They need to be pleasant. At the same time, the prospects of promotion for the best basic workers are very limited. As a result, human resource managers consider relatively high wages a key incentive.

WILL HIGH-ROAD STORES SURVIVE THE RISE OF DISCOUNTERS? CURRENT AND FUTURE TRENDS

Relatively high-wage policies are still alive in classic supermarkets, hypermarkets, and in most stores that employ electrical/electronics sales staff. But the rise of discounters, both in the food sector (with super discount stores) and in the electronics sector (with German specialized stores and the Internet), is challenging these models.

Since the beginning of our case studies in 2004, we have observed that French firms are progressively changing their strategies. Interviews with workers' representatives, top managers, and store managers provide a consistent picture: the medium-term future of cashiers and delicatessen staff in large French food retailers will see a rapid increase of labor productivity. Actually, food retailers are facing not only the development of discounters but also the amendment of the law (in 2006 and again in 2007) that limited price competition. Even though there is not yet a price war, prices are declining slightly; most chains are expanding customer rebates and reducing prices. These mechanisms are eroding profit margins of French groups.

Adapting to Change with Innovations, Investments, and Employment Cuts

Firms have responded by going on the offensive. All classic supermarket and hypermarket chains are seeking to increase their surface areas. After years of poor innovations and increasing administrative procedures, they are innovating and reducing their nonproductive workforce. Thousands of employees in headquarters have been fired or displaced into stores to improve services and reduce administrative costs.

French retailers are experimenting with new concepts for stores. Casino has created super discount areas inside some high-end hypermarkets. Auchan is testing drive-in stores: clients order products in their cars, using a convivial computer, and a worker loads the vehicle. When the profitability of a high-end chain store is too low, it may be transformed into discount stores in the same group. Hundreds of stores have been transferred. When this happens, the workers can either keep their jobs, but with poor bonuses and hence wage cuts, or quit the outlet.

The main innovation comes from the United States: automatic checkout machines. Unlike super discounters, high-end chains are now developing automatic checkout operations. Such equipment was nonexistent at the beginning of our study in 2004, but it is now scheduled for installation over the two next years in about half of the stores in our study. These machines are costly and require heavy maintenance, but managers see two advantages in their use. First, machines can provide more checkout posts, a crucial advantage given massive customer flows. Second, customers using the machines become actors, and so waiting is less boring. Up to 30 percent of checkout positions could be automated.

Officially, labor costs are not the main cause of this trend: a cashier is still necessary for complex payments or for help and control. (One cashier oversees three to four automatic cash registers.) But for unions this technology is likely to reduce the number of cashiers employed by food retailers by about 20 percent, a figure that does not seem exaggerated.[14] So the current strategic choice of firms is to lower labor costs by cutting employment. Top human resource managers believe that the wage equilibrium—the basic minimum wage plus various bonuses—will remain a necessary incentive scheme in high-end stores with a mixed clientele. Consequently, the high-road policy for surviving workers does not yet seem strongly menaced.

This arbitrage in favor of wages and against employment seems relevant to other staff in these outlets as well. Delicatessen vendors and more generally food sales staff are progressively disappearing. For example, one of the chains we studied had decided to suppress all delicatessen positions in its stores in the greater Paris (Ile-de-France) region. On the one hand, hygiene norms have increased the costs of "rayons traditionnels" and skilled butchers are now rare. On the other hand, because customers seek to gain time in stores (and customers cannot reduce the checkout time), they prefer pre-cuts, while, ex ante, their natural wish is to maintain face-to-face services. This is another negative side effect of the restriction of store size in France. Aging is also accelerating this phenomenon, as lengthy shopping time is tiring for older customers.

Finally, high-end chains are seeking to extend opening hours and to open on more Sundays. Currently, except in tourist zones, large outlets can open five Sundays per year. Regulation is changing to allow stores to open probably ten or more Sundays. This development should slightly improve the distribution of customer flows, lengthen hours worked for (past) part-time workers, require hiring, and thus partly compensate for the adverse effects of technological changes on employment.

The End of Restrictive Zoning Rules?

This scenario for the survival of relatively high-road stores supported by innovation could be challenged by potential new regulatory shocks. Actually, pressures by the European Commission, following a claim by Aldi, could induce radical changes in zoning regulations. Brussels considers French regulation anticompetitive and protective of French groups. The French government has begun to reform the

Raffarin law, but the final result is uncertain and depends on the balance between the European Commission and the lobbies in France. If the Raffarin law is repealed, store surface areas may rise exponentially, leading to job creations but also putting pressure on wages in high-end outlets. In addition, with more surface area leading to lower customer flows, working conditions would become less extreme and the compensating wage mechanism less relevant.

MORE LOW WAGES IN FOOD RETAILING AND A BIG BANG IN THE ELECTRICAL AND ELECTRONICS SECTOR?

In any case, super discount stores are likely to gain new market shares, at least gradually, because they meet the needs of poorer customers. Therefore, this development, along with job cuts in classic outlets, should mean that the weight of high-end stores in employment is likely to decline and that the share of workers paid at the rock-bottom minimum wage will grow.

While it is possible to figure out quite robust alternatives for workers in food retailing, the future of electrical and electronics staff is harder to determine. It should be recalled that the case studies provide a positive view of this occupation. Despite having few formal skills, electrical and electronics sales staff have real autonomy and receive high pay. Currently in France, there is no sign of any dangers to this particularly high-road model. The quality and motivation of sales staff are still considered a competitive key for brick-and-mortar stores. For example, Carrefour invests massively to enhance customer assistance and the convenience of electrical and electronics areas in its hypermarkets. Furthermore, the continuous increase of the demand for technical and electronics equipment supports the demand for efficient vendors.

Nevertheless, this model is fragile. The fairly strong—but not cutthroat—competition in this market is still favorable to sales staffs. But tougher competition may make the high-wage arrangement unsustainable. Again, the competition could come from Germany. Two years ago, chains in Belgium had a policy quite analogous to that which currently exists in France. This was the case for FNAC, a very high-end French chain. Since then, the very aggressive strategy of the German company Media Markt (in 2005) pushed FNAC workers to accept significant wage cuts in a referendum. Similarly, it is possible that the stronger competition associated with low profit margins will dramatically change the wage levels of electrical and electronics staff in France.

The French case proves that there is room for high-roads in retail trade. But it also shows that they result from fragile competitive conditions. Changes in retail regulations or the entry of new competitor challenge the survival of relative high hourly wages in this sector.

The research for this chapter was funded by the Russell Sage Foundation and supported by Cepremap. The INSEE trade division has also supported this project through the part-time allocation of Jean-Baptiste Berry and the access to specific data. The authors would like to thank the employees, managers, human resource managers, and union representatives they interviewed; Paule Saint-Léger of the FCD, a French employer organization, for her support; and all participants in the RSF project on low-wage work in Europe, especially Chris Tilly, for their remarks or help.

APPENDIX

Table 6A.1 Regular and In-Depth Case Studies of Food and Electrical/Electronics Retailers

	A: Super-South	B: Hyper-IDF	C: Hyper-South	D: Maxi-South
Store type	Large supermarket	Hypermarket	Hypermarket	Franchise super discount
Food	High-end	High-end	High-end	Low-end
Electrical		High-end	Low-end	
Region	Downtown, Southeast	Suburbs, IDF	Suburbs, large city, Southeast	Suburbs, large city, Southeast
Number of workers	140	620	420	Forty-five
Study type	In-depth	In-depth	In-depth	Regular
Delicatessen	Yes	Yes	Yes	No
Percent of low wages among cashiers	20 to less than 40	Less than 10	Less than 10	100
Union delegates	Yes	Yes, but wife of the mayor of the city	Yes	No, anti-union policy

Source: Authors' compilation.
Note: In-depth study includes various ergonomic observations, analyses, and more interviews. IDF = Ile-de-France.

NOTES

1. Super discounters have a relatively small share of the market; but because they buy basically one good for one need, they represent a potentially important market for suppliers (see the chapter on food industries).
2. Because firms operating in this heterogeneous sector are classified in various industries, it is impossible to obtain relevant overall data on profits or on the evolution of labor's share in value-added.
3. For a detailed history of French zoning regulation, see Askenazy and Weidenfeld (2007).
4. This arrangement was an important source of local corruption in French politics in the 1980s.

Table 6A.1 (*Continued*)

E: Elec-South	F: Hi-fi-Paris	G(a): Super-IDF	G(b): Super-IDF	H: Maxi-IDF
Discount	Electronics	Supermarket	Supermarket	Super discount
		Low-end	High-end	Low-end
Low-end Suburbs, large city, Southeast	High-end Suburbs, IDF	Suburban-rural, IDF	Downtown, IDF	Suburbs, IDF
100	Eighty	Forty	Eighty	Ten to twenty (two stores)
In-depth	Regular	In-depth	In-depth	Via unions
		Yes	Yes	No
n.a.	n.a.	20 to less than 40	10 to less than 20 (2005); 20 to less than 40 (2006)	Less than 50
Yes	No, anti-union policy	Yes	Yes	Yes

5. The period between authorization by the commission and the opening of a store is two to three years, so the consequences of the 1993 freeze and the Raffarin law were delayed.
6. This explains why the stock value of the French retail groups jumped when the Raffarin law was announced.
7. Electrical/electronics staff is not a distinct category in the Labor Force Survey. We use "furniture and household equipment staff" as a proxy for this occupation.
8. The proportion of temporary workers is only 1 percent. In fact, managers consider temps too expensive and believe that using numerous short-term contracts offers a sufficient solution for demand peaks.
9. Note, however, that the notions of productivity in retailing are not particularly robust (Blanchard 2005).

10. Almost all of the managers we interviewed, from low-level managers to national human resource managers, stressed this point.
11. Noncreations of jobs in large outlets overwhelm jobs saved in traditional shops.
12. This is specific training in situ aimed at coping with one's workstation and, in particular, avoiding musculoskeletal disorders.
13. Chains require that their suppliers use systematic, ergonomically designed bar codes.
14. Note also that some managers are expecting massive employment reductions when RFID (radio frequency identification of products) technology becomes available.

REFERENCES

Allain, Marie-Laure, and Claire Chambolle. 2004. "Below-Cost Pricing Laws as Vertical Restraints." Working paper 2004-01. Paris: LORIA.

Askenazy, Philippe, and Katia Weidenfeld. 2007. *Les Soldes de la loi Raffarin : Contrôler le grand commerce* [*The Impact of Raffarin's Law: Controlling Big Retail Chains*]. Paris: Presses de l'ENS/Cepremap.

Bertrand, Marianne, and Francis Kramarz. 2002. "Does Entry Regulation Hinder Job Creation? Evidence from the French Retail Industry." *Quarterly Journal of Economics* 117(4): 1369–414.

Blanchard, Olivier. 2005. "Comments on *Contrasting Europe's Decline: Do Product Market Reforms Help?* by Riccardo Faini et al." Unpublished paper. Cambridge, Mass.: MIT.

Boylaud, Olivier, and Giuseppe Nicoletti. 2001. "Regulatory Reform in Retail Distribution." *OECD Economic Studies* 1(32).

Caisse National d'Assurance Maladie (CNAM). 2005. *Statistiques des accidents et maladies professionnelles 2003* [*Statistics on Professional Accidents and Illnesses, 2003*]. Paris: CNAM.

Canivet, Guy. 2004. *Equilibre entre le grand commerce et les fournisseurs* [*Balance Between Big Retail Chains and Suppliers*]. Report to the Ministry of Economics.

Carré, Françoise, Brandynn Holgate, and Chris Tilly. 2005. "What's Happening to Retail Jobs? Wages, Gender, and Corporate Strategy." Unpublished paper. Lowell, Mass.: University of Massachusetts.

Dousson, Christine, Christian Ferrand, Alain Grossetête, Joëlle Biermé, Messana Amar, Elisabeth Balland, Bernadette Guth, Xavier Royer, and Martine Hours. 2002. *État de santé des salariés de la grande distribution: Epigrandis, une etude descriptive dans le département du Rhône* [*The State of Health in Retail Trade Distribution: Epigrandis, a Descriptive Study in Rhône Department*]. Nancy, France: INRS.

Dube, Arindrajit, Barry Eidlin, and Bill Lester. 2005. "Impact of Wal-Mart

Growth on Earnings Throughout the Retail Sector in Urban and Rural Countries." Unpublished paper. Institute for Industrial Relations, University of California, Berkeley.

Gadrey, Jean, and Florence Jany-Catrice. 2000. "The Retail Sector: Why So Many Jobs in America and So Few in France?" *Service Industries Journal* 20(4): 21–32.

Leclerc, Annette, Jean-François Chastang, Isabelle Niedhammer, Marie-France Landre, and Yves Roquelaure. 2004. "Incidence of Shoulder Pain in Repetitive Work." *Occupational and Environmental Medicine* 61(1): 39–44.

McGuckin, Robert H., Matthew Spiegelman, and Bart van Ark. 2005. *The Retail Revolution: Can Europe Match U.S. Productivity Performance?* Research report R-1358-05-RR. New York: The Conference Board.

McKinney Global Institute (MGI). 2002. *Reaching Higher Productivity in France and Germany: Retail Sector.* Report. Paris: MGI.

Piketty, Thomas. 1998. "Emploi dans les services en France et aux États-Unis: Une analyse structurelle sur longue période" ["Service Sector Work in France and the United States: A Structural Analysis Over a Long Period"]. *Économie et Statistique* 318: 73-99.

Prunier-Poulmaire, Sophie. 2000. "Flexibilité assistée par ordinateur: Les caissières d'hypermarché" ["Computerized Flexibility: Hypermarket Cashiers"]. *Actes de la Recherche en Sciences Sociales* 134: 29-36.

Van der Windt, Danielle A., Elaine Thomas, Daniel P. Pope, Andrea F. de Winter, Gary J. Macfarlane, Lex M. Bouter, and Alan J. Silman. 2000. "Occupational Risk Factors for Shoulder Pain: A Systematic Review." *Occupational and Environmental Medicine* 57(7): 433–42.

CHAPTER 7

Job Quality and Career Opportunities for Call Center Workers: Contrasting Patterns in France

Mathieu Beraud, Thierry Colin, and Benoît Grasser, with the participation of Émilie Fériel

As in the United States, call centers are an emerging tertiary activity in France, characterized by a process of industrialization and flexibility in response to their competitive environment. Their recent and rapid development and the lack of institutional and regulatory frameworks defining the work of call center operators raise questions about job quality. Unions, the media, and research do indeed paint a highly critical picture of operators' working conditions, stressing job insecurity/precariousness and work intensity, for wages that are based on minimum legal pay. Call center operators are also often identified as Taylorist workers of modern times, an image that perhaps highlights characteristics of these new occupations that are little favorable to employees. The proliferation of research and the availability of preliminary quantitative data confirm such first impressions but also qualify them significantly by identifying extremely varied situations. Thus, wages on average are considerably higher than the legal minimum wage (SMIC), the rate of low-wage workers in the industry is relatively low (for example, compared with other European countries like the United Kingdom or the Netherlands), and, above all, low pay is concentrated in independent centers that act as subcontractors for companies that want to externalize customer relations.

There is still relatively little institutionalization in the sector, given the newness of call center activity and its varied nature. Institutions do not therefore seem to be the a priori cause of the limited share of low-wage workers in the sector. In fact, they have a twofold role, as will be shown. First, by fixing a legal minimum wage that is relatively high, national institutions make it difficult for call center economic models to function effectively when based only on price competition. Centers must provide at least some degree of service quality, which in turn creates a complexity threshold for the work to be done. Furthermore, institutions specific to call centers are emerging and, to some extent, beginning to organize a framework for professionalizing operators.

In our initial presentation of the main outlines of the evolution of call centers in France, we stress the institutional factors that partly explain the existence of the contrasting situations we have observed. We then describe the various economic and strategic approaches to exploiting the potential of call centers. These approaches imply specific forms of work and jobs, though without determining them completely; we analyze those forms in more detail in the last section of this chapter.

This research was carried out using existing material, especially quantitative, overall data, while we collected a large amount of qualitative data directly. We began by conducting interviews with leading representatives of employer groups, unions, and public institutions (at the national and local levels). We then wrote up eight monographs: three for in-house call centers in the banking and insurance sectors, three for in-house call centers working for utilities, and two for independent call centers. Overall, we interviewed nearly one hundred people, of whom a large majority were call center operators (see the appendix).

CALL CENTERS: A YOUNG INDUSTRY WITH BLURRED CONTOURS

In this first section, we introduce a description of the sector and its history. We show that the institutionalization is recent and it is still weak.

THE RECENT AND RAPID DEVELOPMENT OF CALL CENTERS

It is important to start by tackling the difficulties of defining and identifying the call center sector from a statistical point of view. About 80 percent of centers belong to companies working in different sectors, either as functional departments or as subsidiaries. They are therefore not statistically visible. A specific call center sector does

Table 7.1 Recent Trends in Call Centers

	2002	2003	2004	2005 (Estimation)
Number of call centers	3,000	3,100	3,300	3,500
Number of employees	191,000	195,000	205,000	210,000
Average size (staff per center)	63.7	62.9	62.1	60

Source: Centre d'Études Stratégiques pour le Moyen-Orient (CESMO) (2003, 2004).

exist, but it comprises only independent centers and was not officially identified by France's National Institute for Statistics and Economic Studies (INSEE) until late in 2003.[1] Consequently, the information provided here comes mainly from surveys conducted by the Centre d'Études Strategiques pour le Moyen-Orient (CESMO) in 2003 and 2004 and the Laboratoire d'Economie et du Sociologie du Travail (LEST) for the Russell Sage Foundation; these surveys include both in-house and independent centers.[2]

Call center activity is growing very rapidly worldwide, and France is no exception, though its sector took off later than elsewhere: the main expansion of centers did not begin until the mid-1990s, when annual growth in the number of centers rose systematically by more than 12 percent (CESMO 2004). In 2005 there were estimated to be about 3,500 centers.

In 2004 the 205,000 employees working in call centers represented 0.75 percent of France's working population. This share is relatively low compared to 3 percent of the workforce in the United States. According to all available data, workers in call centers are young on average and mainly women, and they usually hold post–high school qualifications. (Most have at least two years of higher education or more.)

The size distribution of centers is extremely varied across the sector: while the average center has sixty employees, more staff may be found in independent centers (more than one hundred), while centers in the banking, IT, and telecommunications sectors or in business-to-business (B2B) trade are much smaller (fewer than forty workers).

Some restructuring in the market suggests that the independent call center sector may have started concentrating, via mergers and acquisitions. It may be noted that nearly three-quarters of the turnover by independent centers is generated by the nine largest companies (with 250 employees or more) (INSEE 2006).

Calls may be classified as inbound (the operator receives a call from a customer) or as outbound (the operator contacts a client or a prospect without the latter necessarily soliciting such a contact). Inbound calls account for about 75 percent of call center activity (CESMO 2004). The LEST survey (Lanciano-Morandat, Nohara, and Tchobanian 2004), which fits in with our work (Charlier et al. 2003), notes that in-house centers are more specialized in inbound calls than independent centers. The latter act generally as subcontractors of promotion campaigns aimed at the general public.

The greater Paris region (Ile-de-France) is the main base for centers (24 percent in 2004), though its share is falling rapidly (down from 38.6 percent in 2002). In fact, centers are moving to other regions, especially those that offer labor and cost advantages (real estate and manpower) as well as incentives from public authorities.

As for overseas relocation, 9 percent of the managing directors interviewed in early 2004 stated that they had a project for going offshore (CESMO 2004). The companies mainly involved in such projects handle very high volumes of customer contact and favor countries like Morocco and Tunisia, where labor costs are 20 to 40 percent lower than in France. That said, employment in offshore centers is estimated at only 9,000 to 12,000, or between 4 and 6 percent of all jobs in call centers.[3] While overseas centers are likely to progress, there do seem to be limits to offshoring, as will be discussed later in this chapter.

Even though capital equipment per employee is relatively high for a service-sector activity, call centers remain labor-intensive, and wage bills account for about 70 percent of total costs, according to available research.

Collective Agreements: Marking the Difference Between In-House and Independent Centers

The call center sector is characterized by a complex institutional framework that was built up slowly in the 1990s. This complexity follows from France's diverse industrial relations system, but it also results from the variety of call center types.

In-house call centers are covered by the collective agreements of the branch to which their companies belong. Normally, there are no special measures concerning call center employees at the branch level. Where such measures do exist, they have usually been negotiated at the company or even the establishment level.[4]

As for independent centers, their situation is clearer nowadays, and they may be covered by two different collective agreements.[5] A collective agreement in telecommunications was signed in 1999, and independent centers owned by or working mainly with firms in this sector have increasingly been covered by this agreement. Other independent centers turned to the national agreement of service providers in the tertiary sector, which was negotiated—not without problems—in the early 1990s. It was agreed in 2001 to extend this agreement to cover call centers, though without ratification by the two main labor unions, which consider the agreement to be "socially regressive."[6] Indeed, this national collective agreement improves working conditions only for managers (10 percent of the staff concerned), while merely applying the general measures of France's Labor Code to all other employees.

Call center operators are thus covered by a number of agreements that offer very different levels of protection. The agreement for service providers that covers independent call centers is much less favorable to staff on certain matters (wages and career paths) than the agreements covering banking and insurance employees, or even the agreement for telecommunications workers.

THE EVOLUTION OF INDUSTRIAL RELATIONS

The Convergence of Employers' Views   The Syndicat du Marketing Téléphonique (SMT) is the historical employers' association in the telemarketing and call center sector. It was created in 1978 and has nearly seventy corporate members (see Houéry 2004). Traditionally, its representatives support the idea that jobs should be very flexible, especially in their defense of derogatory labor contracts: the de facto use of short, fixed-term contracts that can be renewed repeatedly without interruption (see chapter 2). SMT representatives also believe that more flexibility should be allowed in terms of hours: for example, that Sunday work should be permitted and the regulation of overtime hours should be relaxed. This association took part in the roundtable talks organized by the French Ministry of Industry in 2004 and thus acquired a greater role in the regulation of the sector. The association was renamed the Syndicat des Professionnels des Centres de Contact (SP2C) in 2005, and its policies have changed notably as it has moved away from demands that are solely focused on quantitative flexibility.[7]

The association has thus moved toward other employer groups that partly acknowledge that the sector has to be better regulated and have agreed to the greater professionalization of operators. This aim is mainly supported by the Association Française de Relation Clientèle (AFRC), an employers' lobby created in 1998 that now has more than four hundred members. In particular, the AFRC has put forward a quality certificate and a code of good practice. Also, in 2002, it set up a monitoring body for call center training and the European Association of Customer Relations Centers (ECCO).

Employees' Representation: Weak and Piecemeal   Unions are present in only half of all call centers, mainly in the telecommunications sector, banking, insurance, and trade. Moreover, unions are far less present in independent centers (less than 30 percent are covered).

The in-house call centers we surveyed usually belong to companies or large corporate groups in which unions have long been present and active. In a majority of cases, however, unions remain peripheral, owing largely to the fact that call center employees are marginal to traditional functions. This does not rule out all union involvement. For example, in one of the strongly unionized companies we surveyed the main union had been involved in issues relating to working conditions and the career opportunities of call center workers within the company after they left the center. In another in-house center, mergers and acquisitions as well as the reassignment of workers had led to numerous different job statuses, and union demands had focused largely on harmonizing in-house employment conditions.[8] There were no unions, however, in the two independent centers we surveyed; even the employers at these two centers regretted that they had no social partner with which to dialogue.

The characteristics of call center employees explain the low union rates fairly well: for instance, operators are young and have little seniority, many come from ethnic minority backgrounds, work is precarious, and the production units (call centers) are small. These are all typical characteristics of non-unionized workplaces. Even more significant probably is the importance workers give to their jobs. In independent centers, work as an operator is rarely considered by employees a real profession; they usually view it as a transitory situation or as work they are doing for want of something else. Being a call center operator is very rarely seen as a choice, and as such, most workers do not see themselves doing the job for long. As a consequence, collective mobilization is limited.

In the large centers that are typical of telecommunications and telemarketing, our interviews with union representatives, as well as our readings of the literature and the press, stressed that industrial relations were very conflictual. Industrial action, sometimes leading to strikes, is pursued by unions at the company level to improve the terms of employment (wages and job status) and working conditions. The unions have noted that certain aspects of call center working conditions have generally improved, thanks to their demands (for example, the size of employees' cubicles). At the same time, "best practice" personnel policies do not exist in this sector, as borne out by the high labor turnover and the frequency of industrial action (where there are unions) protesting against job insecurity and in favor of higher wages or improved working conditions. A review of union tracts explaining union activities at the company level reveals that strong claims are made in most areas (job insecurity/precariousness, wages, working conditions, the frequency of controls, and so on).

THE BEGINNINGS OF AN INSTITUTIONAL FRAMEWORK

Pressure from some of the actors involved is leading to the first steps of an institutional regulation of the sector that would regulate flexibility and professionalize call center work to some degree.

1. *Training schemes are gradually emerging.* France's Ministry of Education has created several high school and higher education diplomas. A vocational high school diploma in customer relations was created in 2000, as was a bachelor's degree in tele- or distance services. A certain number of measures have also been taken by public and private bodies relating to continuing vocational education.[9]

2. Given the rapid rise of customer relations activities and their high potential for creating jobs, *France's regional authorities are seeking to attract companies by offering to support relocation schemes.* They are offering financial incentives to cover training in work oriented to customer relations; for example, the Lorraine region funds 50 percent of such training. Direct financial support is also available for recruitment; in the area of Poitiers, the local authorities have

allocated €4,500 (US$6,420) for every person under thirty years old who is employed. Real estate and property incentives (such as free rent for a year), as well as tax rebates, are also provided.[10] Furthermore, with their capacity to operate free of geographic constraints, call centers can easily benefit from institutional measures to encourage investment in regions with employment problems. In doing so, they can obtain bonuses from regional development policies, which range from €8,000 to €10,000 (US$11,414 to US$14,267) per job created.

3. *Several national measures are aimed at reducing the offshoring of jobs and encouraging job creation.* A national framework agreement covering customer relations centers that was signed in December 2004 strives to encourage various public actors to facilitate recruitment via training and employment support. That year also saw the creation of a "customer relations service center" certificate, the goal of which is to encourage the overall development of service quality, based on a reference framework. In 2005, a "social responsibility" label was created by a committee of independent professionals to be awarded to call centers that pursue best working practices in terms of training, career development, and working conditions.

More detailed analysis shows, however, that the institutionalization of the call center sector is incomplete. For example, a review of training indicates that despite the creation of certified and recognized training programs, these actually involve only a limited number of people.[11] Furthermore, the large majority of training courses in customer relations do not lead to a recognized diploma but only to certificates provided by the training organization. Similarly, only about ten companies have so far acquired a quality certificate, while fifteen companies have obtained the social responsibility label. A mature employment framework specific to the call center sector has therefore not developed as yet, and the cross-cutting nature of the activity is clearly a major obstacle to homogeneous institutionalization.

THE CHOICE OF BUSINESS AND STRATEGIC MODELS

As has been observed in the United States (Batt, Hunter, and Wilk 2003), call centers may adopt different market positioning strategies.

Schematically speaking, call centers may position themselves to compete on price, while seeking to generate large volumes of calls to cut costs. Or they may opt for providing quality services in order to satisfy their customers better and develop customer loyalty. Our observations indicate that there is no predictable connection between centers' strategic positioning and their employment practices. Nevertheless, it is clear that call centers whose primary objective is to maximize hourly productivity growth manifest characteristics of the secondary segment in the labor market in terms of Peter Doeringer and Michael Piore's definition (1971): wages are relatively low, there is a lot of employment flexibility, there are no career prospects, and the external mobility of workers is high. In contrast, call centers that seek to develop their own client relations by creating new services to win customers, nurture loyalty, and increase the value of the services they offer share the characteristics of the primary segment: wages are fairly high, jobs are stable, and employees can progress within the company.

We start this section by stressing that the development of call center activities clearly involves what we could call the industrialization of customer relations. This process has to take into account a technological and competitive environment that pushes companies into different choices concerning the relationship between strategy and employment.

CALL CENTERS AND THE INDUSTRIALIZATION OF CUSTOMER RELATIONS

Call center activities are in a process of industrialization of customer relations in that they are shaped both by rationalization and by the drive for economies of scale. Operations are being standardized, operators' work is increasingly specialized, and the tasks and work pace are ever more narrowly controlled. These industrializing trends are brought on by the intensive use of technology,[12] associated with Taylorist forms of work organization (the exact prescription of work through the use of scripts and time control).[13]

From an economic perspective, industrializing customer relations has a twofold objective. The first is to generate productivity gains (the classic advantage of economies of scale) in traditional activities such as taking customer orders and managing after-sales service, since fixed costs can be spread over a large number of calls. The second objective of industrializing customer relations is to create value, which may take several forms. For example, customer relations activities allow contacts with clients to be maintained and made durable, even if no immediate sale is concluded. (A client who is regularly contacted and informed is likely to turn to the company he or she knows in case of new needs.) These activities also project a certain image of the company and permit information about the company's products and intentions to be publicized. In addition, such customer contacts are a powerful way to improve lists of clients and prospects: each call is an opportunity to update or complete data about clients, thus increasing the economic value of the customer databases available. For these reasons, the value produced by call centers is not limited to the number of contacts or sales made but also includes a non-negligible accumulation of assets in terms of recognition or information acquired. Indeed, handling such contacts poorly may lead to the deterioration of a company's image in the eyes of some clients or prospects. This twofold objective of the industrialization of customer relations therefore contains conflicting forces (both quantitative and qualitative) that the call centers have to handle, in particular by managing employment.

The different approaches to generating value in customer relations are found in varying degrees across call centers. Schematically speaking, it is possible to position centers along a continuum of economic organizational types. At one extreme would be "pure" in-house centers where call center contacts with customers create value and participate in other distribution channels as well (for example, branches in the banking sector). External centers, geared to handling high volumes with low production costs, are at the other extreme. Their goals are quantitative, and the services they provide (for example, offering information on hotlines or fixing appointments) are fairly simple.

The choice between these two business approaches—one based on quantitative productivity, the other on creating value—depends on competitive pressure. It then takes shape as part of the different strategies pursued to integrate the call center into traditional activities.

The Sources of Competitive Pressure

The industrialization of call centers is taking place in a competitive environment driven by technology, market structure, and labor costs.

The low cost of technology strengthens the contestable nature of the market, insofar as investment in call centers can become profitable relatively quickly.[14] Permanent technological developments have numerous implications: extended geographical possibilities for setting up centers in the home country or overseas (through Voice over Internet Protocol [VoIP] technology); the automation of an ever-increasing share of services (using speech synthesis); the increasing integration of telephony and databases (through customer relationship management [CRM] technology); the proliferation of the ways in which the organization of production can be broken down (using programs for managing customers waiting in line, procedures for routing inbound calls, etc.); and so on. The role of technology in a center's competitiveness is not neutral. Modern technologies strengthen price competition by reducing the costs of telecommunications, increasingly offering automation possibilities, and offering several solutions from an organizational point of view. As a result, centers providing services are obliged to seek solutions in order to maintain their profitability and competitive position.

Moreover, the various forms of competition affect call centers in different ways, depending on the markets in which they are active. Referring back to the two extreme cases presented earlier, independent centers are found to specialize in campaigns of outbound calls (a highly competitive market in which offshore companies compete), and these centers are obliged to adopt competitive strategies based on large call volumes and cost minimization. In contrast, for in-house centers in the banking and insurance sectors, the quality of the customer relationship, which strengthens the competitiveness of the company overall, is more important than the characteristics of the service provided. It should be noted that this situation is partly the result of the deregulation of the banking and insurance sectors in the mid-1980s, which reinforced competition and hence the importance of marketing. The banking sector is obviously not the only area in which the regulatory environment has changed in recent years. The regulatory context of utilities, which is also examined here, and especially the distribution and waste treatment of water, has changed as well as controls on tendering procedures in local markets have been strengthened. The new rules for competitive tenders put great emphasis on quality, with companies having to put in bids that relate not just to the price of services but also to quality. As a result, companies in the sector have had to enhance their reactiveness to households using their services. The development of customer relations via call centers has allowed this to occur, and it has also given companies commercial arguments to use with local authorities and municipalities in their efforts to obtain new customers and maintain their loyalty, in the wake of calls for tender.

Lastly, the cost of labor is perhaps the most important factor in determining the positioning strategy adopted by call centers in France. The fact that the legal minimum wage in France is relatively high (see chapter 2) significantly reduces the possibility of adopting strategies based on price competitiveness, for which offshore operators located in North Africa (Tunisia and Morocco) have a clear advantage. As a result of this constraint, independent call centers have adopted one of two solutions: either they shift to high-value-added services, which is made possible by the relatively well-qualified labor in France, or they have increased flexibility in employment and working practices. Some independent centers have indeed chosen to maintain price competitiveness by relocating part of their activities offshore to countries where labor costs are relatively low.[15]

Some in-house centers also send work offshore with the aim of cutting costs, but also for reasons linked to the organization of work and to the institutional constraints on the duration and deployment of time worked. (Offshore centers take over the work of receiving incoming calls in the evening and at nights and weekends.) If offshoring is often presented as a threat, its impact should nevertheless be qualified by the problems related to the low quality of telephone contact in host countries.[16] For a large variety of activities, the sociocultural context of call center operators appears de facto to be a key factor in determining the quality of calls and hence limits offshoring possibilities. Indeed, it is not unusual to see certain operations that were initially offshored being repatriated. That said, offshoring continues to have considerable attractions and retains a competitive advantage whenever call volumes are the main priority. The factors influencing offshoring choices are not therefore fixed definitively. Several strategies are possible, both in terms of company policy (segmenting activities and specifying more clearly the production conditions that lead to offshoring or not) and in terms of meso- and macro-policies (the construction of a skills-based model for this industry that is economically viable in France over the long term). Ultimately, the ever-present potential competitive pressures brought on by the threat of offshoring require national outsourcers to devise strategies based on a certain quality level and to think about the types of employment and skills that are compatible with such strategies.

STRATEGIC POSITIONING AND PROXIMITY TO CORE BUSINESSES

An examination of the details of the industrialization of remote customer relations shows that this is a new activity in technological and organizational terms. This leads to questioning the position of remote customer relations vis-à-vis traditional activities: is this a new way of carrying out customer relations, or are remote customer relations complementary to existing practices? To put it another way: are remote customer relations being fully integrated into core activities, or are they still peripheral? Beyond competitive pressures expressed in terms of costs and prices, proximity to the core business seems to be the key in understanding call centers' relative strategies. Analysis of our case studies allows four different situations to be identified.

In the first situation, remote customer relations are fully integrated into the core activities, inasmuch as it is hard to separate them out. In the banking sector, for example, remote customer relations contribute to the performance of a product, its quality and reliability, in a manner that is similar to customer relations managed through bank branches. This can be explained for legal reasons: for example, only the bank's employees are allowed access to certain types of information. But it may also be explained by the behavior of customers when they remain strongly focused on direct contact with what they think of as their own bank. Lastly, it may be explained on purely technical grounds relating to the knowledge of products, the bank, and its functioning. In this case, the remote customer relationship can be properly carried out only if it is completely integrated into core activities. From this point of view, the development of telephone centers is only a new means (a new tool or a new organization for increasing productivity in particular) for executing a traditional banking function, namely "advising clients."[17]

The second situation arises when an in-house center has a more peripheral status—for example, when remote customer relations are only used to follow up relations that have been first established through direct contact (in an agency or bank branch, in the home, and so on). In this case, call centers may remain in-house for two reasons: first, because a certain level of stability is necessary and an activity cannot be externalized to an independent center; and second, when the in-house call center is used as a place for managing certain job situations, such as redeployment within the company. In this case, the call center activities are quite integrated within the company, even though they do not play a truly strategic role.

The third situation recalls a first category of independent centers, which could be called "quality-service independent centers." Here, call center activities are externalized, that is, they are no longer handled by companies requiring such work. The latter become clients or ordering parties instead, passing orders to independent centers. Such centers are far removed from companies' core businesses, and it may therefore be assumed that their objectives are essentially oriented to reducing costs. However, contrary to this assumption, it may be noted that these independent centers have an interest in developing a new type of specific competence, namely, as service providers for several ordering parties, while adopting an up-market position that stresses quality of service, given cost constraints.

The last situation concerns independent centers whose strategy is mainly based on handling large volumes generated by low unit production costs per call. In some cases, the unit cost per call may be so small that high failure rates are tolerable: this was observed, for example, in one independent center where the aim was to get customers to change their Internet subscriptions. Such centers are highly exposed to offshore competition, with which they must therefore maintain a sufficient quality differential in services in order to generate margins that are high enough to pay for the minimum wage set by French legislation.[18]

Call center work thus needs to position itself between two broad business strategies based on high quantitative productivity, on the one hand, and on seeking out all of the types of potential value creation in customer relations that technology can provide, on the other hand. In France, the former is immediately limited by national institutions underpinning relatively high minimum wages. Companies therefore need to adopt strategies that generate a minimum value-added per call. These choices affect both the complexity of work and the employment models put in place.

CALL CENTER OPERATORS' WORK IS HETEROGENEOUS BUT FEW ARE LOW-WAGE WORKERS

Call center operators may be easily identified as call center employees whose principal job is based on customer contact via the telephone.

This definition actually corresponds to a wide variety of occupations: sales, after-sales advice, service and advice, assistance (for insurance companies and medical services), or work relating mainly to finance and law.[19] Given such variety, it is difficult to describe the typical content of a call center operator's work, and reality is quite different from the mere Taylorization of customer relations. One previous study suggested that contradictory job dimensions probably characterize call center operators work the best (Charlier et al. 2003). On the one hand, operators manifest competencies that imply a high level of skills (situational "intelligence," good oral expression skills, knowledge of products, and so on). On the other hand, their work involves tasks that are traditionally associated with low skill levels (prescribed work, time and result controls, pressure on productivity, and so on).

We will identify the main characteristics of call center operators prior to observing that, for a large majority of them, their pay does not fit into the category of low wages. This is explained by the fact that their work is often more complex than might be thought at first sight, because call center strategies are actually almost never based on costs alone. We will also show that call center wages, which are on average above the low-wage threshold, are tied to fairly contrasting job situations that, depending on companies' strategic choices, may be either very insecure and precarious or integrated into relatively protected internal labor markets. Lastly, call center work is unanimously seen as hard and tiring, owing to its intensive nature and demanding flexibility. This too may explain why average wages are above the low-wage threshold.

Who Are the Call Center Operators?

The first characteristic of call center work is that it is feminized. Female operators account for nearly two-thirds of all staff. The only exception is to be found in the B2B sector, where workers are 50 percent male. Some call centers in our study were almost entirely made up of women, the only exception being the center that specialized in automobile assistance, which had only men. Such high levels of feminization stem partly from what are supposed to be specific female competencies—voice quality, patience, an understanding attitude—but also from the fact that women often accept employment conditions and wages that are less favorable. The private lives of call center operators are varied, but singles and students are overrepresented in independent call centers.

Youth is the second characteristic of call center operators: two-thirds are under the age of thirty. There are, of course, exceptions, especially when workers are redeployed (to work in in-house centers). Another notable exception was the independent call center we studied that recruited "senior" workers in order to stabilize its labor force. Seniority in call centers is generally very low, owing both to the newness of the activity and to high turnover rates. Seniority is highest in in-house centers, where only 20 percent of employees have less than one year's seniority, compared to 40 percent in independent centers.

Lastly, though we have no statistics to support the observation, the share of call center operators from ethnic minorities seemed to be quite high in the firms we studied. The call center sector may well offer employment opportunities for young people who are trained in sales but whose color excludes them from work with traditional contacts to customers, provided they speak with no accent. One call center manager stated, "There's no point in beating about the bush: call centers allow qualified young workers suffering from discrimination elsewhere to enter the labor market."

Formal qualifications vary significantly, depending on the work at hand: workers with no high school diploma may be found in some independent centers, while staff employed in banking and insurance may have gone through two or more years of higher education. Overall, the median qualification level is estimated to be two years of higher education (Lanciano-Morandat, Nohara, and Tchobanian 2004). This fairly high qualification level can be explained by the relative complexity of the work and the competencies it requires.

Overall, employees in call centers demonstrate certain characteristics that are similar to unskilled workers in other sectors of the economy, but their average level of formal qualifications is much higher.

LOW-WAGE WORK IS LIMITED AND CONCENTRATED

Only a minority of French call center employees may be considered low-wage workers: according to INSEE, only 20.3 percent of call center workers in independent centers fell into this category in 2003, while independent centers account for only 20 percent of all call centers. The rate of low-wage workers in in-house centers cannot be measured but is doubtless very small.

The annual average salary for a typical call center operator is €17,940 (US$25,956) (Lanciano-Morandat, Nohara, and Tchobanian 2004).[20] Salaries vary strongly, however, according to the sector and type of market: annual average wages range from €14,980 (US$21,373) in independent centers handling outgoing calls to €21,400 (US$30,532) for centers operating in the B2B sector and IT services. This represents a spread of 35 percent.[21] Pay spreads are less important across different markets, ranging from €17,500 (US$24,968) for mass markets to €19,050 (US$27,176) for activities oriented toward large business operators. In this case, the spread of salaries is far less pronounced in France (9 percent) than in the United States (60 percent). There is no doubt that this is largely explained by the level of the legal minimum wage in France.

Our own surveys confirm such pay levels. Beginner operators earned pay at the low-wage threshold in only three out of the eight cases studied. At the same time, much higher hourly wages were found in some in-house centers (banking and utilities) covered by favorable company or branch collective agreements (classifications based on traditional jobs, bonuses, thirteenth-month salaries, in-kind benefits, working time, and so on).

If call center pay does not fall within the low-wage category, it may be that companies put less pressure on wages than they apply to labor productivity. Also, some call centers strive to limit turnover, which has negative effects on productivity, and this may reduce pressure to push down wages (Delaunay 2003).

Turning to the nature of pay, call centers are increasingly introducing a variable share in wages, with the aim of rewarding and motivating call center workers. This trend is supported by the Association Française de Relation Clientèle (AFRC), and variable pay is commonly believed to be widespread. But in fact, fully 60 percent of call centers have virtually no system of individual pay (Lanciano-Morandat, Nohara, and Tchobanian 2004). Our studies also indicate that while there is a not insignificant trend toward introducing a share of variable pay, it accounts for only a small fraction of total compensation. In the future, the development of sales activities should favor the expansion of individualized remuneration.

An Apparently Simple Activity That Is Actually Quite Complex

Our studies of eight call centers confirm the large variety of operators' work. This variety obviously can be observed between centers operating in different areas. Operators' work, for example, appeared to be less diversified in the call centers managing relations with subscribers to a regional daily newspaper than in banking call centers, where call center operators carried out practically all of the tasks undertaken by advisers working in bank branches.

Such diversity is also to be found among employees in the same center. For example, in one bank work was ranked in four levels. The first level involved customer reception (identifying questions, providing routine information, and fixing appointments). The last level included all standard operations related to current account management (ordering checkbooks, opening accounts, transfers, buying and selling stock, the opportunistic sale of services,[22] administrative tasks, and handling direct marketing activities). In principle, employees reached the last level after two years' seniority, and reaching that level involved acquiring a large share of the competencies required to work as an adviser in a bank network. Another center, in the insurance sector, distinguished between two categories of call center advisers (who did not work at the same site): advisers responsible for traditional relations with policyholders and those involved in sales, to whom calls from policyholders or prospects seeking to take out additional insurance contracts were transferred. Such distinctions between call centers always exist but may be more or less formalized.

Lastly, outsourcers have a very important influence on independent centers. Their demands are incorporated into the definition of scripts, the control of individual and group performance by call center operators, and even training activities.[23] This trend clearly has repercussions on the management of work and employment, as call center activities and the share of variable pay may evolve, subject to the projects being carried out, in such a way as to allow call center operators within the same center to be treated in a differentiated manner.

Call center operators' work is also characterized by very heterogeneous degrees of complexity, depending on the center (Bancel-Charensol and Jougleux 2004; Buscatto 2002; Charlier et al. 2003; Cousin 2002; Pichault 2000). Several factors cause this complexity:

1. *The degree to which the service offered is personalized*: The service may be completely standardized, or it may be personalized using standardized elements. Services offered may be partly creative when specific solutions have to be found. In our case studies, we found that one of the independent centers was partly involved in making standardized outgoing calls. These calls were made in large numbers, using the same product and the same dialogue out-

line for a given type of client. It should be noted, however, that even with standardized calls call center operators must adapt their dialogue depending on the person contacted. For banks and utilities, most calls are incoming, and that makes substantial standardization of communications very hard. Nevertheless, different kinds of cases are identified, and documentation provides guidelines for handling all situations that have been previously identified. Lastly, certain call center operators who provide assistance to callers must give them technical solutions to problems (relating to machinery, for instance, or to law) that have not been classified in advance. Operators must use their own expertise in these cases.

2. *Call center operators' responsibility for failures*: In some cases, the risks from operators' failure are quite limited and go no further than lower success rates (in sales, appointments, increased contacts, and so on). For banks and insurance companies, the risks may be greater, especially for existing clients: poor service, incorrect information, or inappropriate advice might have repercussions that are not negligible.

3. *Different call center operator situations correspond to different levels and forms of competencies deployed*: Three families of competencies may be found all the time: relational skills, commercial skills, and technical skills. Relational skills concern primarily listening capacities: call center operators must translate customer demands quickly into appropriate terms (for banking, insurance, and so on). This is clearly more difficult to do over the telephone than in face-to-face contact. Relational skills must also be expressed in attitude and language, the aim always being to make communication transparent: clients must feel that they are in direct contact with their agency/branch. In independent centers, operators must even "act out a role," using pseudonyms that change according to the outsourcer or ordering party. Relational skills may also serve to manage the critical situations that can arise when clients are unhappy, annoyed, aggressive, or experiencing difficulties.[24] Commercial skills are systematically required in addition to relational skills, insofar as operators are promoting an image, proposing appointments, stimulating customer needs, taking opportunities, selling or altering subscriptions, and so on. Lastly, technical skills fall into two categories: expertise with the equipment and knowledge of the products to be sold. Operators in the banking sector, insurance, and the distribution of water or energy must know the

professions and products of the companies in question and know the customer advisers in agencies/branches. Thus, the actual work is quite different from the stereotype of the call center telephone operator. For example, the use of faxes and emails requires writing skills that are as important as oral skills, not just in terms of the quality of the writing (spelling, vocabulary, and so on) but also in terms of accuracy and conciseness. Furthermore, in our case studies the computer applications used by call center operators frequently caused problems: several applications often needed to be used simultaneously, and there was much room to improve the ergonomics of operators' workstations.[25] Though these three types of skills were sometimes found simultaneously in all the centers studied, their relative importance varied from case to case.

In all situations, analysis of the content of work nearly always identifies a minimum level of complexity. This may be a result of France's relatively high legal minimum wage, while the simplest call center work has been offshored or automated. Whatever the case, it is a factor that explains the relatively small share of low-wage workers in the call center sector.

Types of Employment: Contrasting Choices Depend on Strategies

Diversity Ranging from Job Insecurity to the Type of Work Found in Internal Labor Markets   The employment characteristics of call center operators are heterogeneous and depend directly on the type of center they are working in and the types of calls they handle. The quality of employment and the quality of work usually go hand in hand as a system, according to the strategy adopted by the center.

The call center sector is known for high levels of job insecurity, or precariousness; on average, 25 percent of jobs are temporary, and even more than 50 percent are temporary in independent centers that handle outgoing calls. But arriving at this observation is not easy, and certain situations are misleading. In banking, call center operators benefit from the job security associated with the sector, to which they perhaps accede after a period of working on a fixed, short-term contract or following a vocational training contract (contrat de professionalisation).[26] In contrast, we also came across open-ended contracts that permitted variable working hours: the hours worked changed from week to week, and operators could not work and hence be paid as much as they wished. Furthermore, in the large independent centers involved in telemarketing, open-ended contracts were often accompanied by high turnover rates stemming from the difficulties of the job. Aside the legal aspects of contracts, the most stable forms of employment were found in in-house centers, and the most insecure and precarious jobs were in independent centers.

Call center work is quite suited to part-time work; indeed, 13.8 percent of employees on average (the share running from 6 percent to 32 percent, depending on the sector), work part-time. Once again, care needs to be taken interpreting these figures. Working part-time is clearly a choice for employees in the banking, insurance, and utility sectors. The choice to work part-time is usually made by women seeking to reconcile work and family obligations. Call center work may in this case be considered an opportunity. On the other hand, in the large, independent centers, part-time work is imposed and the result of choices made by the company.

Worker turnover is particularly high in call centers, but it is also central to their functioning. The rate of rotation (turnover plus internal mobility) is on average about 22 percent. This means that call centers have to renew about one-fifth of their workforce every year. Dismissal rates are very low, and absenteeism varies between 4 and 7 percent, the highest rates being found in independent centers and the telecommunications sector. Turnover is obviously linked to difficult working conditions in independent centers, as well as the tiresome nature of the work, even in centers generating high value-added. In some independent centers, high labor turnover is a way of regulating activity, and employers are fully aware of this. Turnover allows them to avoid implementing work enhancement or career management policies. However, when quality of service is important, turnover is clearly considered a cost and above all an obstacle to professionalization. It is indeed hard to invest in training when a significant share of the staff quits the company each year. From this point of view, the existence of internal markets in the banking, insurance, and utility sectors does ensure that firms get a "return" on their investment during employees' careers.

Career development in call centers is strongly constrained by the existence of "flat," three-level hierarchies: call center operators, supervisors, and departmental managers. Overall, management and supervisory staff make up less than 10 percent of all employees, so that the probability of internal promotion is relatively low. On top of this, the work is very tiring and offers little stimulation. Only a minority of workers thus consider making a career in a center. Some companies have created crossover points to allow workers to move into traditional jobs within the firm. In banking, working as a call center operator is automatically seen as an entry-gate into more traditional jobs, and such vertical mobility is indeed organized by companies. Horizontal mobility can also be developed as variation in the types of calls handled leads to new competencies.

Call centers provide employees with an average of 1.3 weeks of training, similar to the national rate. Such training is closely linked to the characteristics of call center work as described so far, and this is all the more so for jobs of a primary segment nature. Training is also linked to the complexity of products and services. Thus, the training of operators in the banking sector is significant (several weeks) and is carried out by training organizations that work specifically in banking. In contrast, training in one independent center lasted no more than seven hours, which included the recruitment interview.

Approaches to Employment Linked to Strategic Priorities When internal call centers are primarily designed as sources of value-added, they are part of a trend to reshape tasks and are increasingly connected to core businesses. The management of human resources then aims at stabilizing the workforce, training workers, and increasing returns to investment. Employment in this type of call center is most similar to employment in traditional internal labor markets (employment statuses are homogenous, pay scales are identical, workers have the same access to further training, and so on). Indeed, such employment is often seen as an entry-gate into the profession. In our case studies, such strategy-employment links were found in the banking and utility sectors.

When companies see call centers mainly as costs rather than as an activity that can generate value directly, the center's positioning may be defined as peripheral, owing to its limited proximity to the core business. In this case, the tensions between the goals of improving customer services and cost minimization lead to less homogenous approaches to managing jobs. Employment is less secure and fulfilling than in the previous situation and is essentially disconnected from companies' internal labor markets. Pay and pay prospects are lower than in the first model. Operators do not have access to the same in-company mobility as other employees do, and mobility is largely horizontal, limited to changing competencies within the same post. The lack of access to internal labor markets, along with low pay and highly constraining, routine work, leads to high turnover rates. Companies may then feel compelled to modify their strategies: decentralizing centers to regions where labor is abundant and unemployment is high, or externalizing work (sometimes abroad) when services are simple and price competition is strong. Call center staff also include company employees whose jobs are being restructured internally. They retain their existing employee benefits. As in the case of nonperipheral, internal centers, such cases are found in banks and utilities. They suggest that, faced with similar economic constraints, companies still have some room for maneuver in choosing their employment strategies.

Both situations may be found in independent centers, depending on their positioning in the market (high-value-added versus low-value-added activities). In one of the independent centers we studied, the positioning in high-value-added services (legal support services, advice in automobile mechanics) was based on the specific and complex work of operators. The search for a certain level of expertise leads centers to employ qualified personnel, which they must attract, then train and retain through relatively favorable employment and working conditions, comparable to those found in in-house centers of the first type. That said, it is hard to organize mobility and career promotion in such independent call centers, especially given their flat organizational structures. The lack of career prospects, along with the lassitude linked to telephone work, greatly hampers workers in investing in their work in the long run. Indeed, workers frequently seek to capitalize on their expertise by moving to companies that work directly in the sectors concerned (in our case studies, legal and mechanical work).

In call centers positioned in relatively simple activities and focusing more on volumes, work was observed to be far more constraining (in terms of procedures and the pace of work) and subject to the permanent pressure of quantitative objectives, which are taken into account in fixing pay (the length of calls, sales opportunities, customer retention rates, and so on). These centers hired relatively qualified workers (usually with a baccalaureate and a certain level of general education) who were not necessarily looking for stable work (for example, students). Immigrants were also found in such jobs, given that they faced job discrimination elsewhere and may have had problems getting work in more traditional sales activities. By employing such staff and situating call centers in regions of high unemployment, companies can keep wages to a minimum, while drawing on external employment and labor flexibility and at the same time meeting minimum service quality standards compared to offshore centers. As a result, the highest turnover and absenteeism rates are to be found in such centers, and more generally workers in this environment are the most likely to fall into the low-wage category.

Overall, despite the existence of various employment situations, working in call centers is very tough because of its intensity and the flexibility required by the work.

FLEXIBLE, INTENSE, AND HIGHLY CONSTRAINED WORK

Generally speaking, the opening hours of call centers are very long. On average, 45 percent of centers are open for more than twelve hours per day (69 percent for subcontractors of incoming calls, 64 percent in the telecommunications sector, and 14 percent in insurance). Only 12 percent of centers—mainly independent centers taking incoming calls—work on Sundays.[27] In contrast, a majority of centers are open on Saturdays. Such national data are confirmed by our various case studies, even including an in-house center that was open seven days a week, twenty-four hours a day.

The long opening hours are possible because work is organized in shifts, which tend to overlap. In some cases, activity cycles are well known and all work can be planned, even for incoming calls. For example, the closing time of traditional agencies/branches generates activity peaks in centers. Similarly, the seasonality of people moving homes or billing by utilities tends to structure activity over time (for example, the opening and cutting off of meters). Some centers use planned schedules to offer their workers very regular hours. Others tend to react more to demand, and activity rates may vary considerably from week to week.

How long operators work each week is also managed in various ways. In one of the centers we studied (the in-house banking center), the working week was fixed at thirty-two hours, spread over four days, and paid on the basis of thirty-six and a half hours. In another center (in-house, utilities), a local agreement had fixed the working week at twenty-six hours, paid on the basis of thirty-five hours.[28] Such favorable conditions result from a compensation process whereby the tiring nature of the work, as well as night and weekend work, is rewarded. Companies may also want to make work in call centers more attractive, especially when centers are situated in peripheral locations. The independent centers studied here organized work, with variable hours for operators, each week. Such variability seemed to be quite well accepted by the workers, who saw it as a means of breaking routine and especially as a way of organizing their own time. In one center in particular, many employees saw their situation as providing supplementary work, or as being temporary, and they therefore appreciated being able to choose days and hours to work. This was especially at the center that was located downtown, where flexible hours could be put to good use.

Operators reply to an average of sixty-eight to ninety-seven calls per day, depending on whether the activity is geared to business customers or the mass market. Average call times run from two to four minutes, though in some cases they may last more than twenty minutes (the opening or cutting off of utility meters) or even fifty minutes (identifying automobile problems over the phone).

Most studies indicate that work is ubiquitously and constantly controlled and assessed (Charlier et al. 2003). New technologies make such control possible, particularly in IT, and it is carried out by listening in on calls. Such listening in may be negotiated or imposed, transparent or hidden. In some cases, it may have real consequences, especially in terms of pay. Our observations show that listening in is also intended to accompany or support operators' work.[29] This is especially the case in centers where the operators themselves record calls they wish to be evaluated or when listening in occurs while supervisors are physically present and is clearly announced.

Performance is often measured using certain indicators, such as the number of calls, the average duration, the number of calls lost, the average waiting time, the number of opportunistic sales, or the number of appointments arranged. That said, it was observed that while performance criteria were dominant in the call centers we studied, many of them preferred to look at indicative target ranges so as to avoid being too heavy-handed and to preserve a degree of service quality. The ubiquity of monitoring screens, which list the number of incoming calls waiting in line as well as waiting times, nevertheless emphasizes the center's objectives and contributes to creating a constraining climate in which operators must guide their customers so as not to exceed recommended call times.[30]

The call center operators interviewed in our studies unanimously stressed the mental fatigue of their work. A recent study by Bernard Dugué and colleagues (2007) confirms this result, stressing that nearly 90 percent of operators are "completely washed out after working." All the tele-operators explained that they felt exhausted at the end of the day. In one center, some women operators, for example, stated that they were incapable of working full-time. The pace of work, the obligation to handle simultaneously a conversation at a distance while using a computer program, the ubiquity of objectives, all lead to fatigue. The physical conditions of the phone call organize a remote, face-to-face situation with a customer in which there is no escape for the operator—not visually (visual scope is limited to the operator's cubicle), not aurally (the headset makes the conversation with a customer exclusive), not intellectually (the path of the discussion is more or less formally structured), and especially not in terms of time (the succession of calls allows only a little breathing space). The operator's full attention is captured by the production process. Work intensity is thus at the maximum level.

Furthermore, the work generates a certain weariness, which everyone stressed (both management and operators). Operators sometimes quite quickly feel that they have learned everything there is to know about the job, which is deemed as routine, if not boring in the long run, even its more complex tasks.

The physical constraints of call center operators' work is mentioned in the literature with respect to different problems: the size of the working space, the temperature, the lighting, and the ventilation (ISERES 2001); the noise levels and the prolonged work in front of computer screens, which may lead to auditory or visual problems (Delaunay 2003); and the ergonomics of workstations. These physical constraints were not mentioned, however, by the operators we interviewed, perhaps for several reasons: whatever the physical conditions, mental fatigue was much more strongly felt than physical discomfort, which was given secondary importance; a majority of workers underlined the efforts made to improve working conditions, such as the "daisy-shaped" organization of workstations, flat screens, ventilation systems, improvements to headsets, workstations that were sometimes personalized, and comfortable rooms for taking breaks; and the physical constraints reflected the initial impact of employers' and unions' declarations in favor of improved working conditions in call centers and their related institutional consequences (for example, the "social responsibility" label mentioned earlier, quality standards, and so on).

Working conditions generate regulations and even resistance. Generally speaking, back-office work (filing, handling mail, replying to emails, enhancing and updating databases), emailing, and when possible making outgoing telephone calls are all means of unwinding. Breaks are also necessary for employees to recover: while they may usually choose when to take a break, time off is regulated and depends on workers achieving the expected objectives, such as a certain number of daily calls or the minimization of waiting lines.

CONCLUSION

Our research qualifies the initial contrast presented between in-house and independent centers. While this contrast remains largely relevant, it is fundamental for this analysis to distinguish call centers according to their proximity to companies' core businesses (the parent company for integrated centers, outsourcers for independent centers). When this criterion is taken into account, it is possible to put forward four business models, or strategic positioning models: the strategic status versus the peripheral status of customer relations for in-house centers, with alternative positions in terms of cost-competitiveness or quality for independent centers. The results of our qualitative survey underline the role of strategic positioning by call centers in determining the working and employment conditions of operators.

Apart from the employment models linked to the strategic choices made by companies, institutions also play a central and complementary role, at two levels. First, the fact that France has a relatively high legal minimum wage automatically excludes competitive strategies based only on costs (see chapter 2). Companies opting for such a strategy are most likely to work offshore, especially as technology reduces the impact of distance and borders. Other firms must include a degree of quality in their performance model, notably in terms of the quality of communication with customers and adaptation to the specificities of the local sociocultural environment. Second, though they are incomplete, the efforts made jointly by public authorities, labor unions, and some employers' representatives have led to embryonic national regulation of work in call centers. This includes aspects of collective agreements as well as some level of training and improved working conditions.

A more institutional regulation of the sector in France thus appears to be a social and economic necessity. It is a condition for a sustainable model to emerge. Indeed, workers' dissatisfaction and demands concerning employment and working conditions are strong and numerous. As a result, call centers have a fairly bad reputation, leading to problems of recruiting and retaining personnel. From an economic point of view, the sector probably needs to be professionalized in order to generalize the content and level of skills compatible with strategies based on service quality.

The call center sector in France differs from the same sector in the United States, not just in its quantitative development but for two other main reasons. The discriminating nature of the presence of unions, and especially its impact on the quality of jobs (stressed by Batt, Hunter, and Wilk 2003), is much lower in France. At the same time, there seems to be no equivalent in the United States to the nascent institutional regulation of the sector in France, which is leading to the professionalization of call center operators. As for convergence, the important impact of strategic choices on the employment relationship stands out, as do similarities in the characteristics of "better jobs": the use of technology stresses the complementarity of workers and machines more than striving for substitution; companies invest in training; there is a team/collective dimension to work; and types of employment are protective.

APPENDIX

Table 7A.1 The Case Study Call Centers

	Presence of Unions in the Call Center	Local Rate of Unemployment[a]	Number of Jobs in the Call Center	Degree of Complexity of the Work	Dominant Type of Labor Contract
Bank 1	No, but strong in the company	8.4%	Sixty (two sites)	Medium +	Permanent
Bank 2	No, but strong in the company	9.1	Ninety (two sites)	Medium +	Permanent
Bank 3	No, but present in the company	9.1	Sixty (three sites)	Medium –/+	Permanent; 25 percent of contracts are temporary
Utility 1	Yes	10.6	120 (two sites)	Medium –/+	Permanent
Utility 2	No, but very strong in the company	10.0	Seventy	Medium +	Permanent
Utility 3	Yes	9.7	Sixty	Medium	Permanent; 20 percent are part-time
EXT1 (telecommunications, press, etc.)	No	9.9	Eighty-five	Low	Permanent contracts with variable hours; two-thirds are part-time
EXT2 (press, mechanical and legal assistance, etc.)	No	8.6	190 (three sites)	Low/high	Permanent; temporary contracts for beginner operators

Source: Authors' compilation.
[a] Institut Nationale de la Statistique et des Études Economiques (INSEE), rate of unemployment (employment catchment area), third quarter 2005.
[b] Data ranked by scale; estimated from available information.

Table 7A.1 (*Continued*)

Weekly Hours for Full-Time Worker	Basic Wage as a Percentage of the Low-Wage Threshold[b]	Total Hourly Pay as a Function of the Actual Number of Hours Worked (as a Percentage of the Low-Wage Threshold)[b]	Average Duration of Initial Training	Career Progression	Work Environment
Thirty-two	114%	145%	Three weeks	++	++
Thirty-five	123	125	Three weeks	++	++
Thirty-five	113	113	Four weeks	−	++
Thirty-five	103	107	Three weeks	−	++
Twenty-six	137	183	Eight weeks	++	+++
Thirty-five	117	159	Eight weeks	+	+++
Thirty-five	92	94	One day	—	−
Thirty-five	101	110	One to three weeks	—	++

NOTES

1. The creation of a sector (coded 74.8H) allowed 320 independent centers—employing the equivalent of 30,500 full-time staff—to be identified. This figure probably understates the real number given the recentness of its definition.
2. Data whose sources are not otherwise specified in this text come from these surveys; see Lanciano-Morandat, Nohara, and Tchobanian (2004).
3. These percentages are calculated on the basis of 210,000 jobs in 2005.
4. Le Crédit Lyonnais, for example, signed a specific agreement for call centers in the banking sector in 1997.
5. A third agreement exists for market-study companies. Independent call centers often referred to this agreement prior to 1999, but today it covers only centers that work specifically in opinion polling.
6. This reflects a French paradox: an agreement that may not be ratified by the main unions is nevertheless applied to all employees of companies in a particular branch (see chapter 2). For the service providers' agreement, two minority unions allowed the agreement to be ratified (the Confédération Générale des Cadres (CGC), the managers union, and the Confédération Françoise des Travailleurs (CFTC), the union of Christian workers).
7. "All actors are conscious of the fact that for jobs to be kept in France, and for our companies to stay in the market, a balance has to be struck. We were putting too much emphasis on cost-cutting," said Laurent Huberti, president of the SP2C, in 2005 (*Revue des Centres d'Appels* 59[November 2005]).
8. The call center was part of a group of more than fifty companies, and employees were covered by twenty-seven collective agreements. Included in the various job statuses were local government employees.
9. "These various training schemes, both in initial and continuing training, will provide the call-center sector with a level of maturity, but they are still insufficiently developed . . . and such insufficiencies are one of the main obstacles to customer relations jobs being fully recognised as a proper profession" (AFRC 2004, 72).
10. Nearly 20 percent of the centers surveyed by the LEST (Lanciano-Morandat, Nohara, and Tchobanian 2004) received tax incentives.
11. Initial training programs notably lack candidates to meet companies' recruitment needs. According to the president of the AFRC, "only 150 young people take the vocational high school diploma each year, even though there is demand for 10,000" (*Le Monde*, September 11, 2004).
12. Call centers in France are less equipped with IT than in the United States: 70 percent use emails or faxes, 18 percent use Internet teleph-

ony, and 16 percent use automatic voice recognition. Centers are developing their tools, from a single voice channel to the use of multiple channels (internet, emails, and so on), but these changes are happening more slowly than in the United States (Lanciano-Morandat, Nohara, and Tchobanian 2004).

13. Scripts are guidelines rather than rigid instructions. But they clearly exist, and they symbolize the separation of conception and execution in the customer relationship.
14. According to Jean-Claude Delaunay (2003), the cost of establishing a call center ranges from €15,000 to €20,000 (US$21,399 to US$28,532) per operator position or workstation.
15. Call centers establishing offshore facilities do so as part of a strategy of being able to provide a whole range of services to their clients. As one manager remarked, "It is important to show our clients that we are based both in France and offshore. In fact, clients very often opt for missions that mix campaigns run from abroad and from France."
16. The quality of a telephone call should be seen here as including a quality relationship, which applies to the relationship between the client company and the call center, as well as to the relationship between the call center and the final customers contacted (either clients or prospects).
17. Indeed, it is interesting to note that most call center operators in this field are usually called "advisers."
18. It should be stressed that an increasing proportion of independent centers seem to take this service quality constraint into account, leading them to revise considerably their approach to human resource management. Numerous references to such quality considerations may be found in the call center trade press.
19. One study identified forty occupations (LAB'HO 2000).
20. In this study, the annual salary includes all forms of performance pay (individual commissions, profit-sharing bonuses, and so on) but excludes paid overtime.
21. A study by ESC Paris (the Paris Business School) indicated a similar spread of 30 percent.
22. "Opportunistic" sales of services are those that arise during a client's telephone call with a call center operator.
23. These features were observed in our study and corroborate results found elsewhere, such as by François Pichault (2000).
24. In independent centers, one criterion by which operators are evaluated is their ability to retain subscribers calling to cancel a subscription. This is actually a contractual objective for them.
25. Information systems are often very old and have evolved through the addition of modules and by successive modifications of new programs.

Such "stratified" systems are not necessarily satisfactory, but they are difficult to improve without being fully overhauled.
26. The contrats de professionalisation are reserved for young people age sixteen to twenty-five. They involve compulsory training, including general subjects, as well as vocational and technological courses. Employees acquire know-how through working in one or several areas with a firm, depending on the qualification they seek. These contracts allow companies to combine vocational training, while benefiting from reduced social security contributions.
27. These patterns may change following the adoption of the decree of August 2, 2005, which allows telephone and telematic help-line services to work on Sundays.
28. The low number of hours worked automatically leads to higher hourly pay rates, increasing the gap vis-à-vis the low-wage threshold.
29. Listening in is legitimized by the fact that it is intended not only to control call center operators but to support them.
30. Some computer programs send out alerts when calls are too long, when not enough customers have been handled, and so on.

REFERENCES

Association Française de Relation Clientèle (AFRC). 2004. *Le Livre blanc de l'AFRC* [*The White Book for AFRC*]. Paris: AFRC.

Bancel-Charensol, Laurence, and Muriel Jougleux. 2004. "Performance du service, autonomie du travail, et système interactif d'aide à la solution" ["Performance of Service, Work Autonomy, and an Interactive System Helps the Solution"]. Communication at the conference "La métamorphose des organisations" ["The Change in Organizations"], organized by Université Nancy 2 and Groupe de Recherche en Economie Financière et Gestion des Entreprises (GREFIGE), 25. Accessed at http://www.univ-nancy2.fr/COLLOQUES/METAMORPHOSE/communications/Bancel-Charensol-Jougleux.pdf.

Batt, Rosemary, Larry W. Hunter, and Steffanie Wilk. 2003. "How and When Does Management Matter? Job Quality and Career for Call Center Workers." In *Low-Wage America: How Employers Are Reshaping Opportunities in the Workplace*, edited by Eileen Appelbaum, Annette Bernhardt, and Richard J. Murnane. New York: Russell Sage Foundation.

Buscatto, Marie. 2002. "Les Centres d'appels, usines modernes? Les rationalisations paradoxales de la relation téléphonique" ["Call Centers, Modern Factories? The Paradoxical Rationalizations of Telephone Communication"]. *Sociologie du Travail* 44(3): 99–117.

Centre d'Études Stratégiques pour le Moyen-Orient (CESMO). 2003. "Le Marché des centres d'appels en France" ["The Call Center Market in France"]. Paris: CESMO.

———. 2004., "Le Marché des centres de contact en France" ["The Contact Center Market in France"]. Paris: CESMO.

Charlier, Myriam, Thierry Colin, Benoît Grasser, Jean-Pascal Higele, Andréana Khristova, José Rose, Régis Rouyer, and Gael Ryk. 2003. *La Construction sociale des frontières entre la qualification et la non qualification* [*The Social Construction of Borders Between Qualification and Non-qualificaion*]. Research report. Paris: DARES.

Cousin, Olivier. 2002. "Les Ambivalences du travail: Les salariés peu qualifiés dans les centres d'appels" ["The Ambivalence of Work: Poorly Qualified Employees in Call Centers"]. *Sociologie du Travail* 44(4): 499–520.

Delaunay, Jean-Claude. 2003. "Centres d'appels: Développements techniques et rôle du facteur humain" ["Call Centers: Technical Developments and the Role of the Human Factor"]. In *Les Centres d'appels: Un secteur en clair-obscur* [*Call Centers: Between Light and Darkness*], edited by Noel Lechat and Jean-Claude Delaunay. Paris: L'Harmattan.

Doeringer, Peter B., and Michael J. Piore. 1971. *Internal Labor Market and Manpower Analysis*. Lexington, Mass.: D. C. Heath Lexington.

Dugué, Bernard, Philippe Maussion, Yves-Alain Durteste, and Béatrice Druelle. 2007. "Stress, TMS, une expérimentation du terrain" ["Stress, TMS, A Ground Experiment"]. *Revue de la CFDT* 81(January-February): 2107.

Houéry, Marc. 2004. *Rapport du groupe de travail sur l'industrie de la relation clientele* [*Report of the Working Group on Business and Customer Relations*]. Paris: Ministry of Industry.

Institut National de la Statistique et des Études Économiques (INSEE). 2006. *INSEE Références: Les services en France (services aux entreprises)* [*INSEE References: Services in France (Services for Businesses)*]. Paris: INSEE.

Institut de Recherches Economiques et Sociales (ISERES). 2001. *Enquête sur les conditions de travail et les relations sociales dans les centres d'appels téléphoniques en France* [*Survey on Working Conditions and Social Relations in Telephone Call Centers in France*]. Les Documents de l'ISERES. Paris: ISERES.

Laboratoire des hommes et des organisations (LAB'HO). 2000. *Un Travail au bout du fil: Les salariés des centres d'appels: Profils, rémunérations, carrières* [*Working Down to the Wire: Employees in Call Centers: Profiles, Compensation, Careers*]. Paris: Groupe Adecco.

Lanciano-Morandat, Caroline, Hiroatsu Nohara, and Robert Tchobanian. 2004. *French Call Center Industry Report 2004*. Aix-en-Provence, France: LEST-CNRS.

Pichault, François. 2000. "Calls centres, hiérarchie virtuelle et gestion des ressources humaines" ["Call Centers, Virtual Hierarchy, and Managing Human Resources"]. *Revue Française de Gestion* 130 (September-October): 5–15.

CHAPTER 8

Summary and Conclusions: Why and How Do Institutions Matter?

Ève Caroli and Jérôme Gautié

This research was motivated by questions about institutions, and we can now draw lessons from our results about the role of French institutions in shaping the low-wage labor market at a global level and in promoting "high-road" management practices at the micro level.

At the macro level, state regulations, particularly the minimum wage and employment protection legislation, play a crucial role and help to shape the French employment model. This model is characterized by a much smaller proportion of low-wage workers than in the United States and in many European Union countries, both at the macro level and in a number of sectors that are typically low-wage-intensive in other countries. This is all the more striking given that French firms have faced changes in their economic environment very similar to those taking place in other developed countries. In particular, competitive pressure has substantially increased in recent years owing to changes in consumption patterns as well as the globalization of production and trade. At the same time, unemployment remains high in France, and no serious improvement seems to be likely in the short run. This raises, of course, one question: does the French employment model boil down to a mere insider- outsider dilemma?

Our case studies suggest that this is not quite the case. In particular, the small proportion of low-wage workers in many sectors is supported by strong work intensification and bad (and worsening) working conditions. Moreover, segmentation in the labor market is strong, not only between insiders (those holding a job) and outsiders (those excluded from employment) but among employed workers as well: some have stable jobs, whereas others experience high precariousness when employed on one of the numerous derogatory work contracts. Eventually, career prospects are few and gloomy for most low-skill, potentially low-paid workers. However, at the micro level, some "good practices" can be seen. Their scope is largely determined by employers' idiosyncrasies, but strong local institutions, such as unions and regional and branch-level collective agreements, also have an impact.

THE GLOBAL PICTURE OF LOW-WAGE WORK IN FRANCE: THE BASIC "INSIDERS-OUTSIDERS" MODEL REVISITED

According to a commonly shared view, someone who has a job in France is well protected, is paid a high salary, and enjoys good working conditions. These privileges may carry a cost: the so-called outsiders are excluded from employment. Consequently, low-wage workers who are employed are much better off in France than in the United States—and many other European countries—thanks to a much more regulated labor market. Many of them, however, are priced out of the labor market.

The picture emerging from the present research is much more nuanced than this received wisdom, for a number of reasons relating to working and employment conditions.

The Model of High Hourly Wages, High Productivity, and Bad Working Conditions

A High Hourly Wage Does Not Necessarily Mean High Monthly Earnings As already mentioned, the French minimum wage is much higher than the American one, in both real and relative terms. But another important feature of the French labor market is that labor supply is highly constrained. Not only is unemployment very high (about 9 percent in 2006), but so is underemployment—workers being employed but not in the desired capacity, whether in terms of compensation, hours, skill level, or experience. Underemployment in terms of skills is widespread among young workers and also among women. In terms of hours, about 8.5 percent of working women are involuntarily part-timers. The implementation of the laws on the reduction of working time has in many instances led to the "annualization" of working time (actual working time defined on an annual rather than a weekly basis), which allows for more variability in weekly working time. For many low-paid workers, the consequence has been a reduction in the number of overtime hours—

which are paid at higher rates than normal hours—and hence a reduction in monthly earnings. Overall, compared to the Americans and the British, it is harder for French low-skilled, low-wage workers to compensate for low hourly wages by increasing the number of hours they work.

High Work Performance but Poor Working Conditions High hourly minimum wages, high capital intensity, and short working times are specific features of the French employment model. But so are high work intensity and bad working conditions. Drawing on the general surveys of working conditions presented in chapter 2 as well as the results of the case studies presented in the industry chapters, we can see that the working conditions of low-wage, low-skilled workers are often poor in France compared to many other European countries. The absence of unions and poor application of the rules seem to have a particularly significant impact in these areas. Moreover, the workers interviewed in the case studies felt strongly that work is intensifying, and that belief helps to explain why their resentment focused on wages more than on working conditions. One comment frequently made (see chapter 3, for instance) was: "We have to work harder, but our wages don't rise in line with the work." These working conditions are surely not specific to France, but they are perhaps more important here than elsewhere.

The high labor productivity in France partly relies on work intensity at the expense of working conditions: this is especially so in many retail and food-processing companies and also in certain hospitals. The backwardness of working conditions in certain sectors has a number of causes, including generational effects and the social and geographic origins of labor. In the food-processing industry, many workers over forty years old come from rural, peasant-farmer backgrounds and are used to hard physical work, whereas younger generations are more demanding about working conditions (chapter 3). In other areas, including housekeeping in the hotel industry (chapter 5) and construction work (which is not covered by this study), immigrants are numerous (and sometimes illegal) and hence more prone to accept bad working conditions and even undeclared work. Apart from the characteristics of labor (but in connection with them), a significant factor has been the lack of importance that unions give to demands for better working conditions. For a long time, their priority has been pay and the possibility of obtaining compensatory bonuses, and that is still their focus in sectors like food processing (chapter 3), hospitals (chapter 4), and retailing (chapter 6). In some sectors (such as food processing), the fear of capital replacing labor has also acted to restrain demands for better working conditions. Last but not least, the high level of unemployment (and underemployment) contributes to the acceptance of poor working conditions.

HIGH DUALISM WITHIN EMPLOYMENT

Permanent Versus Nonpermanent Workers The classical form of dualism between permanent and nonpermanent staff is particularly marked in France (as indeed it is in other Southern European countries). Aside from the "standard" fixed-term contracts—used in two-thirds of all recruitment—and temporary agency work, both of which are strongly regulated, the proliferation of so-called atypical contracts feeds such dualism. Precarious jobs affect low-wage workers in particular, and the industry studies presented in this volume provide many examples of this. Young people, women, and immigrants (or French people of immigrant origin) are found disproportionately among low-wage workers and also among people holding precarious jobs. This segmentation of the labor force flows from company strategies, even in relatively tight labor markets, in which firms use their monopsony power at the expense of targeted segments of the labor force: captive and not very mobile labor such as married women or single mothers (for the most illustrative examples, see chapter 5 on hotels and chapter 6 on retailing). Such strategies are clearly helped, in most cases, by relatively high rates of unemployment in local labor markets.

As a result, there is a continuum of "intermediate" job statuses or situations, ranging from unemployment to full-time employment on open-ended contracts. These situations involve a sort of waiting in line. Hospitals (chapter 4), especially in the public sector, are the most extreme case: some actually keep a pool of candidates recruited according to their daily needs on the basis of fixed-term contracts that may be as short as one day. Hotels (chapter 5) also keep pools of workers who make themselves available anytime in the hope of working even a few hours. In both cases, individuals may work from contract to contract—sometimes over a period of five to seven years in public hospitals—before getting a permanent job. In hospitals, advancement takes place by waiting in line and according to (implicit) rules based on seniority as well as workers' readiness to work. The same is true for hotels, which run hierarchies for housekeepers' contracts, with "extras" at the bottom, followed by "standard" fixed-term contracts and permanent contracts at the top. The latter can be obtained only through seniority and after workers have proven their worth and loyalty. Some employers even admit to not giving employees permanent contracts for fear of losing leverage over them. Advancement not only means moving from more to less precarious contracts but also working more hours and more social and predictable hours: workers move progressively from short, involuntary, part-time, and irregular hours to longer and more regular work. Call centers (chapter 7) and retailers (chapter 6) are more prone to offer permanent contracts directly, but only because harsh working conditions in those sectors induce very high voluntary turnover—and therefore the high employment protection on open-ended contracts is not a problem for these employers.

Precarious jobs are not just a means of putting pressure on workers but also a way for companies to filter and select employees. Most food-processing companies recruit only among temporary workers, and one company even admitted to organizing what it called an "obstacle course" for young recruits, lasting for eighteen months and stretching from temporary agency work to tenure via a fixed-term contract. This is actually common practice among many manufacturing companies in France. Such practices are made possible by the shortage of jobs, but they also result partly from the difficulties (as companies see it) of dismissing workers who hold permanent contracts. Indeed, eighteen months may even be considered a "fast track": the study shows that some women in the food-processing and hotel sectors held seasonal or "extra" contracts for many years and that some of them lost all hope of ever obtaining tenure.

The gender dimension of labor market segmentation stands out clearly in these cases. In some sectors, this is because the occupations examined are nearly always held by women (for example, checkout cashiers, housekeepers, nursing assistants). In others, such as packing operators in the food-processing sector, women work disproportionately in the lowest-paid jobs within a given occupation. Eventually, women are more affected by undesired part-time work, particularly those who work in hospitals and hotels, where many staff work for rather short hours.

The Precariousness of Insiders Access to permanent worker status does not constitute a "step to nirvana" for many low-wage workers.

One of the apparent paradoxes in France is that even alleged "insiders" (workers with much seniority in stable jobs) feel strongly that their job is insecure, even if, on average, the probability of losing their job is relatively low (see European and OECD surveys on subjective security; OECD 2004). But this is not paradoxical if the high probability of becoming one of the long-term unemployed, following dismissal, is taken into account; this probability is especially high for low-skilled workers, and even higher for persons over fifty years old. Except for young workers—who are often victims of firms' churning practices—the French labor market is not fluid: both the probabilities of entering and exiting unemployment are lower than in the United States and other European countries such as the United Kingdom and Denmark.

Low-wage, low-skilled, permanent workers over forty years old tend therefore to "stick" to their jobs—and to defend strong employment protection at the trade union and political levels. In some food-processing companies and in some private hospitals, the turnover rates of permanent workers are so low that employers complain, since they face a loss of "natural" flexibility. This in turn encourages them to resort to precarious employment and reinforces labor market dualism.

In contrast, mobility—both imposed and voluntary—is much more marked among young people, who are also better trained. Young employees tend to avoid certain companies or sectors, which explains the apparent paradox of "labor shortages" in some industries, such as the hotel industry and catering (though this is not true for housekeepers) or the food-processing industry. That said, freedom of choice remains limited, and young people are the first victims of labor market dualism.

In many firms, especially in the retail and hotel sectors (and to a lesser extent in food processing), "exit" and "voice" strategies are quite limited for low-wage workers. "Loyalty" is therefore widespread even if often involuntary.

LOW CAREER PROSPECTS AND FEW OPPORTUNITIES TO GET OUT OF LOW-PAID JOBS

Problems with the poor quality of jobs are diminished if the jobs in question are only temporary in individual employees' careers. This relates to how possible it is for workers to leave low-wage work. From this point of view, the small number of existing studies on wage mobility does not show France to be in a poor position compared to other

European countries. But care should be taken with the statistics, given the compression at the bottom of the wage distribution: the threshold of low wages is close to the SMIC (less than 6 percent higher in the beginning of the 2000s), so that a small rise in pay (due to a seniority premium, for example) may push wages above this threshold. Apart from the call center sector, where labor is often young and staff turnover is high, and hotels, where workers in back-office occupations are older but do more exhausting work, many employees in the other sectors and occupations studied here stay in their jobs throughout their careers. Yet lifetime wage profiles are relatively flat, and the high relative level of the minimum wage as a starting wage may be one cause of this low-(basic) wage "trap." Moreover, in many firms upward mobility on the occupational ladder has decreased for the lowest-skilled because college-leavers are more likely to be recruited into jobs in the middle-ranking occupations. This partly explains why unions are so in favor of the traditional seniority premium, though that premium is being called into question in various sectors (see, for instance, chapter 3 on food processing and chapter 7 on call centers). At the same time, profit-sharing schemes and profit-related pay are spreading, especially in big companies. Overall, all these factors are contributing to the decline of internal labor markets, which used to be a cornerstone of the postwar French employment model.

ASSESSING THE VARIATIONS IN FIRMS' STRATEGIES AND WORKERS' OUTCOMES

Beyond drawing a global picture of low-wage work in France compared to other European Union countries and the United States, this research aims to better understand within-country differences in firms' strategies and workers' outcomes. The case studies were carried out in order to develop a deep qualitative understanding of firms' decisionmaking. Are French firms' strategies the same as American ones, and what is the impact of the national institutional context on these strategies? What can explain variations in firms' strategies in France?

LOOKING FOR THE HIGH ROADS IN THE FRENCH INSTITUTIONAL CONTEXT

American research has pointed out two main types of competitive strategies (Appelbaum, Bernhardt, and Murnane 2003). The first one is focused on reducing labor costs through wage and benefit cuts. It is the consequence of increasing competition on the product market and firms' monopsony power on the labor market (Manning 2003). The second strategy, based on the use of new technologies and new forms of work organization, is to enhance productivity. The second strategy is therefore more likely to develop "high-road" practices with better outcomes for workers. These alternative strategies are pursued in France as well, but they are shaped by a different institutional context. Indeed, because there are more barriers to intense cost-cutting strategies, productivity-enhancing strategies are more likely to be adopted. Outcomes for workers, however, are not always as good as we could expect.

Barriers to Strategies to Cut Labor Costs Two different strategies may be used to reduce the cost of labor (Appelbaum, Bernhardt, and Murnane 2003): keeping the same workers but freezing their wages, cutting their benefits, and increasing their workload; using nonpermanent workers, subcontracting or outsourcing, or relocating the jobs to lower-wage areas. Both strategies can be found among French firms.

In food processing, for instance, the implementation of the thirty-five-hour working week has been accompanied in many firms by wage freezes, suppression of overtime hours, and even, in confectionery, the suppression of the seniority premium for new entrants. In the same subsector, big multinational firms, which used to offer higher wages and fringe benefits, now tend to outsource their production activity to firms where compensation is lower. Public hospitals, facing tighter budget constraints, intensively use nonpermanent workers under different types of contracts —and notably, they also use beneficiaries of subsidized labor market policy schemes. Many hotels use undeclared work (and therefore do not pay mandatory social contributions) and do not pay overtime hours. Moreover, as far as housekeepers are concerned, the threat of subcontracting, at least in big chains, is constant. Not paying overtime hours is also widespread in retailing. As for call centers, many have been offshored to other French-speaking countries, and the threat of offshoring is a constant pressure on French workers.

Nevertheless, the intensity of these so-called social dumping strategies is limited by many features of the French institutional framework. Except for undeclared work, the national legal minimum wage and the mandatory social contributions to the public social security system are strong barriers to wage-cutting. The legal extension of branch-level collective agreements is another key element, especially when compared to the United States or other European countries, such as Germany. Employment protection legislation also puts strong limitations on the use of temporary agency work and fixed-term contracts. It also guarantees, for both types of contracts, that a so-called precariousness premium (amounting to 10 percent of the basic wage) is paid to workers. Nevertheless, firms use these contracts a lot (together with derogatory forms of temporary work) to get more flexibility than would be allowed by permanent contracts. Restrictions on immigration may have also played a role in limiting social dumping strategies: for instance, in food-processing activities, the use of immigrants from Eastern European countries has remained an exception in France so far, while it is widespread in the United Kingdom (where immigrants work as temps) and Germany (where they work as posted workers).

Overall, an important consequence is that the gap between low-paying and high-paying firms in a given sector is probably lower in France than in the United States. The call center sector provides a striking illustration of this: at the aggregate level, while the gap between the average wage of tele-operators is only 9 percent between mass-market service operators and large-business service operators in France, it amounts to nearly 60 percent in the United States.

An Institutional Framework More Favorable to Innovative Practices and Productivity Enhancement? Because of the lesser availability of cheap labor, French firms may be more prone to adopt technology-based competitive strategies. Indeed, as detailed in chapter 2, some empirical evidence at the macro and industry levels (such as the record hourly labor productivity and capital intensity) supports this view. In many sectors, offering higher-quality, higher-value-added products and services appears to be the most reliable strategy to cope with increasing competitive pressures. In this case, the use of nonpermanent workers (as in food-processing activities) or subcontracting (for low-skilled activities such as cleaning in hospitals, housekeeping in hotels, and appointments management in in-house call centers) may be counterproductive in the search for quality, and some firms have reduced or even suppressed this practice.

Beyond those that have an impact on labor costs, other institutional features may foster the adoption of productivity-enhancing strategies. Employment protection legislation and the thirty-five-hour week have led to an increase in functional flexibility (multiskilling and job rotation) as well as internal numerical flexibility (concerning working time). Moreover, the compression of wages resulting from the minimum wage may have had a positive impact on training, according to the mechanism analyzed by Daron Acemoglu and Jörn-Steffen Pischke (1999). Some empirical evidence supports this view in the food-processing sector and in call centers, in which high-wage firms tend to train their workers more, but training remains very low in all sectors at low-wage levels. Overall, it is hard to reach clear conclusions from the industry case studies on this point. Two factors may have played a countervailing role in France: work intensification, on the one hand, and the hiring of young skilled workers in low-skilled, low-wage occupations, on the other hand. These trends have been made possible by the high level of unemployment and the large increase in the educational level of school-leavers since the second half of the 1980s.[1]

But relying on a technology-based, productivity-enhancing strategy does not necessarily lead to better outcomes for workers. In many companies, technological change is used as a cost-cutting strategy and serves to implement lean production processes and computerized control. This has generated work intensification, as is the case in many firms in retailing, food processing, and, to a lower extent, call centers. This "neo-Taylorism," which is widespread in France (Askenazy 2004), is consistent with the global model of high (hourly) wages, high productivity, and poor working conditions. Even in firms that combine technical change with innovative practices in work organization (such as teamwork, total quality management, task rotation, and multiskilling), work intensification and rising stress are increasingly lamented by low-skilled workers.

What Explains Variations in Firms' Strategies?

Even if variations in firms' strategies may appear less important in France than in the United States, there are still differences within each sector, with some firms doing better than others in terms of wages, training, working conditions, or career prospects. The same factors as those reviewed by Eileen Appelbaum and her colleagues

(2003) are at play, but their role is shaped by the features of the French institutional framework.

Unions and Other Forms of Collective Action As in many other Western industrialized countries, French unions have been focused for a long time on the "bread-and-butter" issues of wages and benefits. But once again, because of the role of the legal minimum wage and branch collective agreements, and unlike in the United States, it has not been in the field of compensation that the presence of unions has made the big difference between firms' practices. The role of unions appears to be more important nowadays in the field of work organization and working conditions. The high-end large retail chains offer a striking example of this: the absence or weakness of the trade unions does not prevent these stores from paying much higher wages than the low-end stores, whereas the absence of unions in these stores is acutely felt in the poor working conditions and illegal practices.

The weakness of unions in many activities characterized by low-paid, low-skilled work leads to the emergence of complementary forms of collective actions. "Coordinations" of workers, arising outside the framework of traditional unions, have indeed appeared in some sectors. In the hotel industry, the big strike at one subcontractor where unions were almost nonexistent led the Accor group (the world's leader on the market) to reinternalize its cleaning activities in France.[2] This kind of action is often intensely reported by the media in France. So the threat of a negative commercial image because of bad social behavior may become a major incentive for big companies to reduce bad practices in the coming years.

Regional and Branch-Level Institutions Several regional and local institutions may play an important role in facilitating the adoption of high-road practices. In the food processing industry, two firms in the sample are members of a multi-employer group—an association of employers that "share" permanent workers instead of hiring temporary workers. It should be noted that this type of institutional arrangement is not specific to France. It exists, for example, in the United States (see the San Francisco Hotels Partnership Project; Bernhardt, Dresser, and Hatton 2003). But in France, multi-employer groups are not merely private institutions: they are often supported by public authorities, especially at the local level. Local authorities also intervene a lot in the call center sector—in the funding of training, for instance. In various industries, branch organizations provide expertise to firms investing in training and modernization. Support is also provided by public national and regional agencies dedicated to improving working conditions (the ANACT and the ARACTs), or even by the health insurance system.

Providing expertise is indeed a key factor. Appelbaum and her colleagues (2003) point out that the quality of information available to managers is a precondition for adopting innovative practices—even if not a sufficient condition. In France, on the employer side, branch-level organizations contribute a lot to the spreading of information concerning new practices. But the lack of expertise is particularly felt by trade unionists at the local level. This is a key difference between France and Germany and, even more, between France and the Nordic European countries such as Denmark, where powerful unions provide training and expertise to their members.

Tight Labor Markets From a firm's point of view, the "tightness" of the labor market refers to the alternative options of the workers it would like to recruit or retain. These options are partly determined by social allowances such as the basic income scheme (the revenu minimum d'insertion, or RMI), which have an impact on the reservation wage. The above-mentioned paradox of labor shortage in some sectors (such as food processing, where it is often lamented) while unemployment remains high is often debated in France.

For many French people, the role of the legal minimum wage and social allowances is indeed to force employers to offer decent jobs. This is part of the French model. Indeed, recruitment problems (as in food processing) and high turnover (as in call centers) are a good incentive to adopt innovative workplace practices. But labor shortages may also induce the suppression of certain occupations (like delicatessen sale staff in big retail chains).

THE SUSTAINABILITY OF THE FRENCH MODEL

Overall, France is far from having an optimal set of institutions. Denmark constitutes a contrasting case where, so far, better results have been obtained with far fewer state regulations. The quality of labor relations is particularly bad in France (Blanchard and Philippon 2004), and at the microeconomic level of firms there is a deficit of "arrangements" (in terms of the coordination among actors), which causes all parties to resort to official—and notably state—rules (see Algan and Cahuc 2006). But the latter, because of their general nature, are not adapted to the individual diversity of companies and workers, and sometimes they are not even enforced. This also underlines an important point: even if the labor market is far more regulated in France than in the United States, many determinants of the low-wage workers' situation are actually (and maybe increasingly) related to what is going on at the workplace level—where good practices cannot be implemented only by the law.

Yet the overwhelming presence of the Danish model in French social and political debates in the mid-2000s is a symptom of an increasing pressure on the French model. Indeed, the latter may appear less and less sustainable. Globalization and rising pressure from the European Commission to deregulate markets in order to improve competitiveness may be making the choice of extensive state regulation of both product and labor markets increasingly fragile. But the challenge also comes from internal factors. The persistence of high unemployment and the increasing deficits of the social security system seriously undermine the consensus backing both state regulations (such as employment protection legislation) and the welfare state. At the firm level, the model based on high work intensity and poor working conditions has reached its limits. The issue of sustainable work is also raised by the aging of the labor force. At the macro level, the future of the French "social model" will depend on what emerges at the workplace level to meet these challenges.

NOTES

1. The same has happened in the United States, where manufacturing firms face increased skill requirements: managers have preferred to hire relatively more capable high school graduates rather than train incumbent workers (Appelbaum, Bernhardt, and Murnane 2003, 18).
2. These were previously outsourced to an establishment belonging to the hotel group but presumed to be independent.

REFERENCES

Acemoglu, Daron, and Jörn-Steffen Pischke. 1999. "Beyond Becker: Training in Imperfect Labor Markets." *Economic Journal* 109(February): 112–42.

Algan, Yann, and Pierre Cahuc. 2006. "Why Is the Minimum Wage So High in Low-Trust Countries?" Unpublished paper. Paris: Paris School of Economics. Accessed at http://www.cepremap.cnrs.fr/algan/trust_union.

Appelbaum, Eileen, Annette Bernhardt, and Richard J. Murnane. 2003. "Low-Wage America: An Overview." In *Low-Wage America*, edited by Eileen Appelbaum, Annette Bernhardt, and Richard J. Murnane. New York: Russell Sage Foundation.

Askenazy, Philippe. 2004. *Les Désordres du travail: Enquête sur le nouveau productivisme [Disorders of Work: A Survey on the New Productivism]*. Paris: Le Seuil.

Bernhardt, Annette, Laura Dresser, and Erin Hatton. 2003. "The Coffee Pot Wars: Unions and Firm Restructuring in the Hotel Industry." In *Low-Wage America*, edited by Eileen Appelbaum, Annette Bernhardt, and Richard J. Murnane. New York: Russell Sage Foundation.

Blanchard, Olivier, and Thomas Philippon. 2004. "The Quality of Labor Relations and Unemployment." Working paper W10590. Cambridge, Mass.: National Bureau of Economic Research (June).

Manning, Alan. 2003. *Monopsony in Motion: Imperfect Competition in Labor Markets*. Princeton, N.J.: Princeton University Press.

Organization for Economic Cooperation and Development (OECD). 2004. "Employment Protection Regulation and Labor Market Performance." In *Employment Outlook*, ch. 2. Paris: OECD.

Index

Boldface numbers refer to figures and tables.

absenteeism, 158, 244, 274
accidents, workplace, **57**, 150, 158, 243
Accor, 172, 175, 191, 197, 198, 298
Acemoglu, D., 297
active labor market policy, 19, 69–70, 75, 81n13
AFPA (Association nationale pour la formation professionnelle des adultes), 206n25
AFRC (Association Française de Relation Clientèle), 259, 270
age analysis: call center employment, 269; employment rate, 30–31; hotel sector employment, 178; labor force participation, 31; low-wage work, **38**, **39**; unemployment, 31
Agefaforia, 97–98
agriculture sector, 29, **41**, 98
Aldi, 214, 217, 247
ANPE (National Employment Service), 109, 231
Appelbaum, E., 2, 16, 135, 297, 299
apprenticeships, 34, 61, 81n13, 198
ARACTs (Agence Régionale pour l'Amélioration des Conditions de Travail), 98, 114
artisan shops, 42
Aubry laws, 32, 53. See also thirty-five hour working week law
Auchan, 246
automation, 106–8, 112, 175, 246–7
autonomy, of employees, 234–5

banking sector, 264, 266. See also call centers
barriers to entry, 59–60, 210
basic income program, 18, 69, 71 See also RMI

benefits, 138, 199, **225**
BEP (brevet d'études professionnelles), 198, 199
Bernhardt, A., 2, 16, 168
Bertrand, M., 230
Blanchard, O., 65, 82n17
blue-collar workers: in food-processing sector, 90, 91–92; foreign workers, 40; in hotel sector, 178; temporary employment, 62–63; training, 75; underemployment, 33; working conditions, **54–55**, 56, 111
bonuses: food-processing sector, 94, 110; food retail sector, 223, **224–5**; hospital sector, 138; hotel sector, 200
BP (brevet professionnel), 199
brevet de technicien supérieur (BTS), 199

business strategy: call centers, 275–77, 280; discount stores, 212–13; food-processing sector, 100–103, 114–5; food retail sector, 244–6; hotel sector, 190–1; variations in, 294–9
business-to-business sector, 256, 270. See also call centers
butchers, 247

Cadbury, 91
Caisses Régionales d'Assurance Maladie (CRAMs), 98, 114
call centers: banking, 256, 271, 272, 273, 275; business strategy, 273–7, 280; call classification, 257; career advancement opportunities, 274–5; case study data, **282–83**; collective bargaining agreements, 257–8; competitive conditions, 263–65; cus-

call centers (cont.)
tomer relations, 262–3; data sources, 256; definition of, 255–6; employee characteristics, 259–60, 268–9; employee job skills and qualifications, 268, 269, 272–3, 276; employee turnover, 274; employment statistics, 256; female employees, 268; gap between low-paying and high paying firms, 296; government regulation, 281; historical development of, 254, 255–7; independent centers, 257, 258, 259, 264, 265, 267, 271, 274, 276; industrial relations, 258–60; industry concentration, 256; in-house, 257–8, 259, 263, 264, 265, 266–7, 275; location of, 257; low-wage work, 269–70; market positioning strategies, 261–7; monitoring of calls, 278–79; offshoring, 257, 261, 265, 295; part-time work, 274; regional development incentives, 260–1; research considerations, 255; size distribution, 256; technological change, 264, 284–5n12; training, 260, 261, 275; unions and unionization, 259; in U.S. vs. France, 281; wages and earnings, 254, 257, 269–70; work hours and schedules, 273–4, 277; working conditions, 260, 277–80; work organization, 262–3, 270–3, 277

CAP (certificat d'aptitude professionnelle), 198, 199
capital-GDP ratio, 50–51
career advancement opportunities: call centers, 274–5; hospital sector, 142–4; hotel sector, 186, 196–7, 203, 292
Carrefour Group, 209, 214, 217, 223, 224–5, 248
cashiers: depression incidence, 241; health issues, 242; part-time employment, 220–1; percentage of food store workers as, 234; productivity, 234; training, 232; wages and earnings, 223; women as, 218–9; work hours and schedules, 235–6, 237; working conditions, 234, 237–8

Casino, 214, 217, 246
CDI (contrat à durée indéterminée), 80n13
CES (contrat emploi solidarité), 165n8
CESMO, 256
CFDT (Confédération Française Démocratique du Travail), 63, 177, 204n8
CFTC (Confédération française des travailleurs chrétiens), 204n8
CGC (Confédération générale des cadres), 204n8
CGPME (Confédération Générale du Patronat des Petites et Moyennes Entreprises), 63
CGT (Confédération Générale du Travail), 63, 65, 204n8, 222
chain hotels, 170, **171**, 190–4, 201. *See also* hotel sector
Champion, **224–5**
checkout process, 234, 246–7
child care, 70
child-raising allowance, 70
civil service: in hospital sector, 131, 136; low-wage work, **41**, **42**; as model for French employment, 60–61; percentage of workers in, 60
cleaners, in hotels. *See* housekeepers, hotel
cleaning companies, 195–6
clerks, **54–55**, 62, 75
CNE (contrat nouvelle embauche), 80n13
collective bargaining agreements: call centers, 257–8; coverage of, 63–64; electrical and electronics goods retailers, 226–7; in food-processing sector, 94–97; in food retail sector, 226; hospital sector, 138; in hotel sector, 168, 176–7, 200; national vs. branch-level, 63–64; in Netherlands, 9; role of, 46–47; with wage levels less than SMIC, 47, 50. *See also* unions and unionization
Communist Party, 63

compensation. *See* bonuses; wages and earnings
competitive conditions: call centers, 263–5; confectionary sector, 99; electrical and electronics goods retailers, 213–4; food-processing sector, 89, 99–100, 104–15, 122–3; food retail sector, 7, 214; hospital sector, 152; hotel sector, 7
concentration, of low-wage work, 6–7
confectionary sector: blue-collar workers, 92; case study data, **102**; competitive conditions, 99; concentration in, 91; domestic demand impact, 99; employment in, 91; low-wage work, 42, 43; multinationals, 103, 104; wages and earnings, 95–96, 113; working conditions, **93**, 111
construction sector, **41**
continuous training. *See* training
contract of constant use, 81n14
contracts, employment. *See* employment contracts
cost-cutting practices, 7–8, 104–5, 295–96
cost of labor, 48–58, 59, 295–6
cottage sector model, 190–1
couples with children, 72
CPE (contrat première embauche), 77
CPIH (Confédération des professionnels indépendants de l'hôtellerie), 204n7
CQP (certificats de qualification professionnelle), 97, 114, 124n7
CRAMs (Caisses Régionales d'Assurance Maladie), 98, 114
cross-country studies: advantages of, 3–4; concentration of low-wage work, 6–7; educational attainment, 73–75; hotel sector, 201–3; labor market, 9–12; low-wage work incidence, 5–6; mobility out of low wage work, 6, 44; overview of, 4–12; research considerations, 4–5; retail sector employment, **228**; training, 75; work hours and schedules, 32
customer relations and service, 230, 245, 262–63, 266–7. *See also* call centers

DADS (Déclarations Annuelles des Données Sociales) database, 34, 42, 44, 79n4
Darty, 214
Delaunay, J., 285n14
Délégation interministérielle à la lutte contre le travail illégal, 179
delicatessen employees, 238–9, 243, 247
Denmark: concentration of low-wage work, 7; educational attainment, **74**; employment protection legislation, 61; exit rate out of low-wage employment, 44; flexicurity system, 10; job training, 75; labor market, 10, 73; labor productivity, **52**; low-wage work incidence, 6; low-wage work threshold, 37; mobility out of low-wage work, 6; retail sector employment, **228**; service sector employment, 59; unemployment compensation, 69; work hours, 32
depression, 241
deregulation, 59, 64, 77, 264
derogatory contracts, 62, 81n14
discount stores: business strategy, 212–3; employees, 232; employee turnover, 212; employment statistics, 212; impact on French retailer's profits, 217; market share, 214, 248; part-time work, 245; regulations restricting growth, **216**; store size, 212; unionization, 222; wages and earnings, 219, **224–5**; work hours and schedules, 224, 237
discrimination, 231
distribution sector, 58–59, 59
diversification, 101
Doeringer, P., 142, 262
Dresser, L., 168
dual market theory, 203, 291–3

early retirement, 70, 71
Earned Income Tax Credit (EITC), 71

earnings. *See* wages and earnings
ECCO (European Association of Customer Relations Centers), 259
e-commerce, 214
economic growth, 29, **30**
educational attainment: of call center operators, 269; cross-country analysis, 73–75; of elderly persons, 73; and employment rate, **31**; of food-processing employees, 109; of food retail employees, 218; of hotel sector employees, 178; and labor force participation, **31**; and low-wage work, **38**, **39**; and unemployment rate, **31**; of young workers, 73, 75
elderly persons, 70, 71, 73
electrical and electronics goods retailers: case study data, 250–1; collective bargaining agreements, 226–7; commission, 234; competitive conditions, 213–4; e-commerce, 214; employee autonomy, 234–5; employee health problems, 243; employee recruitment, 231–2; employee stress, 239–40; female employees, 219; future of, 248–9; illegal practices, 233; research considerations, 211; sales strategies, 213; training, 232–3; unionization, 222–3, 226–7; wages and earnings, 210, 220, 248–9; work hours and schedules, 234–5; working conditions, 239–40, 243
emergency services, 151–2
employee benefits, 138, 199, **225**
employee productivity. *See* productivity
employee turnover: call centers, 274; food-processing sector, 109, 120; food retail sector, 243–4; hotel sector, 169; manufacturing sector, 90–91
employers' associations, 63, 64, 76, 176, 258–9
employment contracts: derogatory, 62, 81n14; fixed-term, 61, 80–81n13, 14, 291, 296; flexible, 77; hotel housekeepers, 186–8, 194; open-ended, 61, 80n13; seasonal, 81n14, 96, 117, 118, 121, 187; Tâcheron, 81n14, 117, 120;

temporary workers, 80–81n13, 115; types of, 21, 61, 80–81n13–14
employment models, 288, 289–91
employment protection legislation (EPL), 21, 60–62, 76, 296
employment rates and statistics: age analysis, **31**; call centers, 256; confectionary sector, 91; discount stores, 212; and educational attainment, **31**; food-processing sector, 90; growth rates, **30**; hotel sector, 169, 177–8; by industry, 29; low-skilled workers, 48; meat-processing sector, 91; of men, **31**; service sector, 29; in U.S. vs. France, 58; of women, **31**
Enquête Emploi [French Labor Force Survey], 34, 42
EPL (employment protection legislation), 21, 60–62, 76, 296
ergonomics, 243
European Commission (EC), 43, 247–8, 300
European Common Agricultural Policy, 122
European Community Household Panel (ECHP), 43
European Union (EU), **30**, **52**, 67–68
Eurostat, 45, 227
exit rate, out of low-wage employment, 44
exports, 16, 91
"extra" contracts, in hotel sector, 187–88, 202

factory inspectors, 21, 62
Fillon law, 56
first price products, 100
fixed-term contracts, 61, 80–81n13, 14, 291, 296
flat wage careers, 49–50, 110, 294
flexibility, 8, 145
flexicurity system, 10, 73
FNAC, 248
food-processing sector: automation, 106–8; blue-collar workers in, 90; business strategy, 100–103, 114–5;

characteristics of, 90–91; collective bargaining agreements, 94–97; competitive conditions, 89, 99–100, 104–15, 122–3; data sources, 88–89; domestic demand impact, 99; educational attainment, 109; employee characteristics, 108; employee job satisfaction, 110; employee turnover, 109, 120; employment statistics, 90; hygiene standards, 99; low-wage work, 42, **43**, 88; market differentiation, 100–103; multi-employer groups, 121–2; outsourcing, 105; research considerations, 88–89; sales figures, 89; temporary workers, 90, 91, 96, 115–22, 292; training in, 97–98, 117; unions and unionization, 91, 105; wages and earnings, 93–97, 105, 109–10, 113–4; women in, 90, **92**, 96–97; work hours and schedules, 97, 105, 113; working conditions, 93, 98, 107, 111–3, 121, 123; work organization, 89, 107. *See also* confectionary sector; meat-processing sector

food retail sector: automated checkout machines, 246–47; business strategy, 244–6; case study data, **250–1**; collective bargaining agreements, 226–7; competitive conditions, 7, 214; customer checkout practices, 233–4; employee benefits, **225**; employee characteristics, 210; employee productivity, 227–37, 246; employee recruitment, 230–1; employee turnover, 243–4; foreign workers, 219; future of, 245–9; government regulation, 214–7, 227, 230, 247–8; innovations in, 246–7; low-wage work, **43**; market segmentation, 211–3; part-time work, 220–1, 226, 235–6; as percentage of retail sector, 209; research considerations, 209, 210–1; store hours, 227, 247; training, 232; unions and unionization, 221–7; wages and earnings, 218–21, **224–5**, 226, 245, 247; women in, 218–9, 231; work hours and sched-

ules, **224**, 235–7; working conditions, 236–7, 237–9. *See also* hypermarkets; supermarkets

Force Ouvrière (FO), 204n8

foreign workers. *See* immigrants and immigration

foremen, 40, **54–55**

Fougère, D., 50

franchise stores, 221–2

full-time work and workers, **41**

The Future of Work, 2–3

GDP (gross domestic product), 29, **30**, 50–51

gender differences, employment, 31. *See also* men; women

Germany: distribution sector, 58; educational attainment, 74; employment protection legislation, **61**; exit rate out of low-wage employment, 44; job training, 75; labor market, 9; labor productivity, **52**; low-wage work incidence, 6; low-wage work threshold, 37; "mini-jobs," 9; retail sector employment, **228**; unemployment compensation, 69; work hours, **32**

Glyn, A., 58

government regulation: banking sector, 264; call centers, 281; food retail sector, 214–7, 227, 230, 247–8; hospital sector, 131–2; hotel sector, 200; labor market, 20–21, 300; of overtime, 32, 56; service sector, 59–60; of working time, 32, 53

government work programs, 137, 147, 150

Great Britain. *See* United Kingdom

grocery stores. *See* food retail sector

gross domestic product (GDP), 29, **30**, 50–51

Haribo, 91

Hatton, E., 168

health care. *See* hospital sector

health insurance, 98, **225**

high-road organizations, 3, 114–5, 244–6, 295

hiring process, 230–2
home care services, 154
hospital sector: attractiveness of jobs in, 160–1; career advancement opportunities, 142–4; case study data, **163–4**; characteristics of, 127; competitive conditions, 152; "consumerist" trends, 159; data sources, 129; emergency services, 151–2; employee benefits, 138; employee job skills and qualifications, 132–3, 155–6, 162; financial and budgetary pressures, 152–3; foreign workers, 136; government regulation, 131–2; history of, 129–30; hospital stay length, 154–5, 159; internal labor pools, 145; internal markets, 142, 150; low-wage work, 42, **43**, 128, 136–9; number of beds, 153; outpatient services, 154; part-time work, 140–1; public-private partnerships, 153–4; public vs. private, 129–32; research considerations, 128–29; reserve labor sources, 144–51; restructuring trends, 153–55; subcontracting, 145–46; technological development, 151, 159; temporary workers, 146, **147**, 149, 291; unions and unionization, 132; wages and earnings, 137–9, 160; women in, 136; work hours and schedules, 140–2; working conditions, 158–9; work organization, 132–6, 157. *See also* hospital service workers; nurse's aides

hospital service workers: job design and responsibilities, 134–5, 157, 162; job skills and qualifications, 132–3, 156; limited-term contracts, 149; number of, 156; part-time work, 140; wages, **137**; women as, 136; workload, 158

hotel sector: business strategy, 190–1; career advancement opportunities, 186, 196–7, 203, 292; case study data, **171**, 194; characteristics of, 168, 170–9; collective bargaining, 168, 176–7, 200; competitive conditions, 7; cross-country comparison, 201–3; economy's impact on, 173–4; employee benefits, 199; employee characteristics, 178–9; employee turnover, 169; employment statistics, 169, 177–8; government regulations and incentives, 200; lobbying efforts, 168, 177; low-wage work, 42, **43**, 168, 169, 188–90; marketing strategy, 175; market segmentation, 171–3; subcontracting, 194–6; technological change, 175; temporary workers, 194–6, 292; training, 181, 197–9; unions and unionization, 168, 176–7, 202–3; wages and earnings, 176, 188–90, 199–200; women in, 178, 180–1, 189–90; work hours and schedules, 176–7, 179, 184–5. *See also* housekeepers, hotel

hours of work. *See* work hours and schedules

household services, **41**, 59

housekeepers, hotel: career advancement opportunities, 186, 196–7, 203; characteristics of, 169, 179; employment contracts, 186–8, 194; foreign workers, 205n12; fringe benefits, 199; job design and responsibilities, 181–4, 185, 202; job skills and qualifications, 181, 196; research considerations, 169–70; stress, 184, 202; tips, 185–6; training, 181, 198–9; wages and earnings, 188–90, 199–200; work hours and schedules, 184–5; working conditions, 191, **192–3**, 194, 201; work organization, 185; work recognition, 186

housekeeping, in hospitals. *See* hospital service workers

human capital, 8

hygiene standards, 99, 107

hypermarkets: commercial cooperation contracts, 100; competitive conditions, 214; electrical and electronics goods, 213, 226–7; employee performance, **229**; employee stress, 241; employee turnover, 243–4; female employees, 219; growth of, 89,

99–100; innovations, 246–7; low-wage work incidence, **43**; part-time work, **221**; pressure on suppliers, 100; product offerings, 212; regulations restricting growth, 59, 215, **216**; size of stores, 209, 212; vs. supermarkets, 211; unionization, 222–3, 226; wages and earnings, 219, 223, **224–5**, 245; work hours, **224**; working conditions, 236–7; work organization, 236–7

illegal immigration, 67
illegal practices, 233
immigrants and immigration: educational attainment, 40; employment contracts, 81*n*14; in food-processing sector, 90, 92; food retail employment, 219; in hospital sector, 136; in hotel sector, 178–9, 205*n*12; low-wage work, **38**, 39–40; policy, 66–67, 68; trends, 67–68
imports, 16, 91
income supports, 68–69, 71
income tax, 71
industrial relations: call centers, 258–60; current state of, 20, 299–300; distrust in, 76; in food-processing sector, 91; in hotel sector, 176; role of, 62–64. *See also* unions and unionization
innovation, 246–7, 299
INSEE (Institut National de la Statistique et des Études Économiques), 67, 136, 213, 256
inspectors, 21, 62
insurance sector, 264, 271, 272
internal labor markets, 142, 150
IT (information technology) services, 256, 270. *See also* call centers

job design and responsibilities: call center operators, 268, 270–3; hospital service workers, 134–5, 157, 162; housekeepers, hotel, 181–4, 185, 202; nurse's aides, 133–4, 162. *See also* work organization

job loss. *See* unemployment
job mobility. *See* mobility
job quality, 3, **192–3**. *See also specific components*
job rotation, 52, 107
job satisfaction, in food-processing sector, 110
job security, 14, 22, 75–76, 273, 293
job skills and qualifications: call centers, 268, 269, 272–3, 276; hospital service workers, 132–3, 156; hotel housekeepers, 181, 196; nurse's aides, 133, 156, 162. *See also* educational attainment
job stability, 61
job tenure, 49, 61. *See also* employee turnover; seniority and seniority premiums
job training. *See* training
just-in-time production, 52

Kramarz, F., 50, 230

labor contracts. *See* employment contracts
labor costs, 48–58, 59, 295–6
labor force participation, **30**, **31**, 70
Labor Force Survey, 218–19
labor law, 20–21, 200, 203
labor market: cross-country comparison, 9–12; and employment protection legislation, 21, 60–62, 76, 296; features of, 16; reform of, 76–77; segmented nature of, 66, 291–2; tightness of, 299
labor productivity. *See* productivity
labor's share in value-added, 217, **218**
labor turnover. *See* employee turnover
Leader Price, 217
Lhommeau, B., 44
Lidl, 209, 214, 217
lobbying, 64, 168, 177, 259
lone parents, **72**, 136, 231
Louvre Hotels, 195, 204*n*3
low-price strategy, 212–3

low-skilled workers: employment rates, 48; in food-processing sector, 90; foreign workers, 40; research considerations, 22; unemployment, 19, 30; unionization, 65

Low-Wage America: How Employers Are Reshaping Opportunity in the Workplace (Appelbaum, Bernhardt, and Murnane), 2, 16

low-wage work and workers: age analysis, 38, 39; call centers, 269–70; cross-country comparison, 5–7, 37; definition of, 5–6, 13, 34; and educational attainment, 38, 39; and flat wage profiles, 49–50; food-processing sector, 42, 43, 88; food retail sector, 43; gender analysis, 38; hospital sector, 42, 43, 128, 136–9; immigrants, 38, 39–40; incidence of, 5, 34–45; vs. poverty, 1; research considerations, 28–29; retail sector, 41, 42, 43, 219, 220; temporary work, 40–41, 137; threshold, 34, 35; trap of, 50, 294; unionization, 65; in U.S., 1, 6. *See also specific entries*

managers: in food-processing sector, 90; in hotel sector, 178, 189; low-wage work, 40; training, 75; and workers' health and satisfaction, 242; work hours, 233; working conditions, 54–55

manufacturing sector, 29, 41, 90–91. *See also* food-processing sector

marketing strategy, in hotel sector, 175

market positioning strategy: call centers, 261–7; food-processing sector, 100–103; food retail sector, 211–3

Mason, G., 51

means-tested benefits, 69

meat-processing sector: blue-collar workers, 91–92; case study data, 102; competitive conditions, 99; concentration in, 91; defined, 124n2; diversification, 101; domestic demand impact, 99; employee characteristics, 91–92, 108–9; employment in, 91; foreign workers, 124n3; low-wage work, 42, 43; temporary workers, 117, 119–20; wages and earnings, 95, 96; working conditions, 93

MEDEF (Movement of French Enterprises), 63, 64

Media Markt, 248

median wage: computation of, 34; and SMIC, 49

medical, surgical, and obstetric (MSO) services, 130

medical visits, 240

men: employment rate, 31; labor force participation, 31; low-wage work, 38; part-time work, 32, 33; underemployment, 33; unemployment, 31

"mini-jobs," 9

minimum (basic) income benefit, 18, 69, 71. *See also* RMI

minimum wage: establishment of, 17; in Netherlands, 12; and number of low-wage jobs, 58. *See also* SMIC (minimum inter-branch growth wage)

Ministry of Education, 198

Ministry of Health, 129

Ministry of Industry, 258

Ministry of Labor, 47, 98

minorities, call center employment, 269

mobility: cross-country differences, 6, 44; in food-processing sector, 110; in hospital sector, 142–4; out of low-wage work, 6, 43–44, 110; of young workers, 293. *See also* career advancement opportunities

MSA (Mutuelle Sociale Agricole), 98

multi-employer groups, 121–2, 298–9

multinationals, 99, 101, 103, 104

multitasking, 89, 236

Murnane, R., 2, 16

National Employment Service (ANPE), 109, 231

National Institute of Health Supervision, 57

negative income tax, 71
Netherlands: collective bargaining agreements, 9; distribution sector, 58; educational attainment, 74; employment protection legislation, 61; exit rate out of low-wage employment, 44; job training, 75; labor market, 11–12; labor productivity, 52; low-wage work incidence, 6; low-wage work threshold, 37; retail sector employment, 228; unemployment in, 12; work hours, 32
nurses, 134, 137, 155, 162
nurse's aides: career advancement opportunities, 142–4; career path, 133; growth in number of, 155–56; job design and responsibilities, 133–4, 162; job skills and qualifications, 133, 156, 162; part-time work, 140; wages, 137; women as, 136; work hours and schedules, 140; workload, 158

occupational analysis, 22, 40, 41
occupational health and safety, 56–57, 111–2, 240–3
occupational multiskilling, 174, 200
OECD (Organization for Economic Cooperation and Development), 59, 61, 73, 74, 214
offshoring, 257, 261, 265, 295
O'Leary, B., 51
O'Mahony, M., 51
OMI (Office des Migrations Internationales), 81n14
open-ended contracts, 61, 80n13
organizations, low-road vs. high-road, 3, 114–5, 244–6, 295
outpatient services, 154
outsiders, 289
outsourcing, 67–68, 105, 145–6, 194–6
overtime: and annualization of working time, 289–90; food-processing sector, 105; food retail sector, 226; impact on earnings, 45, 289–90; laws regulating, 32, 56

part-time work and workers: in call centers, 274; characteristics of, 33; in Denmark, 6; in discount stores, 245; in food-processing sector, 90; in food retail sector, 220–21, 226, 235–6; in hospital sector, 140–1; in hotel sector, 178, 186–7; low-wage work, 40, 41; of men, 32, 33; in Netherlands, 12; trends, 32–33; of women, 32, 33, 289; work hours of, 32
pensions, 16, 82n23
personalization, 271–2
Philippon, T., 65, 82n17
piecework, 117, 120, 184, 201
Piketty, T., 58, 70
Piore, M., 142, 262
Pischke, J., 297
poultry sector, 125n14
poverty, 1, 5, 45, 71
precarious jobs, 291–3
price competition, 246
price regulation, 217
private hospitals: competitive conditions, 152; hospital stays, 154; part-time work, 140–1; vs. public hospitals, 129–32; subcontracting, 146; wages and earnings, 137, 139. *See also* hospital service workers; nurse's aides
private label products, 100
productivity: cross-country analysis, 52; in food-processing sector, 106; in food retail sector, 227–37, 246; and high capital intensity, 50–52; and low-wage work, 2; and working conditions, 290–1
profit sharing, 94, 105, 225
promotion opportunities. *See* career advancement opportunities
public employment. *See* civil service
public hospitals: civil servants, 131; competitive conditions, 152; government work programs, 147, 150; hospital stays, 154–5; part-time work, 140; vs. private hospitals, 129–32; role of, 130; subcontracting, 146;

public hospitals (*cont.*)
  temporary workers, 149; unionization, 132; wages and earnings, 137, 139. *See also* hospital service workers; nurse's aides
purchasing power parity, 34

qualifications. *See* job skills and qualifications
quality, 101, 174

Raffarin law, 59, 174, 215, 217, 248
real estate employees, 41
regional development incentives, 260–1
regulation. *See* government regulation
repetitive injuries, 242
REPONSE survey, 223
research considerations: call centers, 255; cross-country studies, 4–5; electrical and electronics goods retailers, 211; food-processing sector, 88–89; food retail sector, 209, 210–1; hospital sector, 128–9; hotel housekeepers, 169–70; low-wage work and workers, 28–29; technological change, 16; in U.S. vs. France, 21–22
reservation wage, 71
reserve labor. *See* temporary work and workers
restructuring, 99, 153–5
retail chain brand products (RCBs), 100, 101
retail sector: customer checkout practices, 233–4; government regulation, 214–7; illegal practices, 233; low-wage work, 41, 42, 43, 219, 220; market forms, 211; occupational health and safety, 240–3; part-time work, 221; share of total employment, 227; training, 232–3; unions and unionization, 221–7; working conditions, 227. *See also* electrical and electronics goods retailers; food retail sector
"RevPar" indicator, 174
RFID (radio frequency identification of products), 252n14

RMI (revenu minimum d'insertion), 18, 69, 71
Robien law, 32
Robinson, K., 51
room attendants. *See* housekeepers, hotel
Royer law, 59, 215

safety, workplace, 56–57, 111–2, 240–3
sales per meter, 230
salespersons. *See* electrical and electronics goods retailers
Saturn, 214
scheduling, of work. *See* work hours and schedules
seasonal contracts: food-processing sector, 96, 118, 121; hotel sector, 187; seniority premium, 117; types of, 81n14
secondary education, 73–75
Senate, 67
seniority and seniority premiums: amount of premium, 44; call centers, 269; food-processing sector, 94, 105, 110; hospital sector, 142, 150; hotel sector, 178; unions' support of, 294
service sector: employment rates, 29; government regulation, 59–60; job deficit in, 58–60; low-wage work, 41. *See also* retail sector
shift work, 107, 140, 277
single persons, 72
skills. *See* job skills and qualifications
small business, 65, 168, 172–3, 213–4
SMIC (minimum inter-branch growth wage): and cost of labor, 48–49; establishment of, 17–18; and food-processing sector, 42; and food retail sector, 228; goal of, 46; and hotel sector, 176, 188–9; increases, 36; level setting, 11, 13, 47; and low-wage cutoff, 35, 47; and low-wage growth, 46–48; and median wage, 49; percentage of workers earning, 47; purchasing power of those earning, 18, 47; real value, 18; and service sector employ-

ment, 58; tenure of workers earning, 49; and unemployment, 14
SMIG (Minimum, Interbranch, Guaranteed Wage), 17
SMT (Syndicat du Marketing Téléphonique), 258
social benefits, 68–72
social contributions, 50, 80n9
social dumping, 104, 114, 295–6
Socialist Party, 63
Sofitel hotels, 191, 199
SP2C (Syndicat des Professionnels des Centres du Contact), 258–9
specialization, 130
sporadic permanent contracts, 81n14
stress: call center workers, 279; electrical and electronics goods retail employees, 239–40; hotel housekeepers, 184, 202; hypermarket employees, 241; increase in, 52–53
strikes, 20
students, 39, 81n14, 218. See also young workers
subcontracting, 67–68, 105, 145–6, 194–6
subsidies, 69
super discount stores. See discount stores
supermarkets: commercial cooperation contracts, 100; employee performance, **229**; employee turnover, 243–4; female employees, 219; growth of, 89, 99–100; vs. hypermarkets, 211; innovations, 246–47; low-wage work incidence, **43**; market share, 212; part-time work, **221**; pressure on suppliers, 100; product offerings, 212; regulations restricting growth, 59, 215, **216**; size of stores, 212; types of, 211; wages and earnings, 219, **224–5**, 245; work hours, **224**; working conditions, 236–7; work organization, 236–7
supervisors: call centers, 274; in food-processing sector, 90; in hospitals, 134; hotel sector, 182, 196–7, 199;

low-wage work, 40; training, 75; working conditions, **54–55**
supply and demand, 33
Surveillance Médicale des Risques (SUMER), 52–53
Syndicat du Marketing Téléphonique (SMT), 258
Syndicat national des hôteliers restaurateurs, cafetiers et traiteurs (SYNHORCAT), 204n7

Tâcheron contracts, 81n14, 117, 120
tax credits, 71
taxi drivers, 60
Taylorism, 262, 297
teamwork, 52, 114
technological change: call centers, 264, 284–5n12; hospital sector, 151, 159; hotel sector, 175; and labor costs, 296–7; research considerations, 16
telecommunication sector, 256, 258–9, 260. See also call centers
temporary work and workers: characteristics of, 119; contracts, 80–81n13, 115; in food-processing sector, 90, 91, 96, 115–22, 292; government regulation, 62; in hospital sector, 146, 147, 149, 291; in hotel sector, 194–6, 292; incidence of, 61–62; low-wage work, 40–41, 137; precariousness premium, 296; and unions, 118
tenure, job, 49, 61. See also employee turnover; seniority and seniority premiums
thirty-five hour working week law, 53, 159, 295
total quality management (TQM), 52
trade, 16
trade associations, 98
trade unions. See unions and unionization
training: apprenticeships, 34, 61, 81n13, 198; blue-collar workers, 75; call centers, 260, 261, 275; cross-country comparison, 75; in food-processing sector, 97–98, 117; in hotel

training (*cont.*)
  sector, 181, 197–9; minimum wage impact, 297; in retail sector, 232–3
tripartite cooperation, 12
trust, 77
turnover, of employees. *See* employee turnover

UMIH (Union des Métiers et des Industries de l'Hôtellerie), 173, 176, 204n7
undeclared work, 36, 179, 295
underemployment, 32–33, 289
unemployment: age analysis, 31; among unskilled workers, 14, 30; and educational attainment, 31; in France vs. U.S., 18–19; growth of, 30; of men, 31; in Netherlands, 12; reasons for, 29; of women, 31
unemployment compensation, 68–69, 70, 71
unions and unionization: call centers, 259; discount stores, 222; electrical and electronics goods retailers, 222–3, 226–7; food-processing sector, 91, 105; food retail sector, 221–7; hospital sector, 132; hotel sector, 168, 176–7, 202–3; lobbying by, 64; low-wage workers, 65; membership statistics, 20, 64, 82n16; at national level, 63–64; protection index, 20; retail sector, 221–7; role and strength of, 11, 13, 19–20, 63–66, 76, 298; temporary workers, 118; and working conditions, 65, 111–2, 298; and work organization, 298. *See also* collective bargaining agreements
United Kingdom: distribution sector, 58; educational attainment, 74; employment protection legislation, 61; exit rate out of low-wage employment, 44; food retail sector, 227–30; job training, 75; labor market, 10, 11; labor productivity, 52; low-wage work incidence, 6; low-wage work threshold, 37; retail sector employment, 228; taxi drivers, 60; unemployment compensation, 69; work hours, 32; Working Families' Tax Credit, 71
United States: call centers, 281, 296; distribution sector, 58; Earned Income Tax Credit, 71; educational attainment, 74; employment protection legislation, 61; employment rate, 30, 31, 58; GDP growth, 30; hospital workers, 127; hotel sector, 202, 203; labor force participation, 30, 31; labor market, 73; low-wage work in, 1, 6; manufacturing sector, 300n1; unemployment, 18, 30, 31; work hours, 32
unskilled workers, 14, 30. *See also* low-skilled workers
utilities sector, 264. *See also* call centers

vocational education, 133, 181, 197–9, 260

wage bargaining. *See* collective bargaining agreements
wage inequality, 18
wages and earnings: call centers, 254, 257, 269–70; of cashiers, 223; confectionary sector, 95–96, 113; discount stores, 219, **224–5**; electrical and electronics goods retailers, 210, 220, 248–9; flat profile, 49–50, 110, 294; food-processing sector, 93–97, 105, 109–10, 113–4, 119; food retail sector, 218–21, **224–5**, 226, 245, 247; hospital sector, 137–9, 160; hotel sector, 176, 188–90, 199–200; mobility trends, 44–45; and overtime work, 45, 289–90. *See also* collective bargaining agreements; minimum wage
Wal-Mart, 209, **229**
women: call center employment, 268; cashiers, 218–9; employment rate, 31; food-processing sector employment, 90, **92**, 96–97; food retail sector employment, 218–9, 231; hospital sector employment, 136; hotel sector

employment, 178, 180–1, 189–90; labor force participation, 31, 70; low-wage work, 36, 38; part-time work, 32, 33, 289; retail sector employment, 218–9; temporary workers, 119; underemployment, 32; unemployment, 31
workers' committees, 65
workers' representatives, 222
work hours and schedules: call centers, 273–4, 277; cashiers, 235–6, 237; cross-country analysis, 32; discount stores, 224, 237; electrical and electronics goods retailers, 234–5; food-processing sector, 97, 105, 113; food retail sector, 224, 235–7; hospital sector, 140–2; hotel sector, 176–7, 179, 184–5; irregular schedules, 53; laws regulating, 21, 32, 53, 56; of managers, 233; of part-time workers, 32; and productivity, 51; trends, 32. *See also* overtime
working conditions: across occupations, 53–56; blue-collar workers, 54–55, 56, 111; call centers, 260, 277–80; cashiers, 237–38; confectionary sector, 93, 111; electrical and electronics goods retailers, 239–40, 243; food-processing sector, 93, 98, 107, 111–3, 121, 123; food retail sector, 236–7, 237–9, 242; in hospital sector, 158–59; hotel housekeepers, 191, 192–3, 194, 201; and productivity, 290–1; retail sector, 227; and unions, 65, 111–2, 298; and young workers, 111–2
Working Families' Tax Credit (WFTC), 71
working poor, 22, 45
working week: call centers, 277–8; food-processing sector, 113; food retail sector, 226; hospital sector, 141–2, 159; hotel sector, 177; thirty-five hour working week law, 53, 159, 295; variable hours, 289–90
work intensification, 52–53, 297
workload, 158–59
work organization: call centers, 262–3, 270–3, 277; food-processing sector, 89, 107; food retail sector, 236–7; hospital sector, 132–6, 157; hotel housekeepers, 185; trends, 52; and unions, 298
workplace accidents, 57, 150, 158, 243
work shifts, 107, 140, 277
Wrigley, 91

young workers: active labor market policy, 69–70; contrat première embauche (CPE), 77; educational attainment, 73, 75; employment statistics, 31; in food-processing sector, 90, 91; job mobility, 293; low-wage work, 39; temporary contracts, 62; working conditions, 111–2

zoning regulations, 215, 227, 230, 247–8